THE
MIDDLE
PATH
COOKBOOK

BY THE SAME AUTHOR

Let There Be Lite!

THE MIDDLE PATH COOKBOOK

A Vegetarian Awakening

JAY DISNEY

THE OVERLOOK PRESS
WOODSTOCK & NEW YORK

First published in the United States in 2002 by
The Overlook Press, Peter Mayer Publishers, Inc.
Woodstock & New York

WOODSTOCK:
One Overlook Drive
Woodstock, NY 12498
www.overlookpress.com
[for individual orders, bulk and special sales, contact our Woodstock office]

NEW YORK:
141 Wooster Street
New York, NY 10012

EXCERPTS WERE REPRINTED WITH PERMISSION FROM THE FOLLOWING:
A Zen Forest, Sayings of the Masters, translated by Soiku Shigematsu, Inklings,
Weatherhill, Inc., 1981.; *Cage of Fireflies, Modern Japanese Haiku*, translated by Lucien
Stryk, Swallow Press, 1993; *The Dumpling Field, Haiku of Issa*, translated by Lucien Stryk
with the assistance of Noboru Fujiwara, Swallow Press, 1991; *Haiku Harvest*, translation
by Peter Beilenson and Harry Behn, The Peter Pauper Press, 1962; *Haiku Master Buson*,
Yuki Sawa & Edith M. Shiffert, Heian International, 1978; *Lotus Moon, The Poetry of the Buddhist
Nun Rengetsu*, translated/introduced by John Stevens, Weatherhill Press,1994; *Mountain Tasting,
Zen Haiku by Santôka Taneda*, translated by John Stevens, Weatherhill Press, 1980; *Ryôkan, Zen
Monk-Poet of Japan*, translated by Burton Watson, Columbia Press, 1977; *Saigyô, Poems of a
Mountain Home*, translated by Burton Watson, Columbia Press, 1991; *Tao Te Ching, Lao-tzu*,
translated by Stephen Mitchell, Harper & Row, 1988.

Library of Congress Cataloging-in-Publication Data

Disney, Jay
The middle path cookbook: a vegetarian awakening / Jay Disney
p. cm.
Includes index.
1. Vegetarian cookery.
TX837 .D54 2002   641.5′636—dc21   2001056047

Book design and typeformatting by Bernard Schleifer
Manufactured in the United States of America
FIRST EDITION
1 3 5 7 9 8 6 4 2
ISBN 1-58567-260-2

For Luigi—who else?

CONTENTS

• •

Acknowledgments

A very special thanks to:

My parents, Don and Naida Disney,
who, when their 18-year-old son said he
was "going vegetarian," let him.

And in wry amusement at my nephew,
Scott Mitchell Henderson,
who since his birth has staunchly refused to eat meat.

As well as
Hermann Lademann, "The Jamón King."

INTRODUCTION

● ●

Gather knowledge and discern; the process of being is all there is.

SOAPBOX OPPORTUNITIES

In today's world, where we move at an ever-increasing pace, the idea of moderation in all things shines as a beacon of welcome above the scattered dust of our harried lives. "Moderation, yes," you may say, "but who has the time?"

I suppose that's the point—we must make time and space for Life. When time is scant, we are presented with the danger of relying on "experts" to tell us how best to utilize our lives—how to organize our closets, to keep within our budgets, or to get a healthy meal. But there is a hidden catch to this mode of living, namely that we begin to associate styles of living and eating habits as being either "right" or "wrong"; we begin to assign "superior" or "inferior" judgments to what were intended as guidelines. We consult experts to diagram the healthiest way to exercise and/or eat, but how much attention have we paid to the practicability of it? And why should we attach a morality of right and wrong to eating, the very mainstay of our existence?

To illustrate, I was once invited to speak about low-fat cookery to a group of adults taking a nutrition class, and during the discussion a student asked my opinion as to how to get X grams of protein for breakfast with the least amount of fat, utilizing beans and grains. I was rather taken aback with wonder as to why she (or anyone for that matter) should care about her intake of protein, since most Americans get more than double the amount of protein they need on a daily basis with no difficulty whatsoever, vegetarian and carnivore alike. I could sense that the questioner felt she was a bad person because she found the nutritionist's guidelines for breakfast difficult to incorporate into her life-style. My answer went something like this:

> Breakfast is one of those bugbears we all face; we all know how important it is, yet few of us have or take the time to get what is commonly referred to as a good breakfast. Some people simply aren't hungry in the morning, let alone willing spend twenty minutes preparing a "healthy" breakfast when they're late for a meeting. And since each of us is psychologically, physically, and metabolically unique, it's important to recognize our own body's needs and requirements, regardless of what any nutritionist may suggest.

Probably it was at this point I made an enemy of the nutritionist. However, since I had the floor, I continued:

> The point I'm making is, get as much nutritional information as you can, and perhaps even try out new regimens for a while, then see how you can *easily and logically* fit any of it into your life-style while simultaneously listening to your body for any advice it may give. For you [pointing to a classmember], a cup of coffee and toast may be fine, since the rest of your day's meals are balanced and nutritious. If you feel fine and perform your morning duties efficiently on just toast and coffee in the morning, what's wrong with that? Am I *advocating* a cup of coffee and toast as a healthy breakfast? Of course not—but it's better than not eating breakfast at all.

After the class, the nutritionist informed me that many of the students had (in her words) "atrocious eating habits" and she was trying to illustrate the pinnacle of nutritious menu planning so that they could get "on the right track." I asked her, "Aren't you making all this terribly complicated? If you're trying to make too abrupt a change in their eating habits too quickly, how many of them will find it practical? Isn't it better to give them a *realistic* view of nutrition and eating rather than the most optimum, high-tech view? Why not simply give them the information and let *them* make the decisions and alter their diets as they see fit?"

She didn't much like my approach. Not being able to stop once I was securely perched atop my soapbox, I added, "And what about quality of life? Should optimum nutrition always take precedence over the quality of life? What if through this intensive examination of food, you've turned the very act of eating into a chore, and now your students hate the idea of meal planning because they can't get the equation of X grams of protein to X grams of fat correct? What if you've turned the creative and spiritual act of feeding oneself into an algebraic assignment? What, if in the interest of 'better nutrition,' you've made food, the most basic necessity of life, their enemy?"

(At this point I received a strong impression that the nutritionist would never ask me to speak to her class again, an accurate prediction to this day.)

I didn't even touch on the idea that the nutritionist was making her students feel inferior simply because they couldn't quite get a handle on this "optimum, high-tech" life-style. I saw the confusion on their faces as they struggled with combining bean products with grains to give them the highest carbohydrate-to-protein ratios with the least fat—and all of this first thing in the morning! No wonder they were frustrated!

The crux of this story is that most of us know what foods are commonly considered to be "good" or "bad," but we needn't kick ourselves in the head if we eat something that isn't necessarily "good" for us. Even the labels "good" and "bad" are erroneous, since butter, a solid saturated fat, is not "bad" for you as long as you don't eat massive quantities of it. There are no bad foods. It is imperative to look at one's diet as a whole, cohesive, connected unit, and to judge the healthiness of your diet by looking at what is ingested over a weekly period (or, if necessary, a daily period), rather than obsess on one serving at one meal on one particular day. It's helpful to incorporate as many healthy habits as you can without cursing yourself for not being "better." You are who you are. If you are in the process of adapting your lifelong eating habits, accept the fact that you're in transition and that there's nothing wrong with being in transition. It drives me to distraction when I hear people say, "Oops! There goes my diet! I had a wonderful piece of chocolate cheesecake at lunch." "Did you enjoy it?" I ask. "Of course," they reply. "Then good for you!" I respond.

> Be content with what you have;
> rejoice in the way things are.
> When you realize there is nothing lacking,
> the whole world belongs to you.
> —Lao-Tzu

Why, if this is a "moderation" book, are there no moderate amounts of meat?

Moderation! We can find happiness in our diet through common sense and moderation, yet this is a difficult concept for many of us to grasp. And how much of the confusion is abetted by weekly reports of "new information" regarding foods mankind has eaten for thousands of years? Yes, it is important to take a good look at your diet and keep it healthy, but in the interests of both physical and mental health, there is nothing wrong with the occasional indulgence.

The "moderation" I'm speaking of refers not to the moderate use of flesh (for reasons outlined below in *The Vegetarian and The Carnivore*), but the moderate use of what would be considered "unhealthy" foodstuffs, such as cheese, butter, oils. Many decades ago, the popular notion was that vegetarian diets were healthier merely because they eliminated meat and thereby most cholesterol; but it was quickly apparent that the substitution of high-fat items such as nuts, cheese, eggs, and dairy more than made up for the simple elimination of flesh fats. Some of the recipes in this book will be low in fat, some not. The point of *The Middle Path* is to illustrate how moderate amounts of foods (both low in fat and high in fat) can aid in a healthy, balanced life-style.

If fat is a problem, the recipes can easily be altered to fit into a low-fat life-style by substituting lower-fat items, such as nonfat sour cream for sour cream. Some people are thinking, "The best of all would be a nonfat vegetarian diet." There's no such thing as a nonfat diet—our bodies must have fat to survive.

What does the "Middle Path" have to do with cooking?

In a word, moderation. Moderation not only in fat quantities, but in the philosophy of how you approach cooking and eating. Subsisting (or attempting to subsist) on a bowl of rice a day is not moderation, it is ascetic torture. Neither deprivation nor overindulgence lead to a balanced, holistic approach to cooking and eating. And, of course, one must be moderate in everything, including moderation.

The most important food-oriented advice I can give is: Gather as much nutritional information as you can. Incorporate as many healthy habits into your life as possible. Feel good about yourself and allow yourself the luxury of enjoying your life, including the occasional indulgence.

THE VEGETARIAN AND THE CARNIVORE

It is my view that the vegetarian manner of living by its purely physical effect on the human temperament would most beneficially influence the lot of mankind.
—ALBERT EINSTEIN

Nowhere is the division between the vegetarian and the carnivore more apparent than with guests! For the carnivore host, it seems absurd not to serve meat, and to vegetarian hosts, it seems hypocritical to serve flesh since they don't eat it themselves.

Where does this leave the good host and hostess who want to please their guests? Nowadays there are many people who don't eat beef, pork, lamb, shellfish, or fish, so even the issue of what kind of meat to serve is difficult. One easy answer when in doubt as to your guests' eating habits is always to serve vegetarian meals. Carnivores aren't averse to eating wonderful vegetable entrées (though they may grumble to themselves en route home), so by ignoring the issue of meat entirely you've solved the problem by preparing a meal that all can enjoy.

Although this is a vegetarian cookbook, it is neither my goal nor purpose to proselytize for vegetarianism, since I think what a person decides to eat is his choice and his concern. I prefer a vegetarian diet because it suits my temperament better than a meatbased existence. On a vegetarian diet I don't feel as angry, stressed-out, or hyperactive as when I include small portions of meat; for some reason, vegetarianism keeps me on a more even keel mentally, emotionally, and physically.

For people not thus affected, why not eat lots of vegetables and small amounts of meat? The most obvious answer is that people elect vegetarianism for health reasons. Certain types of vegetarian life-styles have been suggested to lower cholesterol levels, reduce stress, and enable one to live a cleaner, simpler life.

Another reason is that of conscience: an individual may not wish to live by eating animal flesh, that is, "to live by consuming death." This motive encompasses religious prohibitions as well as moral ones—the massive slaughter and commercialization of animals as food, for example.

Yet another reason why one would wish to cut back on meat products (in addition to the issues of cholesterol and fat content) would be the toxins, chemicals, antibiotics, steroids, hormones, and, in the case of some fish and shellfish, mercury and deadly bacteria strains sometimes embedded in their flesh. These are not unwarranted worries, since every year people acquire debilitating illnesses and even die because of meat-based food poisoning.

But the most important reason why meat is a dubious food product is because flesh is the "lowest point" on the food chain. To illustrate, think about what is normally considered food: vegetables, fruit, dairy products, and meat (including poultry and fish). Vegetables and fruit are plants, and as such consume only soil, air, water, and sunshine. If you wish to judge whether fruits and vegetables are healthy or not, you need to observe how they were grown and if they were sprayed with pesticides and fertilized with chemicals (a good argument for organic gardening). Even if an apple were handled with dirty hands, a quick wash of the apple will make it sanitary. To analyze dairy products, meat, and poultry, however, you must look at the animal; was it healthy when it was slaughtered? Was the milk handled and processed in a sanitary manner, or was it exposed to dangerous bacteria? Was it refrigerated properly? Was the chicken given large doses of hormones to produce eggs? Was the cow given antibiotics to cure an infection? Did the fish come from polluted waters? Aside from all of this, the questions linger once the animal has been killed: has the flesh been handled properly? How old is it? Has it been exposed to any toxins or bacteria? Does it have parasites? Has it been frozen and refrozen? Was it accurately and competently inspected by government inspectors? What were the sanitary conditions at the slaughterhouse?

It is undeniable that flesh products contain residues of whatever went into them and what came in contact with them. A fish, living in a polluted lake, for instance, may contain those same pollutants lurking in its flesh, and when you eat the fish you're eating the pollutants (perhaps made more concentrated by the cooking process) as well. Next think of a cow. Two hundred years ago, cows used to spend their days roaming through fresh fields, eating hay and grass, getting milked and petted by their owners. The fresh grass was organic and contained no toxins; they weren't exposed to high levels of radiation or injected with antibiotics. Cows were organic (and also had diseases, namely tuberculosis). Nowadays, though, cows are injected with antibiotics to keep them "healthy" and to increase their growth, a side effect of regular exposure to low-dose antibiotics. Additionally, some cows are given Bovine Growth Hormone (rBGH) to increase their milk yields, which increases the risk of infection to the cow's udders (mastitis), thereby making it necessary to give the cow *more* antibiotics to cure the infection caused by the growth hormone!

Meat, then, is the end of the road insofar as foodstuffs are concerned. Each piece of flesh has a link to whatever that animal was exposed to during its life, and if the animal you're eating also was a carnivore, then the cycle is doubled and redoubled every time that animal ate another animal. As you can guess, when you eat the flesh of a carnivore the dangerous link of exposure to toxins grows exponentially.

Health-minded vegetarians use this mode of thinking with regards to vegetables as well, which is why many insist on organically raised produce. For just as a fish or cow is a repository of whatever went into it, an orange or a carrot is a repository of whatever it was grown in or was sprayed with. With fruits and vegetables, you are eating a food for the first time; they are *living* foods.

There is one more reason why some elect vegetarianism, and it is one that almost no one believes (or wants to believe), namely "I don't like the taste of meat." Incredible though it may seem to carnivores, there *are* people who don't like the texture and flavor of flesh products. Why this should be a mystery is a mystery itself, since it is commonplace for people to object to the taste of items such as Brussels sprouts, okra, or beets. Why should meat be the lone exception? It isn't for some.

So take a good long look at your diet. You may find vegetarianism is neither as difficult nor as radical as you thought. At the very least, try it for a week or two and see how your body feels. You just might surprise yourself

RULES AND REGULATIONS

For those of you new to the world of vegetarianism, there are only a few (but vital) rules to keep in mind, and the most important concern protein and vitamin B-12.

Protein

There is a great deal of discussion and confusion on vegetable protein, so it is a matter worth covering in detail.

Protein is made up of chains of amino acids, but not all of the protein we consume contains each and every amino acid in its molecular chain. This is not a problem except when one is considering the nine essential amino acids the body needs to function but cannot produce by itself. Meat, dairy products, and eggs contain all of the essential amino acids, so these are called "complete" proteins. However, not all proteins contain all nine essential amino acids; these are called "incomplete" proteins; rice is one. For example, let's hypothetically say that rice is strong in six of the nine essential amino acids, hence, although it contains protein, it is only a partial protein. This fact has caused many people to suggest that vegetable proteins are inferior to meat proteins, which is absolute rot. Beans and grains *in combination* contain all nine essential amino acids. Although rice may be weak in a few of the essential amino acids, beans are strong in those amino acids in which rice is deficient; ergo, when eaten in tandem, a complete protein, containing all nine essential amino acids, is digested.

When discussing "complete" versus "incomplete" proteins, one must keep in mind one thought: that the *lowest common denominator* wins. Let's say you've got a single vegetable protein that has all nine essential amino acids (methionine, threonine, tryptophan, isoleucine, leucine, lysine, histidine, valine, and phenylalanine). In this protein, amino acids #1 through #8 are all weighing in at 15 grams, but amino acid #9 is only weighing in at 1 gram. Since the nine essential amino acids are in a sense linked, your body will only process *one gram's worth* of each of those nine essential amino acids, despite the fact that amino acids #1 through #8 are 15 grams! Your body will process however much *complete* protein there is, and in this case, since there is only 1 gram's worth of all nine amino acids, that is the amount your body will process. Thus, if amino acids #1 through #8 were 15 grams and #9 was 5 grams, then your body would process 5 grams' worth of protein. The lowest amount of the nine amino acids "wins." This amount could also be called "usable" protein.

As a result, some studies suggest that many vegetable sources commonly thought of as "incomplete" proteins are in fact "complete," but this "completeness" is by definition only, not in practice. Some so-called "incomplete" proteins *do* in fact contain all nine essential amino acids, but the levels of some of these components are so low that their protein is ostensibly rendered incomplete. In other words, you'd have to eat an *enormous* amount just to get a decent serving of protein. Bean-grain combinations are nature's perfect complement to each other for getting quick, simple, *complete* vegetable protein.

But insofar as the body is concerned, protein is protein is protein; whether it is animal or vegetable protein is immaterial. (Some studies suggest, though, that one's minimum amount of protein can change depending on circumstance, such as age, if you're a professional athlete, if you're under huge amounts of stress, and so forth.) Almost all Americans consume around 100 to 120 grams of protein per day, which is roughly *twice* the RDA guideline. Protein deficiencies are commonly seen when severe health problems exist or when a radical crash diet is involved. The real problem with the average American diet is not that we aren't eating enough protein, but that we are eating too much; we would be hard pressed to limit our protein intake to the RDA guidelines!

Combining legumes and grains to get a complete vegetable protein is quite simple when you keep in mind that all you need to do is serve at the same meal something made *from* the bean or grain, not the *whole* bean or grain. Flour products count as a grain: oat cakes, wheat rolls, barley bread, or cornbread. Miso, tofu, tempeh, and chick-pea flour all count as legumes since they are bean-based.

Protein cannot be stored by the body, which is why "complete" protein must be eaten often. Below is an abbreviated list of legumes and grains. Combining one component from each column would constitute a complete vegetarian protein.

LEGUMES	GRAINS
Beans (e.g., Anasazi, azuki, black, Great Northern, kidney, lima, navy, pinto, soy)	Amaranth
	Barley
	Buckwheat
Dried bean curd sheets (yuba)	Corn
Flour made from legumes	Flour made from any grain
Garbanzo (chick-peas)	Millet
Lentils (any variety)	Oats
Split peas (any variety)	Quinoa
Tofu, tempeh, miso	Rice (all varieties)
	Rye
	Seitan (wheat meat or wheat gluten)
	Teff
	Wheat (includes most pasta)

Vitamin B-12

Being a healthy vegetarian is simple if your diet includes milk, milk products, eggs, cheese, and assorted other dairy products. Strict vegans (those who eat only vegetable products and no eggs, dairy, or cheese) must pay heed to vitamin B-12, as this is mostly found in foods of animal origin; the notable exceptions are: fortified nutritional yeast, B-12 fortified soy (or other vegetable) milk, Marmite/Vegemite, tempeh, and/or B-12 supplements.

HOW TO GET A "MEATY" TASTE FROM YOUR VEGETABLES

For those uninitiated into the world of vegetarianism, the concept of doing without meat or meat by-products seems daunting. "Will it taste any good without all that rich, meaty stock?"

First of all, vegetables aren't meat. What is the point of trying to make vegetables seem like what you're trying to avoid? Vegetables are vegetables; and as such, have their own characteristics and qualities that should be highlighted, appreciated, and treasured, not beaten and tortured into submission in a vain attempt to render them like animal flesh. Meat and vegetables are vastly different, and one should cherish these differences rather than attempt to make them more similar.

Here are a few things to think about when you want a "meatier" taste.

- Add some yeast products, like nutritional yeast (preferably toasted first), Marmite, Vegemite, or smoked torula yeast. This yields a hearty, richer taste.
- Brown your vegetables. This gives a deeper, more complex taste, particularly if you're browning onions and mushrooms. Avoid browning large amounts of sweet vegetables (carrots, sweet potatoes, winter squash), as browning these will concentrate and caramelize their natural sugars.
- Use tamari or some store-bought "herb/spice" mixes instead of salt.
- Increase the amount of vegetables in stocks to concentrate the flavor.
- Grilling or broiling vegetables and soy products gives an outdoorsy, richer taste. Similarly, roasted vegetables yield a different note to an otherwise routine entrée.
- Don't forget to add wine—this gives another layer of taste.
- Add a bit of smoked cheese instead of pure "regular" cheeses (such as Swiss, Cheddar, mozzarella, and the like). The smokiness of the cheese will add a deeper note to the character of the entrée, sometimes suggesting the inclusion of bacon or smoked meats.

- I f you are new to the vegetarian game, you may want to check out some of the packaged vegetarian meals and foodstuffs available in your natural grocery store. Many times they'll have vegetarian hotdogs, hamburgers, and even vegetarian cold cuts, like pastrami, "turkey" or "beef"! Unquestionably these vegetable-based substitutes aren't fooling anyone into believing they are truly meat, but if you are in transition with your diet, they can ease the mental craving for meat while keeping you meat-free. Also, you can add these alternatives to recipes as you wish, such as vegetarian sausages in paella, or bits of vegetarian hamburgers in a stir-fry.

TRANSITIONAL VEGETARIANISM

"But I've been eating meat my whole life. How can I just give it up?"

"One bite at a time," is the answer. And parenthetically, "Only if you want to."

Vegetarianism is no different from any other form of diet modification: you can elect to eat or not eat any food, be it fish, meat, vegetable. If you can't stand the taste of raw onions, you don't have to eat them. If you don't like green bell peppers, don't buy them. If you don't wish to eat pork, then don't—no one is forcing you to abandon anything you want to eat. Putting political and/or religious dietary restrictions aside, this is all vegetarianism amounts to, because you're electing to eat only vegetable products. No one is forcing you not to eat meat.

One of the greatest mistakes beginning vegetarians can make is to decide meat products are strictly taboo, which creates an aura of temptation around meat. If, while you're in transition into vegetarianism, you decide that you really want a chicken breast, then by all means have a chicken breast. After having it, you may decide it wasn't worth all that effort and discover that a tempeh stir-fry tastes better anyway.

For those long-term carnivores interested in vegetarianism but unsure how it will fit into their life-styles, the practice of transitional vegetarianism comes to the fore. What does this term mean? It means nothing more than eating vegetarian meals as often as you like, perhaps with the goal of ultimately eating no meat at all, but exerting no pressure to force a strict dietary regime on your life regardless of circumstance. You can set and modify the rules, because you will be in transition from one method of eating to another, and these rules are based on your life at the moment. There are no rights and wrongs, and you should be comfortable eating whatever seems appropriate at the time. Eventually the concept and practice of vegetarianism will be as familiar as a bowl of soup, and the habit of using meat will disappear. There is no pressure to "stay on the vegetarian wagon," since: a) there is no "wagon" (vegetarianism is not like alcoholism), and b) you are the one choosing to eat (or not eat) meat. Eating meat during the period when you're learning about vegetarianism is part of what will make the switch to vegetarianism simpler.

"How does one begin a life of vegetarianism?"

Again, one bite at a time. Depending on your goals, you can slowly wean yourself from the habit of meat products by having (say) "one vegetarian day" per week, and then gradually increase to two vegetarian days, then three, and so on. Or perhaps have vegetarian breakfasts and lunches, but fish with dinner. Since your body isn't literally addicted to meat, the transition is the period when you're replacing one set of eating habits with another. Eventually you may find that you enjoy the variety of vegetarian meals, coupled with many assorted health benefits, and decide that you want to opt for such meals as frequently as possible.

"What happens if I eat meat after being a vegetarian for months and months?"

I think it is important to look at one's diet holistically—and by that I mean you must look at your diet over a period of months, not a period of hours. If you've eaten vegetarian meals for ten months and then have a shrimp kabob, that shrimp kabob does not negate the previous ten months of vegetarianism.

So, the simplest way to become a vegetarian is always to maintain the option of eating meat if you want. There are no pressures, and you can rest assured you can always have a burger if you crave one. But you probably won't crave one. And the reason you won't is because no one is forcing you not to have one; you're simply not having one.

> *The first morsel is to destroy all evils,*
> *The second morsel is to practice all good deeds,*
> *The third morsel is to save all sentient beings—*
> *May we all attain the Path of Buddhahood.*
> *—The Verse of the Three Morsels of Food*

SOUPS

● ●

ABOUT VEGETABLE STOCKS

There are several trains of thought as to what should go into vegetable stock, with some cooks suggesting that any scrap you have around the kitchen is fair game (from gnarly carrot tops to onion skins to fibrous celery roots), and other cooks saying you should use only the freshest, finest vegetables available. I've always found that stocks made from odds and ends taste exactly like that—gnarly carrots, onion skins, and celery roots (and usually a healthy dose of dirt as well). It stands to reason that whatever goes into the stock is what it will taste like, so why use inferior ingredients? Use the inedible scraps for your compost heap, not your soup.

This does not mean, however, that you can't use sundry leftover pieces of vegetables for soup stock. Many times I'll have a few sticks of carrots or celery from a crudité lying around, so I put them in a sealed plastic bag in the freezer; within a month I've accumulated enough good, initially edible scraps to make stock. Many things can go into this catchall bag; tomato juice from canned tomatoes, Swiss chard stems, parsley stems and the woody stems from other fresh herbs, bean juices, mushroom stems, slightly old gingerroot knobs, and the like, anything that is ordinarily edible but you'd probably throw away. Two things need to be said about this stock: 1. tomatoes and tomato juice tend to overpower everything else, so if you have more than a small amount of tomato you'll wind up with tomato stock (which is fine, if that's what you want), and 2. cabbage family vegetables (turnips, broccoli, cabbage, kohlrabi, cauliflower, kale, parsnips, rutabaga) overpower other flavors, so if you have turnips and tomatoes in a big pot, you'll end up with tomato-turnip stock—completely edible, of course, but not very versatile. Usually I put the cabbage family scraps into the compost heap and leave everything else for the soup stock.

Vegetable stocks are by nature more delicate, subtler, and lighter in taste than traditional meat stocks, so some adjustment may be needed if you're only used to beef or chicken stocks.

CANNED STOCK AND BOUILLON CUBES

Although some major soup manufacturers have finally discovered that the entire world doesn't eat meat and have produced vegetable stock in a can, I wish I could say this is a great improvement. However, these stocks usually taste like salt, turnips, and metal. I've seen frozen, 100 percent natural, salt-free vegetable stocks too—and they, unfortunately, taste of watery turnips in dire need of salt! Also available is liquid shiitake stock in a small brown bottle found in health food stores—very expensive and rather disappointing in taste, truth be told. There is also the route of vegetable bouillon cubes; these are available in health food stores as well as major supermarkets. Unfortunately, vegetable bouillon cubes, whether the health-food store variety or supermarket variety, usually contain hydrogenated vegetable oils, lots of salt, MSG, and/or yeast extracts. (Yeast extract in itself isn't bad, but sometimes the term *yeast extract* includes not only yeast but MSG as well.) Though vegetable bouillon cubes usually contain hydrogenated and/or partially hydrogenated fats, the amount is typically so small that fat really isn't the issue—the problem is the MSG and massive amount of salt. (Knorr Vegetarian Vegetable Bouillon cubes, for example, contain only 2 grams of fat per cube but a whopping 1820 milligrams of sodium!) However, if you look carefully and read the information provided on the package, you'll find some vegetable stocks in cube or powder form that aren't loaded with salt and fat. And brace yourself if you go to the health food store looking for vegetable bouillon—it isn't cheap.

Do I advocate the use of powdered or cubed vegetable bouillon cubes? That's a tricky question to which I answer: "Sometimes." (Has the theme of moderation whacked you over the head yet?) I'm keenly aware that not everyone has the time to prepare homemade vegetable stocks, and purchasing a little box of instant bouillon is easy, and one must never underestimate anything that is easy! Bouillon cubes sit on the pantry shelf indefinitely without harm, and when you're in a hurry these products suffice perfectly well. I don't think they're the best alternative, but they're certainly not the worst. You will undoubtedly note that I've listed vegetable bouillon cubes in a few recipes, usually in rice or bean recipes, and since vegetable bouillon cubes contain lots of sodium, I've on occasion tossed in a cube *instead of adding salt*; the results have been quite satisfactory.

There are several vegetable bouillons that are "clean" in their ingredients, two of which are Vogue Instant Vege Base, and The Organic Gourmet Wild Mushroom Stock and/or Vegetable Stock, all available in health food stores. The Vogue stock is a powdered bouillon containing no MSG or hydrogenated fats, and you don't have to be a chemical engineer to read the ingredients list. It also has no added salt, a great boon for those watching their sodium intake. The Organic Gourmet stocks are "wet," that is, they are concentrated paste stocks available in small jars. They, like their counterparts, are not inexpensive, but they are quick, simple, and tasty.

On other fronts, some chefs use fresh vegetable juices for stocks and sauces, which is undoubtedly a bonus if you happen to have a fancy vegetable juicer around and want to juice twenty dollars' worth of vegetables just for soup stock. Juicers are great machines, but it takes an enormous amount of vegetables to get a small amount of fresh juice, and the copious amount of ground-up vegetables left (which could be put into a compost heap) added to the hassle of cleaning the juicer strainer and blades makes me wonder if it's all worth the trouble. If you have a juicer and want to experiment with fresh juices, please do so; for myself, I'd rather spend my extra time gardening or reading than cleaning juicer parts.

*A dumb man has eaten
a bitter cucumber.*

Vegetable Stock

● ●

*This is an all-purpose vegetarian stock. It is mildly flavored and will not
intrude upon the flavors of any kind of soup. For a truly "universal" stock, do
not use the herbes de Provence; then the stock will be suitable for any type of
cuisine, Chinese, Thai, Japanese, or other. It is pale yellow in appearance (like
chicken stock), so it is the stock of choice if you're making a soup that needs to
be pale in color.*

3	large onions, peeled and roughly chopped
3	large carrots, peeled and roughly chopped
2	stalks celery, chopped
1	clove garlic, peeled and mashed or chopped
1	teaspoon herbes de Provence, optional: see above
5	cups water
1 to 2	teaspoons salt
1	teaspoon whole black peppercorns
1	teaspoon whole allspice berries
1	bay leaf
½	cup dry white wine

Put the ingredients in a large stockpot and bring just to the boil;
reduce the heat to low and simmer for 30 minutes. Turn off the heat
and allow the stock to cool. Strain first through a large sieve, squeezing out any extra juices from the vegetables by pressing them
against the sieve with the back of a spoon, then strain the stock again
through a fine-mesh sieve or through cheesecloth to remove any
herbs or other floating debris. Refrigerate or freeze the stock.

If you have these things lying around, feel free to include any
of them: parsley stems, fresh herb stems or fresh herbs, potatoes
(sweet, white, or baking), summer squash (zucchini or crookneck),
winter squash, beets (these will turn the stock red), green beans.
Bell peppers may be added, but as with tomatoes and turnips, they
have a tendency to overpower the other tastes.

Things not to include: cabbage family vegetables, eggplant,
onion skins, very delicate vegetables such as lettuce, carrot tops, or
parsley tops.

*Store the whole world
in a grain
of millet!*

Japanese Broth

ABOUT 4 CUPS STOCK

● ●

*This is amazingly flavorful for a pure vegetable stock; it is perfect for clear
broths as well as miso soups and chawanmushi.*

¼	cup dried arame or hijiki (see Ingredients, page 251)*
1	6-inch piece dried kombu (see Ingredients, page 254)
4	cups water
2	tablespoons sake
2	tablespoons tamari
1	¼-inch slice gingerroot
1	green onion, or 2 to 3 tablespoons chopped white or yellow onion
4	dried shiitakes or dried Chinese black mushrooms
2	tablespoons mirin or 1 to 2 teaspoons sugar

Place everything in a pot and bring to the boil; reduce the
flame and barely simmer the mixture for 5 minutes. Turn off the
heat and cover the pot; allow it to sit for at least 30 minutes.

After the stock has steeped, strain it through cheesecloth or a
very fine mesh strainer. You may use the stock immediately or
refrigerate or freeze it.

Additionally:
- You could remove the rehydrated shiitakes and cut off the
  tough stems; slice the mushrooms into ⅛-inch thin pieces and
  either use them in another recipe or return them to the stock.
- If desired, remove some of the arame from the sieve and
  return it to the stock.

**Arame and hijiki are somewhat difficult to measure, as they are dried pieces of seaweed
and don't fit easily or conveniently into a measuring cup. However, give it a shot and do
the best you can. It's not terribly important to be accurate.*

*Eyes wide, enter
the boiling water
—with dignity!*

Mushroom Soup Stock
ABOUT 4 CUPS STOCK

● ●

*This stock is the "meatiest" in taste and appearance of the vegetable based
stocks. It uses a large amount of mushrooms, but the result is undoubtedly
worth it. Although it is brown, like beef stock, its taste is much more closely
linked to chicken stock.*

1	*large onion, peeled and roughly chopped*
2	*cloves garlic, peeled and roughly chopped*
2	*tablespoons olive oil*
2	*pounds white mushrooms, cut into chunks*
1	*tablespoon tamari*
1	*teaspoon thyme*
1	*teaspoon whole black peppercorns*
1	*bay leaf*
½	*teaspoon ground cumin*
4	*large dried shiitakes, Chinese black mushrooms,*
	a handful of dried Chilean mushrooms,
	or 1 tablespoon Chilean mushroom powder
1	*carrot, peeled and roughly chopped*
½	*cup white vermouth or white wine*
6	*cups water*
	Salt to taste

In a large, deep skillet or pot, sauté the onion and garlic briefly
(a minute or so) in the olive oil over a moderate flame. Add the
white mushrooms and turn the heat to high. Sauté until the mushrooms have begun to brown lightly, stirring often. After 3 to 5 minutes, the mushrooms will have exuded their juices: there will be a
deep brown liquid in the bottom of the pot. Add the remaining
ingredients and bring the mixture to the simmer, uncovered,
allowing the stock to cook for 30 minutes. Turn off the heat and
allow the stock to cool naturally. Strain the stock into a bowl.
Squeeze out the cooked mushrooms and carrots by pressing them
against the colander with the back of a large spoon. Refrigerate or
freeze until needed. After the stock has been refrigerated, you can
defat it by scooping off any floating oil on top. Simple!

Need fire?
Best strike a flint.
Water?
Dig a well.

Browned Onion Stock

ABOUT 4 CUPS STOCK

● ●

*This stock may seem a bit labor-intensive, but it is worth the effort. It is rich
and hearty, giving an unbeatable foundation for stews, thick soups, and rice
dishes (such as pilafs and risottos).*

*It is also a wonderful liquid for poaching: eggs, vegetables, perhaps fish
(if you eat fish), as well as a robust base for chawanmushi, gravies, and sauces.
Don't forget, too, to use this as the liquid for rice dishes, such as pilafs and
risottos, remembering that it will tint the rice a nutty brown hue.*

     4   **large onions, peeled and thinly sliced**
     2   **tablespoons olive oil**
 1 to 2   **teaspoons salt or to taste**
     ½   **teaspoon sugar (to help the onions caramelize)**
     1   **cup white vermouth or very dry white wine**
     ½   **cup dry port or Madeira**
     1   **teaspoon thyme**
     1   **bay leaf**
     1   **tablespoon tamari**
     4   **cups water**

Peel and thinly slice the onions (this is easier if you have a
mandoline-type slicer—otherwise refrigerate the onions before
you slice them to lessen the smell).

Place the olive oil in a large, heavy pot over a moderate flame;
when it is hot, add the onions. Toss them in the oil, then cover the
pan and cook for 5 to 10 minutes, until the onions have softened.
Uncover and sprinkle in 1 teaspoon of salt and ½ teaspoon of
sugar; turn the flame to medium low and continue to cook and stir,
scraping the bottom occasionally, for 20 to 30 minutes, until the
onions are deep brown and have reduced to a fraction of their original quantity. They will begin to stick to the bottom, so scrape with
a wooden spoon or spatula as necessary. When the onions have
completely caramelized, add the wines, thyme, bay leaf, tamari,
and water; bring the stock to a simmer and cook, partially covered,
for 30 minutes. Stir occasionally, scraping along the bottom and

sides to remove any remaining browned bits of onion. Remove from the heat.

Allow the stock to cool to room temperature. Strain it and refrigerate or freeze. After the stock has been refrigerated, it is simple to remove the fat; merely take a spoon and scrape off any fat floating on the top.

However priceless,
a piece of gold
In the eye
is nothing but grit.

Tomato Stock

ABOUT 4 CUPS STOCK

● ●

Any kind of vegetable stock to which a large quantity of tomatoes or tomato juice has been added ends up being tomato stock. But for those of you who don't like leftover vegetable pieces lying around in a plastic bag in your freezer, here's a quick and easy way to make tomato stock.

1 to 2	teaspoons olive oil
1	large onion, peeled and chopped
1 to 2	cloves garlic, peeled and chopped
1	28-ounce can chopped or crushed tomatoes
2	stalks celery, chopped
1	cup chopped fresh fennel bulb, optional but recommended: or 1 teaspoon fennel seeds
½	cup white wine or vermouth
4	cups water
	Salt or tamari to taste

Heat the oil in a 2-quart pot over a moderate flame. Add the onion and garlic, and sauté for 2 minutes. Add tomatoes (including their liquid), celery, fennel, wine, and water. Bring the mixture to the simmer and cook for 30 minutes.

Strain the stock and taste for seasoning, adding a bit of salt or tamari as needed.

Asu wa kuru
to iu ame no fuki
o nite oku.

Tomorrow I'll come
Cooking wild vegetables
For your visit.

—SANTÔKA

Tomato Herb Soup

SERVES 4

● ●

I originally called this recipe Tomato-Dill Soup, but one evening when I was in a rush to prepare an impromptu dinner I realized that I did not have any fresh dill, and after a last-minute dash to the supermarket, I learned that they didn't have any fresh dill either. I substituted cilantro and found it to be every bit as good, but totally different. Although the execution of the recipe remains identical, I consider them to be independent soups. Guests who have the Tomato-Dill version might not recognize the Tomato-Cilantro Soup as a near cousin.

Unless it is the height of summer, when you can get delicious fresh tomatoes for a song, I usually use a mixture of fresh and canned tomatoes. Since canned tomatoes are packed in tomato juice, it is unnecessary to have the requisite four cups; a 28-ounce can will usually suffice if you add the juice as well as the tomatoes. The addition of some fresh tomato brightens the taste of the soup and gives a distinct flavor that cannot be achieved by using only canned tomatoes.

1 to 2	tablespoons olive oil or butter
2	cloves garlic, peeled and minced
1	cup minced onion
4	cups chopped fresh tomatoes (peeled and seeded) or a combination of fresh and canned tomatoes
½	teaspoon herbes de Provence
1	cup dry white wine or dry vermouth A few tablespoons of finely chopped parsley, optional
2	cups Vegetable Stock Salt and pepper to taste
1	cup sour cream (regular, light, or nonfat)
¼	cup chopped fresh dill or cilantro (see above) Sprigs of fresh dill, fresh cilantro, or parsley, and/or more sour cream, as garnish

In a heavy saucepan, heat the olive oil or butter over a medium flame, then add the garlic and onion. Cover and let the onion cook for a few minutes until fairly translucent and "sweated." Add the tomatoes and the herbes de Provence and keep covered over heat for a few more minutes, until the tomatoes have begun to cook through. Add the white wine and let the mixture come to the simmer. Remove and let cool for a few minutes.

Put the mixture in a food processor and blend in short off-and-on spurts until it is fairly smooth but still retains small recognizable chunks of onion and tomato.

Place the processed mixture back in the saucepan and return it to the heat. Add the finely chopped parsley and vegetable stock and bring to a simmer. Taste for seasonings, adding salt and pepper as necessary. The soup can cook for a few more minutes if you like, or you may cover it and let it stand until about 15 minutes before you're ready to serve.

Fifteen minutes before serving, bring the soup back to the simmering point. Blend the sour cream with a whisk to get out any lumps and add it to the soup, blending again with the whisk. Add the chopped fresh dill or cilantro and taste—it should be delicious. When the soup is just under the simmering point, take it off the heat. Ladle it into heated bowls, and add an additional dollop of sour cream and sprigs of fresh parsley, dill, or cilantro as garnish.

Waters, however rapid,
never carry off the moon.

Chinese "Sick" Soup

SERVES 4

● ●

No, this isn't a soup from China that makes you sick.

While staying with us, my friend Wang Chi-Mei from Taiwan made this wonderful recipe one frigid December day. She told me that it was typical of the kind of soup the Chinese would make if you were sick or feeling under the weather—it was soothing, nutritious, easy to digest, and satisfying. I was surprised at how rich and full-flavored it was for being so simple to make.

1	onion, peeled and diced into ¼- to ½-inch pieces
1	large or 2 small potatoes, russet, red, or Yukon gold, washed and scrubbed
2	stalks celery, sliced into 1-inch pieces
1 to 2	cloves garlic
1	tablespoon grated or finely chopped gingerroot
4 to 5	cups water or Vegetable Stock
1	small turnip, peeled and cut into small cubes, optional
1	teaspoon toasted sesame oil
1 to 1½	cups peeled, seeded, and chopped tomatoes
1 to 2	tablespoons tamari
	Salt to taste
	Cilantro sprigs, for garnish

Place the onion, potato, celery, garlic, and gingerroot in a large soup pot. Add the water and bring the mixture to the simmer, then reduce the heat so that it remains at the simmer, cooking for 20 minutes. Add the optional turnip, sesame oil, and chopped tomatoes. Simmer for an additional 15 to 20 minutes until the potato and turnip are tender. Add the tamari and salt to taste. Serve immediately in big bowls with sprigs of cilantro on top.

*The biggest bowl
fills last.*

Soothing Potato Soup

SERVES 4

● ●

One brisk October evening I had a yen for potato soup, and this is what I came up with—an inspired creation for its delicacy and simplicity, if I do say so myself. It is subtle, satisfying, and will stick to your ribs—a perfect meal with a loaf of hot French sourdough bread slathered with butter.

Although the Mushroom or Browned Onion stock would give this soup a richer taste, both are deep brown in color and would render this soup rather unattractive.

1 to 2	tablespoons butter
½ to 1	cup chopped onion, the smaller amount for a very delicate soup
1	clove garlic, minced, optional (do not use if you want a delicate flavor)
2	large baked or steamed potatoes, skins included if you like*
2	cups milk (skim, regular, or soy milk)
½	cup sour cream, regular or nonfat
2	cups full-flavored Vegetable Stock
1	cup grated sharp Cheddar cheese, regular or reduced fat
⅓	cup Parmesan cheese
1 to 2	easpoons thyme
½	teaspoon marjoram
	Salt and pepper
	Finely chopped fresh parsley

Use regular baked russet potatoes, or steam some cubed russet or red/white/Yukon gold potatoes in a steamer for 20 to 30 minutes until soft when pierced with a small knife. Cool and set aside.

Melt the butter over moderate heat in a large, heavy pot. Add the onion and optional garlic; sauté until the onion is translucent and soft (about 4 minutes). Remove from heat.

Put the onion mixture in a food processor and process briefly. Add the cooked potatoes (in a few batches if your processor is small), processing until you have a smooth mixture. Add some of the milk if this is particularly thick.

Return the thick paste to the pot. Add the remaining milk, sour cream, and stock; mix with a whisk until everything is incorporated and you have a fairly thin broth. Add the cheeses and herbs; mix well and bring to the simmer, stirring all the time to melt the cheeses evenly. When the soup reaches the simmering point, taste for seasoning; add salt and pepper to taste. If desired, cook for another 20 to 40 minutes over a very low flame to blend the flavors well.

Serve hot with a sprinkling of chopped fresh parsley and another sprinkling of Cheddar cheese if desired.

> A no-ear banana,
>   hearing thunder roar,
>   opens its leaves;
> A no-eye sunflower,
>   seeing the sun,
>   turns its head.

O-Miso Soupu

SERVES 4

● ●

Miso soup, in addition to being quintessentially Japanese, is extremely nutritious. Miso, like yogurt, contains active cultures that are enormously beneficial for the digestive system. Since miso is a "live product," it is of paramount importance that once the miso has been mixed in, the soup never comes to a boil or you will kill its beneficial properties. Miso soup is perfect dairy-free fare for those with head or respiratory colds or those with stomach disorders. But don't wait until you're sick to try it, for it's great any time of the year

Red miso is saltier and more robust than white miso, so if you're using mellow white miso, you may wish to increase the salt slightly.

2   tablespoons hijiki or arame seaweed
        or whatever remains from making the stock)
½   cup chopped, blanched fresh spinach
        (about 3 cups fresh spinach)

2   *green onions*
4   *cups Japanese Broth (see page 27)*
¼   *cup sake*
4   *white, brown (crimini), oyster, or*
       shiitake mushrooms, sliced into thin strips
¼   *block firm tofu, cut into ¼ to ½-inch squares,*
       optional
3   *tablespoons red or white miso, in a small bowl*
4   *thin lemon slices*
       Sprigs of cilantro, as garnish
       Toasted sesame seeds, as garnish, optional

Place the hijiki in a small bowl and add hot water to cover. Allow the seaweed to soak for 30 minutes, then remove it from the water. (If you're using the seaweed from the Japanese soup stock, eliminate this step and proceed.)

Remove the stems from the spinach and wash the leaves in a colander. Bring a kettle of water to the boil and pour the boiling water over the spinach, turning once or twice to blanch the spinach evenly. Rinse the now bright, green spinach in cool water; squeeze out any excess water and chop into ½-inch bits. Divide the blanched spinach into equal portions among four serving bowls.

Chop the green onions into fine rings; divide 2 teaspoons of the raw green onions among the serving bowls with the spinach. Place the remaining onions in a soup pot.

Pour the Japanese Broth into the pot with the chopped green onions and add the rehydrated hijiki, the mushrooms, and optional tofu. Bring the mixture to a simmer and cook for 5 minutes. Remove the pot from the heat.

Using a ladle, remove ½ cup of the hot soup stock from the pot and pour it into the bowl with the miso; stir the hot soup with the miso until you have a smooth paste. Add the thinned-out miso to the soup pot and stir. Divide the soup among the 4 bowls and float a slice of fresh lemon on top of each, adding a sprig of cilantro (and perhaps some toasted sesame seeds) as garnish. Serve immediately.

*Rich food
doesn't tempt
the man who has eaten.*

Rasam Stew

● ●

I love this soup. Rich and thick, it contains a complete vegetarian protein, and is complex in taste and spiciness.

2 to 3	cups cooked kidney beans, puréed
2	teaspoons whole cumin seeds
1	tablespoon ghee or flavorless oil, such as canola
2	teaspoons black mustard seeds
	Pinch of hing (see Ingredients, page 253)
2	whole dried red chile peppers
8	fresh curry leaves*
½	teaspoon turmeric
3 to 4	cups water, or Mushroom Soup Stock or Vegetable Stock
¼ to 1	cup leftover cooked brown basmati rice, optional
1	cup chopped tomatoes, fresh or canned
1	tablespoon tamarind paste, or 1 tablespoon lime juice mixed with 2 teaspoons sugar
2	teaspoons sugar
1 to 2	tablespoons rasam powder (see Ingredients, page 255)
	Salt to taste
	Sour cream or yogurt (regular, light, or nonfat)
	Mint or cilantro leaves, for garnish

Put the cooked kidney beans in a food processor and blend to a smooth paste. Set aside.

Spread the whole cumin seed in a small sauté pan and place over moderate heat; toss and stir the cumin until it has roasted and emits a lovely, warm, toasted smell. Remove from the pan and set aside.

Place a large soup pot over a moderate flame; tilt the pot to one side so that one edge is directly over the flame; add the ghee and allow it to melt if it is hard. Once the ghee is hot, add the mustard seeds. Turn the heat to medium high and continue to cook until the

*Fresh curry leaves are available in Indian markets. Despite their name, curry leaves taste nothing like curry powder. If you cannot find fresh curry leaves, eliminate them entirely and increase the proportion of black mustard seeds from 2 teaspoons to 1 tablespoon.

mustard seeds begin popping; immediately cover and take the pot off the heat until the popping subsides, about 15 seconds. Add the roasted cumin, hing, whole red chile peppers, fresh curry leaves, and turmeric; return the pot to medium heat for 30 seconds, cooking the spices. Add the puréed beans, water or stock, cooked rice, tomatoes, tamarind paste, and sugar, and bring the mixture to a simmer. Simmer for 20 to 30 minutes. Add the rasam powder, stirring well, and taste for seasoning; it will probably need salt. When you are satisfied with the seasoning, ladle the soup into deep bowls. Place a dollop of yogurt or sour cream on top of each serving along with a sprig of fresh cilantro or mint. Serve immediately.

Chant poetry
to your best friend!
Drink wine
with your true friend!

Asian Noodle Soup

SERVES 4

● ●

1 to 2	*tablespoons ghee or flavorless oil, such as canola*
1	*large onion, peeled and minced*
3	*cloves garlic, peeled and minced*
1	*tablespoon gingerroot, peeled and minced*
½	*teaspoon turmeric*
½	*teaspoon cayenne*
1	*teaspoon garam masala*
4	*cups Vegetable Stock or water*
½	*cup unsweetened coconut milk, optional*
1	*large red or white potato, chopped into 1-inch cubes*
1 to 1½	*cups chopped tomatoes, fresh or canned*
2	*tablespoons tamari*
	Salt to taste
4	*ounces fresh egg noodles*
2	*cups chopped fresh spinach or chard*
	Chopped cilantro, for garnish

Heat the ghee in a soup pot over a moderate flame. Add the onion and garlic, stirring for 3 to 5 minutes, until the onion just begins to brown on the edges. Add the gingerroot, turmeric, cayenne, and garam masala, stirring and cooking for another 30 seconds. Add the vegetable stock, coconut milk, potato, tomato, and tamari, and bring the mixture to a simmer. Cook for 30 minutes, or until the potato is just tender when tested with a small knife. Taste the broth for seasoning, adding salt as needed. (The soup may be made ahead of time and refrigerated at this point. Bring the refrigerate soup back to the simmer before proceeding.)

Add the noodles, cooking for 2 minutes or so until they are just done. Add the spinach and stir once, then take the soup off of the heat.

Ladle the soup into deep bowls, garnishing with cilantro. Serve immediately.

> An errand boy
> with a bottle
> buying village wine,
> Back home,
> dressed up, becomes
> the master.

Bean and Barley Stew

SERVES 4

● ●

Another comfort food specialty, this stew is rich, flavorful, and looks for all the world as if you've used beef stock. Even though the alcohol in the wine cooks away, feel free to use alcohol-free wine if you wish—the results are nearly identical.

1	teaspoon olive or canola oil and Pam
2	cups finely diced onion
1½	cups finely diced celery
1	cup peeled and diced carrot
1 to 2	cups sliced mushrooms, optional
1 to 2	small new potatoes, washed and cut into ½ inch cubes, optional
1	teaspoon nutritional yeast or Marmite or Vegemite
3 to 3½	cups Browned Onion Stock or Mushroom Stock
1	cup dry white or red wine
1	bay leaf
1	teaspoon thyme
¼	cup barley
2	cups cooked white beans
	Approximately 1 teaspoon salt or approximately 1 tablespoon tamari, to taste
¼	cup chopped parsley

Place a large pot or Dutch oven over a moderate flame; when it is hot, add the oil and spray with Pam. Put in the onions, tossing once, and allow them to sauté for 5 to 10 minutes until they are soft and may have begun to brown, stirring occasionally. Add the celery, carrot, and optional mushrooms and potatoes, sautéing for another 5 minutes. If using nutritional yeast, sprinkle it in now and sauté for 1 minute; if using Marmite or Vegemite, add it with the liquid. Pour in the stock and wine, bringing the mixture to the simmer. Add the bay leaf, thyme, barley, and beans; simmer for 30 minutes with the lid ajar. Stir the soup several times during the cooking so the beans and barley don't stick to the bottom.

If you like, purée 1 cup of the beans and add to thicken the soup, leaving the other cup of beans whole. Or, if you want a smoother soup, you could purée all the beans.

Serve the soup hot with a sprinkling of fresh parsley on top, accompanied by hot crusty bread.

Ripe heads of barley
bent down by a rain,
narrow my pathway
—Joso

Dahl Soup

SERVES 4

● ●

1	cup toor (toorval) dahl or yellow split peas, washed
4	cups water
½	cup very finely diced onion
1	tablespoon ghee or flavorless oil, such as canola
2	teaspoons whole black mustard seeds
1	clove garlic, minced or put through a press
1	teaspoon cumin seed, whole or ground
10	fresh curry leaves*
½	teaspoon ground or crushed (not whole) fenugreek seeds
½	teaspoon turmeric
1	cup chopped fresh or canned tomatoes
2	fresh green chiles, minced
1	teaspoon sugar
1	teaspoon salt
1¼	cups unsweetened coconut milk (about 1 can)
¼	teaspoon garam masala, optional
	Cilantro, for garnish

Wash the dahl, place it in a soup pot, and add the water. Bring the mixture to a simmer, then reduce the heat to low. Cook for 45 minutes with the lid ajar, stirring occasionally.

After 45 minutes, add ¼ cup of the onion, reserving the other ¼ cup for later. Cook for another 15 minutes.

Place a small saucepan over a moderate flame; tilt the pot to one side so that the edge is directly over the flame; add the ghee and allow it to melt if it is hard. Once the ghee is hot, add the mustard seeds. Turn the heat to medium high and cook until they begin popping; immediately cover and take the pot off the heat until the popping subsides, about 15 seconds. Add the garlic, cumin seed, fresh curry leaves, fenugreek seeds, turmeric, and the remaining ¼ cup onion; return the pot to medium heat for 1 to 2 minutes, cooking the spices and stirring until the onion has just begun to brown. Add the spice mixture, along with the tomatoes, green chiles, sugar, salt, and coconut milk. Bring the mixture to a simmer, and cook for 15 to 20 minutes. Remove the pan from the heat. If desired, add the garam masala just before serving.

Serve immediately, garnished with cilantro.

> A parrot cries,
> "Green tea!"
> Give it to him, but he doesn't
> know what it is.

Santa Fe Corn Chowder

SERVES 4

● ●

There are many corn chowders around, with New England corn chowder probably being the most famous. This one, however, takes a Southwestern turn, but doesn't try to blow the top of your head off with jalapeños. It is mild and simple, utterly delicious in its modesty. If you want to add some spice, go ahead and throw in a few red chiles just before serving.

The name of this chowder stems from the appearance of the soup—it has an earthy, adobe tan color speckled with deep reds, faded yellows, and a few splashes of bright green cilantro. It would feel right at home in Santa Fe.

For you vegans out there, use olive oil instead of butter and use soy cheese instead of regular cheese.

  1   dried ancho chile, roasted and rehydrated
  4   ears fresh sweet corn
  2   tablespoons olive oil or butter
  2   teaspoons cumin seeds
  1   medium onion, cut into 1/4-inch dice
2 to 3   cloves garlic, peeled and minced or put through
         a press
  2   cups mushroom slices
  3   tablespoons flour
1 to 1½   cups soy milk or regular milk
2½ to 3   cups Vegetable Stock or bouillon
         Salt to taste
1 to 2   fresh red chilies, finely minced, optional
         Grated Cheddar and smoked Gouda cheese
         Cilantro leaves

Roast and rehydrate the ancho chile as directed on page 251.

Husk the corn and wash under running water, removing as much corn silk as possible. Strip the corn kernels from the cobs with a knife or a corn kernel removing gadget, and set the kernels aside.

Heat the olive oil in a soup pot over a moderate flame; add the cumin seeds and onion and cook and stir for 3 to 5 minutes, until the onion begins to brown. Add the garlic and mushrooms, stirring and cooking for another 2 minutes. Sprinkle the flour in the pot, coating everything and stirring for 30 seconds. Add the ancho chiles and soaking water, the milk, and vegetable stock. Bring to a simmer, scraping any bits of flour from the bottom and sides of the pan. Add the corn kernels. Keep the mixture just at the simmer for 20 minutes, with the cover ajar.

Taste for seasoning, adding salt as needed. If desired, add the red chiles 5 minutes before serving.

Serve in bowls with a sprinkling of grated cheese and cilantro leaves, accompanied by hot bread.

Variations:
- Add sour cream as needed.
- Remove half of the soup mixture and put into a food processor or blender: blend until smooth and return to the pot.
- Add a small potato, cut into ¼-inch dice while you're cooking the onion.
- For a bit of bright red, add 1 cup chopped fresh tomato just before serving, cooking it long enough to warm but not to become mush.

Harvesting barley—
even corner-stones
drip with sweat.
*—*ISSA

Mushroom Soup with Fresh Cream

SERVES 4

● ●

This unquestionably is not diet food, but who cares? It's rich and delicious, an incredible first course to a formal dinner or perfect for a brunch. As this soup is not served hot but warm, it is a great boon for the cook, since it can be sitting on the stove while you attend to your guests.

1	tablespoon butter or olive oil
1	cup finely diced onion
2	tablespoons all-purpose flour
3	cups mixed sliced mushrooms (shiitake, white, oyster, crimini, or any available mushroom)
2	cups Vegetable Stock or Mushroom Soup Stock (mushroom stock will make the soup darker brown in color)
1	cup milk (regular or soy)
1	teaspoon thyme
1	tablespoon tamari
¼	teaspoon freshly ground nutmeg
	About 1 teaspoon salt
	White pepper to taste
½ to ⅔	cup heavy cream or sour cream
2 to 3	tablespoons finely chopped fresh chervil, or
1	tablespoon finely chopped fresh thyme or tarragon
	Additional chervil sprigs, for garnish
	Sour cream, for garnish, optional

Heat the butter in a soup pan over a moderate flame. Reduce the flame to low and add the onion, sautéing for 2 to 3 minutes, or until soft and nearly cooked. Add the flour, cooking and stirring with the onion for 1 minute. (This will be a bit sticky.) Add the mushroom pieces and turn the heat to medium high; stir constantly, being sure to scrape the bottom of the pan, until the mushrooms have begun to exude juices. Remove the pan from the heat and allow it to cool for 1 to 2 minutes. (This helps release the flour from the bottom of the pan.) Place the mixture in a food processor and blend to a pastelike consistency. Return this paste to the soup pot.

Using a whisk, add the stock and milk by cupfuls, blending well. Bring the mixture to a simmer, continuing to stir and scrape the bottom of the pan with the whisk, until the soup thickens slightly. Continue to stir while the mixture simmers for 1 to 2 minutes. Add the thyme and tamari and continue to simmer for 15 minutes over low heat. Add the nutmeg, salt, and pepper. If the soup seems a trifle salty, don't worry; the cream will sweeten the soup later. The soup may be made ahead of time and refrigerated or set aside, covered, at this point.

When ready to serve, bring the soup to the simmer. Blending with a whisk, add the cream; taste for seasoning. Remove from the heat and add the chervil. Taste again for seasoning.

Ladle into bowls, garnishing each with a chervil sprig, and if desired, a small dollop of sour cream.

The pile of
Fallen leaves
Separates my hermitage
Further and further
From the world of woe.
—RENGETSU

French Onion Soup

SERVES 4

● ●

OK, so this recipe is slightly reminiscent of the Browned Onion Stock recipe. This is by far one of the best completely vegetarian French onion soups I've ever had, and the double duty of browning massive amounts of onions for both the stock and soup is unquestionably worth the effort. I certainly wouldn't put myself through the trouble if the end result didn't warrant the extra work.

> ½   **teaspoon ground cumin**
> 3   **white or yellow onions, peeled**
> 1   **tablespoon olive oil**
> ½   **teaspoon sugar (to help the onions caramelize)**
> 4 to 5   **cups Browned Onion Stock (page 29)**
> ½   **teaspoon thyme**
> 2   **tablespoons brandy or Cognac**
>   **Croûtons**
> ⅓   **cup grated Gruyère or smoked Gruyère**
> 2   **tablespoons freshly grated Parmesan cheese**

Put the ground cumin in a small sauté pan and set over a medium flame; stir and dry-roast the cumin until it emits a roasted smell, has darkened slightly in color, and may have begun smoking a bit. Remove the cumin to a small bowl.

Peel and slice the onions into thin slices (this is easier if you have a mandoline-type slicer and if you have refrigerated the onions before you slice them). Put the olive oil in a large, heavy pot over a moderate flame; when it is hot, add the onions. Toss them in the oil, then cover the pan and cook for 5 to 10 minutes, until they have softened. Remove the cover and sprinkle in the sugar; continue to cook and stir, scraping the bottom occasionally, for 20 to 30 minutes, until the onions are deep brown and have reduced to a fraction of their original bulk. Midway through the browning process, add the roasted cumin. The onions will begin to stick to the bottom, so scrape with a wooden spoon or spatula as necessary. When the onions have completely caramelized, add the stock and thyme; bring the soup to the simmer and cook, partially covered, for 30 minutes. Stir occasionally, scraping along the bottom and sides to remove any remaining browned bits of onion. (You may stop at this point and refrigerate the soup for up to 2 days. To continue, merely bring it back to the simmer.)

Add the brandy and cook for 5 more minutes. Taste for seasoning. Spoon the soup into bowls, add some croûtons, then sprinkle on Gruyère and Parmesan cheeses. Serve immediately with hot French bread and a salad.

Variation:
- If you have four small ovenproof crocks, you may put the soup in the crocks, place a large piece of dried toast on top, then sprinkle the cheese on top of the bread. Broil the hot soup for 3 minutes or so until the cheese has browned.

Each time you show it,
each time
it's new.

Sopa de Calabaza
Pumpkin Soup

SERVES 4

● ●

In contrast to the following recipe, this soup shows a South-of-the-Border
influence. If you have the ingredients on hand, this soup can be whipped up
in less than 30 minutes.

Sopa de calabaza is delightful when the first onset of autumn arrives and
you begin to see fresh pumpkins at the market, carefully placed in every pro-
duce section from October through November. Instead of the giant Halloween
pumpkins, purchase small, 8-inch diameter baking pumpkins—they're sweeter,
fresher, and you won't have nearly as much pumpkin purée left over. An aver-
age 8-inch pumpkin will yield about 3 to 4 cups of purée, enough to make one
recipe of this soup and one recipe of Fresh Pumpkin Pie *on page 222. Try*
serving it with Spiced Corn Bread, *page 232.*

1	*tablespoon olive oil*
½	*cup finely minced onion*
4 to 6	*cloves garlic, minced or put through a garlic press*
2 to 3	*cups strong Vegetable Stock or 2½ cups liquid*
	(such as water, whey, or a combination of
	water and milk), plus 1 or 2 vegetable
	bouillon cubes
1½	*cups fresh pumpkin purée (see page 222)*
1	*cup cooked white beans (navy beans, soy beans,*
	Great Northerns, lima beans, or butter beans)
1	*teaspoon ground cumin seeds*
½ to ¾	*cup diced (¼-inch) roasted red bell (use either*
	your own roasted bell pepper or bottled)
½ to 1	*cup grated Cheddar, mozzarella, or Monterey*
	Jack cheese
1	*cup chopped cilantro*

Heat the olive oil in a large pot over a moderate flame. Add the
onion and garlic and cook for 2 to 3 minutes. Add the vegetable
stock, pumpkin purée, cooked beans, ground cumin, and roasted bell
pepper. Bring the mixture to the simmer and cook for 10 minutes.

Add the grated cheese and ½ cup of the cilantro, stirring well,
and continue to simmer for another 10 minutes.

Once the cheese has melted and is incorporated into the soup, serve the soup garnished with the remaining chopped cilantro.

> Year's end—
> who drinks not,
> gains not.
> —Issa

Pumpkin Soup

● ●

Pumpkin soups are creamy, bright orange affairs that are loaded with vitamin A and beta-carotene. Since pumpkins are mildly sweet, these soups are best delicately spiced, creating a soothing and unusual first course or dinner. One brisk autumn evening, serve this soup with hot, fresh pumpernickel bread and butter on the side.

1	*small, sweet pumpkin or 1 acorn squash (about 2 cups steamed pumpkin)*
1	*tablespoon olive oil or butter*
1	*cup finely minced onion*
1	*tablespoon grated gingerroot*
½ to 1	*teaspoon cinnamon or cumin seed*
¼	*teaspoon freshly grated nutmeg*
3 to 4	*cups Vegetable Stock*
⅛ to ¼	*teaspoon cayenne pepper*
2	*tablespoons tamari*
1	*tablespoon sugar or honey, optional*
½	*cup yogurt or sour cream (regular, light, or nonfat)*
	Salt to taste
3	*tablespoons chopped fresh parsley or sage*

Cut the pumpkin in half and scrape out the seeds and stringy innards. If possible (and some pumpkins can be very stubborn), peel the skin off with a vegetable peeler. If the pumpkin won't peel easily, don't worry.

Using a heavy, strong knife, cut the cleaned pumpkin into ½-inch slices. Place the slices in a vegetable steamer and steam for 20 minutes until tender. To check for doneness, insert a small knife into the flesh of the pumpkin—if the knife enters easily, the pumpkin is done. Pumpkin will change in color from a bright, raw yellow orange to a more subdued, richer orange yellow when cooked. Remove from the steamer. (If you weren't able to peel the pumpkin, wait a little bit for it to cool and then remove the peel with a small knife.)

Place the cooked pumpkin in a food processor and purée until it is fairly smooth. Leave the purée in the processor bowl.

Place a soup pot over a medium flame; when it is hot, add the oil and minced onion, cooking until the onion is soft and tender, about 5 minutes. If necessary, reduce the heat to medium low if the onion seems to be browning. Add the gingerroot, cinnamon, and nutmeg; sauté for 1 minute. Add the onion mixture to the food processor and purée with the pumpkin until smooth. Return the purée to the soup pot.

Add the vegetable stock, cayenne pepper, tamari, and optional sugar; bring the mixture to a simmer, blending everything well. Allow the soup to cook over low heat for 15 minutes.

Just before serving, blend in the yogurt or sour cream and salt to taste. Serve in deep bowls garnished with a lovely sprinkling of fresh herbs.

> Drive off the ox
> from the farmer!
> Snatch the food
> from a hungry man!

Potato Bisque

SERVES 4

● ●

Potato bisque is a delicate, mildly creamy comfort food. It is great served with freshly baked herb bread on the side.

6 to 8	small new potatoes, peeled or unpeeled, washed and cut into ¼-inch cubes
½	sweet potato, peeled and cut into ¼-inch cubes (about 1 cup)
1	tablespoon butter
1	medium yellow or white onion, peeled and chopped into ¼-inch dice
3	stalks celery, cut into ¼-inch dice
3½ to 4	cups Vegetable Stock
4 to 6	dried shiitake mushrooms, stems removed, tops thinly sliced
1	cup milk or soy milk
1 to 2	cups grated sharp Cheddar cheese
¼	cup chopped fresh parsley

Place the chopped potatoes in a steamer and steam until they are soft, about 15 minutes. Set aside.

While the potatoes are steaming, put the sweet potato cubes in a small saucepan; cover with water and bring to a simmer. Cook until the cubes are tender, after 15 minutes. Drain and set aside.

In a soup pot, melt the butter over moderate heat. Add the onion, reduce the flame to low, and gently cook the onion for 5 to 10 minutes, until soft and translucent. Add the celery, new potato cubes, and sweet potato cubes. Add the vegetable stock and bring the mixture to a simmer. Once the soup is simmering, add the sliced dried shiitakes. Partially cover, and simmer for 20 minutes.

Turn off heat and let the soup cool for 5 minutes. Remove half of the soup to a blender or food processor and purée until it is completely smooth. Pour the purée back into the soup pot and return the soup to the simmer. Add the milk and let the soup cook for another 15 minutes.

Taste the soup for seasoning; it should be quite delicate. (If you're using a low-sodium stock or have made your own soup stock, you may need to add salt to taste.) When ready to serve, ladle the soup into bowls and sprinkle the grated Cheddar cheese and parsley on top. Serve immediately.

Shôshô	*From the thicket*
to furu muzu	*To the pot:*
o kumu.	*One bamboo shoot.*
	—SANTÔKA

Chili

SERVES 4

● ●

A complete protein, great either for cold nights or summer days. Serve with fresh corn bread.

> 1   ancho chile, roasted and chopped
> 2   cups Vegetable Stock (page 26), Browned Onion
>   Stock (page 29), or Mushroom Soup Stock
>   (page 28) or water
> 1   tablespoon olive oil
> 1   medium onion, peeled and diced
> 2   cloves garlic, minced or put through a press
> 1   cup diced mushrooms
> ½ to ¾   cup each chopped green and red bell peppers

1½	cups cooked beans (black, pinto, or kidney)
1	18-ounce can chopped tomatoes, including juice
½	cup red or white wine
1	tablespoon Worcestershire sauce
½	cup raw bulgur wheat or cooked brown rice
2	teaspoons cumin, whole or ground seeds
¼ to 1	teaspoon cayenne
1	tablespoon ground coriander
2	teaspoons chili powder
½	teaspoon oregano
¼	teaspoon curry powder
1	teaspoon Marmite or Vegemite
1 to 3	tablespoons sugar, to taste, optional
	Salt or tamari
	Chopped cilantro, for garnish
	Sour cream (regular or light), for garnish
	Grated Cheddar or Monterey Jack cheese, optional, for garnish

Roast the ancho chile over an open flame until it is hot and slightly charred. Remove the stem, discard the seeds inside, and chop the roasted chile into small pieces. Place the chopped chile in a small bowl and add ⅓ cup of the vegetable stock. Let stand for 15 minutes to rehydrate.

In a large pot, heat the olive oil over a medium flame. Add the onion and garlic and cook for 5 minutes or so, until the onion is soft. Add the mushrooms and bell peppers and sauté, stirring occasionally, for 3 minutes. Raise the heat to medium high and lightly brown the vegetables. Reduce the flame to medium low and add the rehydrated ancho chile (this will splatter—be careful!) and remaining vegetable stock. Add the remaining ingredients except the garnishes and bring the chili to the simmering point. Reduce the flame to very low and let the mixture simmer for 30 to 40 minutes, then taste for seasoning, adding salt or tamari as needed. (You may stop at this point, and cover and refrigerate or even freeze the chili.)

When ready to serve, return the chili to the pot and reheat gently. Serve hot with chopped fresh cilantro and a dollop of sour cream. If desired, sprinkle some grated cheese on top as well.

Coals under ashes—
just now starting to boil,
the stuff in the pot.
—BUSON

PASTA

• •

TYPES OF PASTA

One would think that pasta is pasta is pasta; 99 percent of it is made from durum wheat, and subsequently all unembellished pastas should taste the same. Taste notwithstanding, the dozens of shapes and textures of pasta are part of what is appealing about it; it is ever changing, ever new, and always welcome.

angel hair pasta - see cappellini

bow-tie - see farfalle

cannelloni - very large, round tubes, usually about 4-inches long and 1- to 1½-inches in diameter; perfect for stuffing. Sometimes cannelloni are blunt-cut on the end, sometimes they are cut on an angle, much like the negligible difference between penne and ziti. Deep-fried cannelloni are frequently seen in bakeries stuffed with whipped cream and dusted with cocoa.

cappelleti - the name refers to a peaked hat resembling a bishop's mitre. This stuffed pasta begins its existence as a square piece of pasta which is stuffed and folded, with the result being a small, roundish "hat." See also tortellini.

cappellini - very, very thin spaghetti, commonly referred to as "angel hair pasta."

farfalle (also **bow-tie pasta** or **butterfly pasta**) - 2-inch wide pieces of pasta, usually cut with a jagged edge, that are crimped in the center to resemble bow-ties. The butterfly pasta is exactly the same as the bow-tie except that it has rounded edges.

fettuccine - about ⅛- to ¼-inch wide, flat, long noodles.

fusilli - small, 2-inch long spiral pasta, more delicate than rotini. A personal favorite of mine since it cooks fairly quickly while maintaining its shape and texture.

linguine - one of my favorites. Very thin, slightly flattened noodles. Somewhat like spaghettini that has been run over by a steam roller.

macaroni (elbow pasta) - small, curved, circular pasta. No discussion is needed on this omnipresent pasta.

orzo - small, grainlike pasta shapes. Orzo is perfect as a side dish when you would ordinarily use rice. It cooks in a different manner, however, so some practice is called for if you're unfamiliar with it.

penne (and penne rigate) - penne is exactly the same as ziti except it is cut on an angle, with the pasta having pointed ends (like the tip of a fountain pen). Penne rigate has a ribbed, textured exterior.

ravioli - stuffed pasta pillows, about 2 inches across, stuffed with anything from meat to cheeses to spinach.

risi - small pasta shapes that look much like rice, hence the name. Risi is a miniature version of orzo.

rotini - spiral pasta, larger than fusilli. I find rotini gets mushy by the time it is done in the center and thus prefer fusilli.

spaghetti - round, long noodles.

spaghettini - round, long, thin noodles. A bit more textureed than spaghetti.

tagliatelle - extra-wide fettuccine, anywhere from ½- to ¾-inch in width.

tortellini - exactly the same thing as cappelleti except the stuffed pasta is originally formed with a circle, rather than a square. The result is a roundish, folded pasta.

tortelloni - miniature ravioli.

ziti - macaroni ¼-inch diameter by 2 inches long.

HOW TO COOK PASTA PROPERLY

Pasta, as we all know, can be mushy and soft. Overcooked pasta is nasty. Pasta should have a lovely firm texture, not unlike rice, and it should have body and firmness. I keep coming back to that word *firm* because it is the key to understanding the term al dente. The best way to learn how to cook pasta properly is to cook it; you will learn by your mistakes, both by undercooking and overcooking. While you're standing over the boiling pot of pasta, you will occasionally stir the bubbling mass and pick out a piece and taste it, testing it against your teeth to see whether it is done. Underdone pasta is perfectly simple to detect; it is hard and inflexible. It is the next phase that is most important, that of judging exactly when the pasta is *nearly* done, but not quite. All foods continue to cook after they have been removed from the heat source, and pasta is no exception. You must remove the pasta from the boiling water just 30 seconds *before* you think it is done, since it will cook a bit more while you are draining and plating it.

Be sure to experiment with different kinds of pastas and shapes. My personal favorites are: linguine, fusilli, cappellini, and penne rigate. Bowtie pasta, while festive and entertaining to look at, is frustrating because by the time the crimped inner portion is done the outer "wing" is overdone. I'm not crazy about spaghetti or spaghettini, since they are completely round noodles; by the time the innermost section of the pasta is cooked the outermost part is gummy.

Store-bought dried pasta should be made with 100 percent durum wheat, water, and maybe salt. That's it. Unless, of course, you're having spinach pasta or herbed pasta.

Many Italian cookbooks have recipes for egg noodles using regular all-purpose flour and eggs, but since this topic has been covered extensively, I will refrain from adding yet another egg noodle recipe to this already overburdened canon.

WHAT ABOUT STORE-BOUGHT FRESH PASTA?

There are two kinds of store-bought fresh pasta: edible and inedible.

The edible kind: this fresh pasta is made daily on the premises in an Italian market. They don't make more than they can sell in a day's time, and there will be a huge pasta machine somewhere within view. If you can watch them make it and buy it seconds later, so much the better.

The inedible kind: the packaged pasta you'll find wrapped and sealed in plastic containers in the supermarket's refrigerated section. This pasta is designed to have a lengthy shelf life and is quite dreadful. Commercially made, prepackaged, "fresh" pasta is like a sponge—whatever sauce you put on it is absorbed instantly. So if you've labored lovingly over a delicious pasta sauce, once it touches this pasta you'll be left with a dry, underseasoned, bland meal that no amount of doctoring will save. I think regular old dried pasta is a thousand times better than this impostor.

ONE TECHNIQUE FOR LOWERING THE FAT IN PASTA

Some pasta recipes call for enormous amounts of fat, particularly if you're tossing cooked pasta in a flavored oil. One easy way to cut some of the fat is to utilize the hot stockpot in which you've just cooked the pasta.

To wit, after you've cooked and drained the pasta, place a small amount of oil in the hot pot and add a bit of water. Turn on the heat again and the water will begin to boil and separate this oil into thousands (if not millions) of tiny oil particles. If you toss the cooked pasta in this, you'll coat it sufficiently with the thousands of oil particles to get a wonderful taste without its being fat-laden and heavy.

HOW TO MAKE YOUR OWN FRESH PASTA

Pasta isn't a difficult thing to make, but it does take several steps.

The following recipe is for a hand-crank pasta maker, found easily in gourmet or Italian markets. These machines usually have one smooth side for rolling the dough into a uniform thickness and another side fitted with "blades" to cut the pasta into (most frequently) linguine or fettuccine.

And if you've never cooked fresh pasta before, please note that the cooking time is drastically reduced; fresh linguine or fettuccine will cook in less than 3 minutes after it has been added to the vigorously boiling water, whereas fresh ravioli will be done in less than 5 minutes.

Plain Semolina Pasta

This type of pasta is akin to what you'd find dried in every supermarket. If you look at the ingredients of most Italian-made pastas, they are either exactly what you see below, or even simpler, such as: semolina flour, water.

> 2   *cups semolina flour*
> 2   *teaspoons salt*
> ⅔   *cup warm water*
> 2   *tablespoons extra virgin olive oil*
>   *All-purpose flour for dusting*

Place the semolina and salt in a food processor fitted with a plastic S hook (as opposed to the metal S blade). Mix the warm water and olive oil in a measuring cup. Turn on the processor and gradually pour in the water and oil mixture through the chute in the lid. Run the processor for 10 seconds or so, then check the dough, flipping it in the bowl if the dough is wet on top but still completely dry on the bottom. Avoid adding extra water at this point, as the semolina hasn't quite absorbed all the liquid you've added yet. Continue processing for another 20 to 30 seconds, until the dough forms a ball. Remove the dough and wrap it in plastic wrap or waxed paper. Allow to rest for 10 minutes before proceeding. Note: Depending on the weather conditions and dryness of the semolina, it may be necessary to add a small amount of water if the dough is quite dry and crumbly; usually after the dough has rested and absorbed the liquid it will hold together once kneaded through the pasta machine a few times. However, on rare occasions, a small amount of additional liquid may be required. The dough should hold together as a ball, but not be sticky or wet. If you squeeze a little of it between your fingers it will look a bit dry and sandy, but will hold together.

Set up a hand-crank pasta machine by clamping it to the side of a counter or table top. Put the crank into the flat rolling section of the machine, with the opening set at the widest setting (usually a 1 out of 6). Have some all-purpose flour handy on a flat surface for dusting the dough.

Once the dough has rested, cut it into 4 equal pieces. Keep the remaining quarters wrapped while you work with the first quarter. Note: Lightly dust the dough with all-purpose flour anytime it seems necessary during the rolling/kneading process. Once you've made a few lengths of pasta, it will become apparent how much flour you'll need.

Knead the dough for 30 seconds with your hands. Flatten it out slightly and dust it lightly with flour. Insert one end of the dough into the pasta machine (between the smooth rollers) and crank it through the widest opening. When it comes out the bottom it will be a rough, ragged flat strip. Fold the dough over in thirds (as you would fold puff pastry), lightly dust with flour again, then roll it through the machine at the same setting. The first few times the dough is put through the rollers it will still be grainy, rough, and ragged; as you force it through again and again it will become smooth and soft. (This initial rolling takes the place of kneading the dough entirely by hand.) Continue in this manner until you have folded and rolled the dough through the machine 10 times. By the tenth time the dough should be smooth and gently elastic. (This will take about 2 to 3 minutes tops.)

Set the rollers up one notch (from a 1 to a 2). Fold the dough into thirds again and roll it through the machine once. Set the machine to 3. Lightly dust the dough and again fold it into thirds, rolling it once through the machine. Set the machine to 4. Continue as before. When you get to 5, fold the dough *in half* and roll it through the machine. If there are any breaks, holes, or ragged stretch marks in the dough, fold it in half and roll it through the same setting until you have a smooth, unbroken length of pasta about 4 to 5 inches wide and 18 to 24 inches in length. Note: You can stop at number 5 if you want a thicker pasta, or continue to number 6, the thinnest setting.

Lightly flour the strip of dough, set it aside, and let it rest as you repeat the procedure with the next quarter of pasta dough. Once the second quarter has been rolled to the same thickness as the first, you can use the first length as follows:

For Lasagne Noodles: Roll out *all* of the dough and place on a flat surface to air-dry for 30 to 60 minutes before cutting into appropriate lengths for your lasagne pan. Lightly boil the pasta, for 1 minute, before using.

For Fettuccine or Linguine: After you have rolled out the second quarter of dough and are letting it dry, you can cut the first length by inserting it in one of the cutting slots of the pasta machine and cranking it through. Be sure to catch the noodles as they leave the other side of the machine, as you will want to hang these noodles on a rod to let them air-dry while you continue rolling the third and fourth quarters of dough. (Or you could lay the separated noodles flat on large sheets of waxed paper.)

For Ravioli: Place the first length of dough over a floured ravioli plaque (available at a gourmet or Italian market). Lightly press down the dough to fill the receptacles of the mold. Fill the sections of ravioli with a filling of your choice, being careful not to overfill them. Moisten the dough by lightly spraying it with a hand-held atomizer filled with water. Lay the second length of dough on top of the first, making sure you have sealed all edges. Dust the top layer of dough with flour and roll over the mold with a rolling pin to seal each ravioli. Cut off any excess dough (which can be rerolled for more ravioli or used for other pastas) and rap the mold against a hard surface to release the ravioli. Place the ravioli on waxed paper, being careful that they are all lightly dusted with flour and aren't sticking together.

Continue rolling the dough as above until it is used up. Cut or use the dough as desired, after it has air-dried somewhat to keep it from sticking together.

Variations:
- For herb pasta: add 2 tablespoons dried herbs (such as basil, oregano, or herbes de Provence) to the semolina flour.
- For tomato pasta: add ⅓ cup tomato paste to the semolina, reducing the water from ⅔ cup to ½ cup.
- For garlic pasta: add ⅓ cup Roasted Garlic purée (see page 210) to the semolina, reducing the water from ⅔ cup to ½ cup.
- For lemon pasta: add ¼ cup finely grated lemon zest to the semolina flour.
- For orange pasta: add 2 tablespoons finely grated orange rind to the semolina flour.

Spinach Pasta

½	cup chopped frozen spinach, thawed, or
½	cup blanched, chopped fresh spinach
1¾	cups semolina flour
2	teaspoons salt
½	cup warm water
2	tablespoons extra virgin olive oil
	All-purpose flour for dusting

Squeeze out as much liquid as possible from the spinach and place it in a food processor bowl fitted with the metal S blade. Process the spinach a bit, pushing it down with a spatula as needed, until it is almost puréed. Add the semolina flour and salt; blend the mixture briefly.

Combine the water and oil; add to the spinach flour while the processor is on; when the dough forms a ball in the bowl, stop the processor (after about 1 minute). Turn the dough out onto a lightly floured board and knead it slightly, then wrap it in plastic wrap or waxed paper.

Roll and cut the dough exactly as you would Plain Semolina Pasta.

Basic Pasta

● ●

*This is about as basic as it gets while still tasting great. There's nothing diffi-
cult here, but as soon as the pasta is cooked, speed is vital, as the final preparation happens in less than one minute.*

2 to 3	large cloves garlic, peeled and minced or put through a press
¼	cup extra virgin olive oil
2	tablespoons finely chopped fresh rosemary, optional
12 to 16	ounces dried pasta
¼	cup water
¾ to 1	cup freshly grated Parmesan cheese
	Freshly cracked black pepper
	Salt to taste

Place the minced garlic in a small bowl. Add the olive oil and the
rosemary (if you like), mixing briefly. Set aside.

Bring a large stockpot of salted water to a boil; add the dried pasta
and cook until just al dente. Drain in a colander or a large sieve.
Immediately return the hot stockpot to a medium flame and add
the garlic mixture; sauté for 30 seconds until the garlic has cooked
and may have toasted lightly. Add the water; it will sputter and
splatter, possibly making a mess. Turn off the heat and immediately add the drained, cooked pasta, tossing it in the garlic mixture. When the pasta has been coated with the garlic oil, place
equal portions on heated plates and garnish with Parmesan cheese
and black pepper. Serve immediately.

Variations:
- Eliminate the fresh rosemary and toss the cooked pasta
  with 1 cup (or more) of freshly chopped basil.
- Use some melted butter along with the olive oil.
- Use an assortment of cheeses, such as ¼ cup Parmesan
  cheese, ¼ cup grated smoked Gruyère, and ¼ cup Bel Paese
  or Derby sage.
- Use fresh, homemade pasta.

Incredible Cream Sauce for Pasta

There's nothing low-fat about this dish, which is probably why it's absolutely delicious.

THE BASIC CREAM SAUCE:

3	tablespoons butter or olive oil
½ to 1	teaspoon fennel seeds
½	teaspoon red pepper flakes, optional
2 to 4	large cloves garlic, peeled and minced or put through a press
1	pint heavy cream
½	cup sour cream, optional
¼	teaspoon freshly grated nutmeg
¾ to 1	teaspoon salt, or, to taste
¼ to ½	teaspoon freshly ground black or white pepper
½	cup highest quality Parmesan or Romano cheese

OPTIONAL SEASONINGS:

1	teaspoon dried basil, or 2 tablespoons chopped fresh basil
1	tablespoon chopped parsley
½	teaspoon dried oregano, or 1 tablespoon chopped fresh oregano
½	teaspoon herbes de Provence
¼	cup chopped fresh tomatoes, added at the end
¼	cup pitted, chopped Kalamata olives
¼	cup toasted chopped walnuts

GARNISHES:

Additional Parmesan and/or Romano cheeses
Chopped parsley and/or fresh basil
Chopped black olives
Freshly ground black pepper

Place a heavy saucepan over moderate heat. Add the butter; once it is hot, add the fennel seeds, the optional red pepper flakes, and the garlic. Sauté until the garlic has cooked but has not browned, about 1 minute. Add the heavy cream, the sour cream if you wish, the nutmeg, salt, and pepper, and bring to just under the simmering point. Lower the heat to low. Cook the sauce for 10 to 15 minutes or so.

Place the pan over the lowest possible heat and add the cheese. Do not let the sauce simmer or boil; keep it at a constant low and even heat so that the cheese will melt but not stick to the bottom. (It may be necessary to use a Flame Tamer or heat-diffuser to achieve this very low heat.) Stir the sauce often until the cheese is incorporated and the sauce is noticeably thicker—this may take up to 30 to 60 minutes, depending on the heat. Taste for seasoning. You can prepare the sauce up to this point a day ahead, and return it to just under the simmer before continuing.

When you're ready to eat, cook the pasta and keep the sauce warm. Add some of the optional herbs (but not all those listed) to the sauce. Add tomatoes, olives, or walnuts of you wish, cooking the sauce just long enough to heat through. Spoon over hot, al dente pasta. Garnish and serve immediately.

> *Early-wheat harvest time—*
> *what is it that has frightened*
> *the chicken on the roof?*
> —BUSON

Bonnie's Quick-5 Pasta

SERVES 4

● ●

The title of this recipe sounds like a lottery. My dear friend Bonnie Leslie once said to me, "I wish you'd write some quick pasta recipes. You know, something that's pretty basic but you change depending on whatever you've got on hand." Here you go, Bonnie!

This recipe is one basic idea with variations. The first part remains the same for all the variations.

BASIC PREPARATION:

2	tablespoons extra virgin olive oil
2 to 3	cloves garlic, peeled and minced or put through a press
1	pound dried linguine, penne rigate, or fusilli

Place the olive oil in a small bowl and add the garlic. Prepare the sauce ingredients as directed for the variation you select. Once that is done, return to this point.

Bring a large pot of lightly salted water to a boil; add the pasta. Cook until it is al dente, then drain it in a colander.

Return the large pot (now empty) to a medium flame and add the garlic and olive oil; sauté for 20 to 30 seconds, or until the garlic is tender and may have begun to lightly brown. Turn off the flame and immediately add ¼ cup water (keeping your face averted) and the drained pasta. Using one or two large forks, toss the pasta evenly to coat with the garlic oil. Continue with whichever preparation you have chosen.

THE PASTA SAUCES

Pasta Mediterráneo

This is a raw tomato sauce that should be made with deliciously ripe tomatoes. A nice break from the traditional cooked tomato sauce.

3	cups fresh, ripe, raw, peeled, seeded, and chopped tomatoes
2	tablespoons chopped fresh rosemary
½	cup chopped Italian parsley
¼	cup pitted and roughly chopped Kalamata olives
¼	cup chopped, lightly toasted walnuts
2	cloves garlic, peeled and minced (either raw or lightly sautéed), optional
½ to 1	cup freshly grated Parmesan cheese
	Salt or tamari to taste

Mix the first five (or six) ingredients in a large bowl. Cook the pasta as directed, then toss with the sauce. Sprinkle with Parmesan cheese as desired, and season to taste.

No-Cream Pasta Primavera

1 to 2	tablespoons olive oil
1	cup sliced onion
2	cups ¼-inch pieces of mushrooms
1	red bell pepper, sliced into thin strips
1	zucchini, sliced into thin rounds
2	carrots, cut into thin (⅛-inch x 2-inch) strips
1½	cups broccoli florets

1   *cup thawed frozen peas*
¼   *cup white wine or dry vermouth*
⅔   *cup grated smoked Gruyère or smoked Gouda*
       cheese
    Chopped fresh basil or parsley

Heat the olive oil in a large sauté pan over a moderate flame. Add the onion and cook, stirring often, until it just begins to brown, about 8 to 10 minutes. Add the mushrooms and turn the flame to medium high; the mushrooms will begin to exude juice, then they too will begin to brown. Continue tossing and stirring. Once the onions and mushrooms have brown edges, add the bell pepper, zucchini, carrots, broccoli, peas, and wine; stir the vegetables for 60 seconds until they are barely cooked. Turn off the flame.

Cook the pasta as directed, then toss with the sauce. Sprinkle with cheese as desired, garnishing with chopped fresh basil or parsley.

Pasta au Courante

3   *green onions, sliced into 2-inch lengths*
1   *red bell pepper, sliced into thin 2-inch pieces*
1   *small zucchini, sliced into thin half-moons*
2   *cups mushroom slices*
1 to 2 *tablespoons olive oil*
¼   *cup port or Madeira*
1   *cup shredded radicchio*
¼   *cup chopped pepperoncini (pickled Italian pepper)*
½   *cup chopped Italian parsley*
½   *cup chopped fresh basil*
        Grated Parmesan cheese, to taste
        Salt and freshly grated black pepper, to taste

Sauté the green onions, bell pepper, zucchini, and mushrooms in the olive oil over a moderate flame for 2 to 3 minutes, until everything begins to cook through. Add the port and continue to cook for another minute. Turn off the flame, cover, and keep warm.

Cook the pasta as directed. Add the sautéed vegetables. Add the radicchio, pepperoncini, parsley, and basil to the garlic-coated pasta, then toss everything well. Sprinkle with the Parmesan cheese as desired, and add salt and black pepper.

Pasta Russo

4   green onions, chopped into 2-inch lengths
    Pam
2   cups broccoli florets or chopped rapini (broccoli rabe)
¼   cup white wine or dry vermouth
½ to ⅔   cup sour cream
½ to ⅔   cup cream, half-and-half, or milk
½ to 1   teaspoon thyme or basil
    Salt and pepper to taste
1   large ripe tomato, peeled and seeded, and cut into
       ¼-inch dice
¼   cup chopped fresh parsley
½   cup grated Parmesan cheese and/or Derby sage

Heat a large sauté pan over a moderate flame and spray it with Pam. Add the green onions, stir-frying for 2 minutes until they are limp and cooked. Add the broccoli and wine, and cook for 2 to 4 minutes until the broccoli is tender and most of the wine has cooked away. Add the sour cream, cream, and herb, and bring the mixture to a simmer. Add salt and pepper as desired. Add the chopped tomato, cover, and turn off the heat, keeping the mixture warm.

Cook the pasta as directed, and divide it among four warm plates. Spoon the sauce evenly over the pasta servings. Sprinkle with parsley and the Parmesan or Derby sage cheese as desired.

Thai-time Pasta

1   tablespoon finely grated gingerroot
¼   cup fresh lime juice
⅔ to ¾   cup unsweetened coconut milk
2   tablespoons sugar
1 to 3   teaspoons red pepper flakes, depending on how
       much heat you like
4   green onions, sliced into 2-inch lengths
1   green or red bell pepper, sliced into thin strips
2   cups bean sprouts
1   tablespoon flavorless oil, such as canola
1   cup pea pods (snow peas)
2 to 3   tablespoons tamari, or to taste
½   cup chopped cilantro and/or mint
¼   cup dry roasted peanuts

Mix the gingerroot, lime juice, coconut milk, and sugar in a small bowl and set aside.

Cook the pasta as directed and toss with the garlic oil. Set aside.

In a large skillet, stir-fry the pepper flakes, green onions, bell pepper, bean sprouts, and pea pods in 1 tablespoon oil over a medium high flame until everything is nearly done, about 3 minutes. Add the gingerroot mixture, and bring everything to a boil; taste for seasoning, adding tamari as needed. Add the cooked garlic pasta, tossing well.

Serve in four warm bowls with a garnish of chopped cilantro or mint and chopped peanuts.

Living in a valley, you have nowhere to go but up.
Living on the mountaintop, you have nowhere to go but down.
Living midway up the mountain, you can appreciate both
the summit and the valley.

Pesto

ABOUT 1⅓ CUPS

● ●

Pesto is one of the most popular and enduring of summer sauces. It cannot be made without lots of fresh basil, an item that makes it prohibitively expensive during cold months, unless, of course, you freeze your own homemade sauce to enjoy year around.

I love pesto except when the cook gets carried away with the garlic; raw garlic is a potent and powerful seasoning, and in my opinion, a little goes a long way. However, many people adore raw garlic, and I have adjusted the quantity accordingly—use the lesser amount if you're not a huge garlic fan, the larger amount if you are. Additionally, you can include a cup of fresh parsley in the pesto in an attempt to help mask the garlic; parsley is a deodorant of sorts, so its inclusion may help reduce "garlic breath."

Pesto can be frozen by placing it in a tightly sealed container, and you can, if desired, pour a thin layer of olive oil on top. Refrigerated or frozen pesto will discolor slightly, turning from bright green to a dull green, but it will still taste wonderfully pungent. It is best to thaw frozen pesto in the refrigerator overnight, but many times I've just taken a knife and whacked off a chunk for a pesto cream sauce without any noticeable harm.

> 4   cups tightly packed fresh basil leaves
> 1   cup fresh parsley leaves, optional
> 1 to 4   cloves garlic, peeled
> ⅓   cup extra virgin olive oil
> ¼   cup lightly toasted pignoli (pine nuts), or
>   toasted, chopped walnuts
> ½ to ⅔   cup grated Parmesan cheese
>   Freshly ground black pepper
>   A few scrapings of nutmeg
>
> Pasta: linguine, fusilli, bow-ties, fettuccine
> (fresh homemade pasta strongly recommended)

Place the washed and stemmed basil in a food processor. (If you're adding parsley, add it now as well.) Process a few times in short spurts. Add the garlic, olive oil, and pignoli; process the mixture until smooth, scraping down the pesto from the sides of the bowl with a spatula as necessary. Add the Parmesan cheese, pepper, and nutmeg; process for 15 seconds to mix thoroughly. (The pesto may be made ahead of time and refrigerated, tightly covered, until needed.)

Bring a large pot of salted water to the boil; add the pasta and cook until it is just al dente. Drain and shake off any excess water. Place the hot pasta in a large bowl and add pesto to taste, tossing well. (Sample amount: ½ pound pasta to ½ cup pesto. Pesto is pungent, so it is best not to get carried away with adding too much—otherwise you'll probably overdose on it in one sitting.) Serve immediately.

Variations:
- Toss 2 to 5 tablespoons of softened, unsalted butter with the hot, cooked pasta and pesto.
- For those who cannot abide raw garlic, sauté it in some of the olive oil until just tender. Cool and use as above.

Laying down chopsticks—
enough.
I'm grateful.
—SANTŌKA

Pesto Cream Sauce

SERVES 4

● ●

I find that pesto by itself can sometimes be overpowering, but a pesto cream sauce isn't. It couldn't be easier to make (especially if you have some fresh or frozen pesto on hand) and is quick and delicious—but not terribly low in fat.

½ to ⅔   **cup Pesto**
1½   **cups heavy cream**
       Salt to taste
       Fresh parsley, for garnish
       Freshly ground black pepper
       Parmesan cheese, grated, for garnish
1   **pound fresh or dried pasta**

Place the pesto and cream in a saucepan and bring just to the simmer; taste for seasoning, adding salt as needed.

Bring a large pot of salted water to the boil; add the pasta and cook until it is just al dente. Drain and shake off any excess water.

Place the pasta on warm plates and spoon the sauce on top. Garnish with fresh parsley. Serve immediately with freshly ground black pepper and additional Parmesan cheese, as desired.

Variations:

- For a bit more color, you could peel, seed, and dice a ripe tomato, adding it to the sauce just before serving, or use it as garnish.
- Reduce the heavy cream to 1 cup and add ½ cup sour cream to the sauce.

> *Brow to cliff,*
> *he drinks*
> *clear water.*
> —Toyojo

Skippy Noodles

SERVES 4

● ●

This side dish is derived from a Chinese restaurant in Minneapolis, Minnesota, that served a special noodle recipe with peanut butter: hence, "Skippy Noodles"—I couldn't think of a better name, so even though this isn't their recipe, I have requisitioned the title.

These noodles are great hot or cold; if served cold, be sure you thin out the sauce more than usual before tossing with the cooked noodles, keeping in mind that the pasta will absorb some of the liquid.

1 to 2   *teaspoons flavorless oil, such as canola*
    3   *cloves garlic, peeled and minced, or put through*
        a press
1 to 2   *tablespoons minced gingerroot*
    ½   *teaspoon red pepper flakes, or more*
        depending on how much spiciness
        you like
    ¼   *cup tamari*
    ¼   *cup red wine vinegar*
    2   *teaspoons sugar*
   1¼   *cup chunky peanut butter or toasted sesame*
        butter
½ to ¾ *cup water*
    ½   *teaspoon toasted sesame oil*
8 to 10 *ounces soba noodles (buckwheat noodles)*
        or regular pasta noodles
    ¼   *cup chopped cilantro*

Place a sauté pan over medium heat; add the oil, garlic, gingerroot, and red pepper flakes, and cook for 1 minute or so, until the garlic has begun to toast slightly. Add the tamari, vinegar, and sugar (be sure to avert your face when adding the liquids as they will sputter and sizzle); bring the mixture to the boil, scraping the garlic and ginger off the bottom of the pan. Reduce the heat to low and add the peanut butter and water (start with the smaller quantity of water), stirring until the peanut butter has blended with the liquid and has formed a thick sauce. Add the sesame oil and taste for seasoning; it should be rather potent. Remove the sauce from the heat and keep it warm.

For soba noodles: Bring a large stockpot of water to the boil; add the noodles. As soon as the water returns to the boil, add 1 cup of ice water. Stir the noodles, and once again, allow the water to return to the boil. Add another cup of ice water. By the time the water boils for the third time, the soba noodles should be done. (Soba noodles are firmer than regular pasta; don't judge their doneness by appearance, take a strand and eat a bit of it to be sure it's tender.)

For regular pasta noodles, cook as usual until al dente.

When the noodles are done, drain them in a colander and shake off any excess water.

Place the noodles in a large bowl and pour the warmed peanut mixture on top, tossing well. If for some reason the noodles seem a bit dry, add ¼ cup of hot water to smooth out the sauce. Sprinkle chopped cilantro on top, toss briefly, and serve.

Cat dozing on the stove—
is there one thing
he doesn't know?
                    —FUSEI

Spinach-stuffed Ravioli

MAKES ABOUT 36 RAVIOLI

• •

When you're in the mood for something truly special, make these elegant ravioli. They're more labor-intensive than plain pasta, but the result is worth it. Pillows of handmade pasta filled with a fragrant mixture of spinach, lemon, and cheese, tossed in garlic butter. Who could ask for anything more?

I've specified frozen spinach for the filling, but you could just as easily blanch and chop fresh spinach—but then you'd be adding yet another step to a rather step-laden recipe. And in all honesty, since the spinach is coupled with garlic and cheeses, the difference between using frozen and fresh spinach would be negligible once the ravioli are cooked and served.

1	*10-ounce package frozen chopped spinach, thawed*
1	*egg*
½	*cup ricotta cheese*
1 to 1½	*teaspoons freshly grated lemon zest*
¼	*teaspoon freshly grated nutmeg*
1	*teaspoon dried basil*
	Salt and pepper
¾	*cup grated Parmesan or a mixture of Parmesan and Romano cheeses*
1	*recipe Plain Semolina Pasta (see page 53)*
	Flour for dusting
3	*tablespoons butter*
2	*tablespoons olive oil*
3 to 4	*cloves garlic, peeled and minced or put through a press*
1	*teaspoon freshly grated lemon rind, optional*
½ to ¾	*cup shredded Parmesan cheese*

Squeeze out as much liquid as possible from the thawed spinach and set aside. If you've bought frozen leaf spinach, chop it into ½-inch pieces.

Place the egg and ricotta in a medium bowl. Using a whisk, blend until completely smooth and creamy. Add the lemon zest, nutmeg, basil, a dash of salt, and about ¼ teaspoon freshly ground black pepper, mixing well. Add the spinach and cheese, blending well. Refrigerate the mixture.

Make the pasta according to the directions.

To fill the ravioli: Place the first length of dough over a heavily floured ravioli plaque (available at a gourmet or Italian market). Lightly press down the dough to fill the recesses of the mold. Fill each of these ravioli recesses with about 1½ teaspoons of the spinach mixture, being careful not to overfill them. Moisten the dough surrounding the spinach by lightly spraying it with a hand-held atomizer filled with water, or by gently dabbing the edges of the dough with moistened fingertips, or with a wet pastry brush. Lay the second length of dough on top of the first, and seal all edges with your fingertips. Dust the top layer of dough with flour and roll a rolling pin over the mold, sealing, sectioning off, and cutting each ravioli. (Sometimes the cutting edges on the ravioli plaque don't quite cut through—in this case, turn the plaque over and cut the ravioli into squares.) Remove any excess dough (which can be rerolled for more ravioli or used for other pasta) and rap the mold against a hard surface to release the ravioli from the plaque. Place the ravioli on floured waxed paper, being careful that they are all lightly dusted with flour and are separate. Put the completed, uncovered ravioli in the refrigerator until ready for use. Continue until you've used up all the dough and/or spinach. You'll have about 36 to 40 ravioli. The ravioli can be made ahead of time and kept refrigerated for 2 days, or frozen for several weeks.

Bring to a boil a large pot of lightly salted water. Meanwhile, melt the butter in a small saucepan with the olive oil and garlic. Reduce the flame to low and allow the garlic to cook for 3 minutes or so, until it is tender but has not begun to brown. Add the optional lemon zest. Remove the pan from the heat but keep warm.

As soon as the water has come to a vigorous boil, gently add the ravioli. Fresh ravioli will take less than 5 minutes to cook. As soon as the pasta is added, the water will stop boiling; once it returns to the boil, reduce the flame somewhat and continue to cook the ravioli until the pasta has lost its raw look. Cooked ravioli (usually) float to the surface of the water. Remove one and taste for doneness if necessary. As soon as they are done, drain them in a colander.

(Although you want to be careful not to overcook the pasta, you need to heat it through thoroughly, so "sacrificing" one for testing purposes is a good idea until you are an old hand at ravioli cooking. Besides, it gives you a sneak peek at what's to come!)

Place the warm garlic butter in a large bowl. Add the drained, cooked ravioli and toss gently with a spatula. Add the shredded Parmesan cheese, briefly tossing again. Serve the ravioli immediately on warmed plates, topping with additional freshly ground black pepper as desired.

> *Kore ga saigo*   *Eating this,*
> *no Nihon go gohan*   *The last Japanese meal,*
> *o tabete iru ase.*   *They sweat.*
> —SANTŌKA

Viva Italia Orzo

SERVES 4 AS A SIDE DISH

• •

The name for this dish comes from the colors of the Italian flag—red, green, and white. This is an attractive, interesting side dish or a lovely first course.

½   **pound green beans (preferably small, delicate beans, not big, woody pods)**
2   **cups diced (¼- to ½-inch) white mushrooms**
3   **cloves garlic, peeled and minced or put through a press**
1   **red bell pepper**
3   **tablespoons butter**
½ to 1   **teaspoon dried basil (and/or 2 to 4 tablespoons chopped fresh basil)**
½   **pound orzo**
   Salt and freshly ground black pepper
⅓ to ½   **cup grated Parmesan cheese**

Wash the green beans and trim off the ends. Slice the beans on the diagonal into ¼-inch pieces and set aside. Wipe off any dirt from the mushrooms, cut them into ¼- to ½-inch chunks, and set aside. Peel the garlic, mince it and set aside. Wash the bell pepper, remove the core and seeds, and slice the pepper into ¼-inch strips, then slice the strips diagonally into ½- to 1-inch pieces. Set aside.

Melt the butter in a large sauté pan over moderate heat. Add the garlic and cook for 30 seconds, then add the green beans and mushrooms. Sauté the vegetables for 2 to 3 minutes, until the mushrooms are beginning to cook and the green beans are bright green. Turn off the heat. Put the bell pepper in the pan along with the dried basil. (If you're using fresh basil, add a small amount of dried basil now and later add the fresh basil along with the Parmesan cheese.)

In a large pot, bring 2 to 3 quarts of water to the boil (you may salt the water if you wish); add the orzo and stir. When the water returns to the boil, reduce the flame so that you have a steady simmer, not a rolling boil. Continue to stir the pasta for 5 to 7 minutes, testing it occasionally, until it is nearly done but still has a barely hard center. Turn off the flame and allow the pasta to sit in the hot water.

Return the green beans, mushrooms, and red bell peppers to medium heat; allow them to get thoroughly hot but not over-cooked. Turn off the flame.

Drain the orzo in a colander or sieve, shaking to remove any excess water. Place the hot, cooked pasta in the pan with the vegetables; stir and season with salt and pepper and the fresh basil, if using it. Sprinkle in the Parmesan cheese and toss; serve immediately.

Variations:
- Toss with ½ cup heavy cream or sour cream just before serving.
- Add ¼ cup chopped Niçoise or Kalamata olives along with the Parmesan cheese.

*This brimming wine
in the golden bowl:
Don't hesitate—drink it
to the last drop!*

Viva Italia Penne

SERVES 4

● ●

Interesting how one idea can evolve into something else; in this case, I was experimenting with the preceding orzo recipe and came up with something nearly identical but quite different. Unlike the orzo, this is a main course.

1   *pound green beans (preferably small, delicate
     beans, not big, woody pods)*
2   *red bell peppers, roasted, peeled, seeded, and
     thinly sliced*

3   cups ¼-inch slices white mushrooms
3   cloves garlic, minced and peeled or put through
        a press
3   tablespoons olive oil
¼   cup white wine
1   teaspoon dried marjoram
      Salt to taste
½   cup sour cream (regular or nonfat)
½   cup half-and-half
1   tablespoon Pesto
1   pound penne
      Salt
      Freshly ground black pepper
½   cup or more grated Parmesan cheese

Wash and trim the green beans. Slice into 2-inch lengths, then slice the pieces into thin strips. (If you have a French-cut green beaner gadget, put the whole beans through the bean cutter and then afterward cut them into lengths.)

Place the whole bell peppers over (and sitting in, if possible) an open flame and roast, turning periodically, until they are completely black and charred on the outside. (If you don't have a gas flame, roast the peppers under the broiler in an electric oven.) Remove the peppers from the flame and wrap them in a paper towel, then wrap the paper towel in a cloth towel. (You may also place the roasted peppers in a paper or plastic bag, sealing well.) Let the hot peppers steam for at least 20 minutes.

While the peppers are steaming, brush and slice the mushrooms and peel and mince the garlic. In a bowl, mix the sour cream, half-and-half, and pesto.

After the peppers have cooled, remove them from their wrappings. Using a fresh paper towel, remove the blackened charred outer skin by brushing it off—you will need to turn the paper towel occasionally, or use a fresh one. Some black spots should remain; this gives a nice, smoky flavor. When all the skin has been removed, cut out the cores and seeds, then slice the peppers into ¼-inch by 2-inch lengths.

Bring a large pot of water to the boil and add the penne; stir and cook until it is just done. (This will take about 10 to 14 minutes after the water has come back to the boil, so time the finish accordingly.)

While the pasta is cooking, heat the olive oil over a medium flame in a large sauté pan; add the garlic and mushrooms, tossing and frying, for 1 minute, until the garlic has cooked and the mushrooms may have browned lightly. Add the green beans and roasted bell pepper; toss and stir for 30 to 60 seconds, then add the wine and marjoram. Salt the vegetables lightly and continue to cook for another few minutes until the green beans are nearly done, cooking off some of the wine. Add the cream and pesto mixture, stirring once. Turn off the heat.

When the pasta is done, drain it in a colander or sieve, shaking off any excess water. Immediately put the pasta in the sauté pan with the vegetables and toss to incorporate everything. Place the pasta and vegetables on warm plates and sprinkle with Parmesan cheese and a grating of black pepper. Serve immediately.

> Farmer,
> pointing the way
> with a radish.
> —ISSA

Blue Penne

SERVES 4 AS A SIDE DISH

● ●

This cold pasta salad is creamy and unusual, a refreshing light lunch, first course, or side dish.

8	ounces penne
1	tablespoon salt
1	large head of broccoli, broken up into florets
3	cloves garlic, minced or put through a garlic press
1	teaspoon crushed red pepper flakes
2	tablespoons olive oil
1	cup sour cream (regular, nonfat, or a mixture)
1	cup crumbled blue cheese (Danish blue or Roquefort would be excellent for this)
1	cup slivered toasted almonds*
½	cup chopped parsley
	Salt to taste
	Freshly ground pepper, to taste
4	large lettuce leaves
	Paprika for garnish
	Parsley sprigs for garnish

*To toast almonds: place the almonds in a toaster oven (or a regular oven) at 350° for 10 minutes or so until they have begun to brown lightly and give off a lovely, roasted smell. Allow them to cool before you use them. You can roast whole, slivered, or sliced almonds in this manner.

Bring a large pot of water (3 to 6 quarts) to the boil; add the pasta and salt. Cook the pasta until it is just done, about 13 minutes, then drain it in a colander and rinse under cool water. Shake off any excess water and refrigerate.

Place a steamer basket in a pot and add 1-inch of water; bring to a boil and add the broccoli. Cover the pot and steam the broccoli until it is just done, about 3 to 4 minutes. Remove the broccoli from the steamer and rinse under cool water for a bit, then shake off any excess water. Set aside.

Place the garlic, red pepper flakes, and olive oil in a sauté pan; heat the pan over a moderate flame and cook for 1 minute, or until the garlic has just begun to brown lightly. Remove the pan from heat and add the broccoli pieces, tossing well. Allow to cool.

When the broccoli has cooled, add it to the cooked pasta, tossing well. Stir in the sour cream, blue cheese, toasted almonds, and chopped parsley. Add salt and pepper to taste.

Place the pasta salad on lettuce leaves; garnish with a sprinkling of paprika and sprigs of parsley.

Variation:
- Of course you can use any variety of pasta other than penne, but I'd avoid long, thin noodles in favor of the shorter, easy-to-handle varieties like penne, rotini, fusilli, or tortelloni, for example.

Sato naruru	*The twilight cuckoo*
tasogaredoki no	*now quite at home in our village—*
hototogisu	*I pretend not to hear,*
kikazugao nite	*hoping to make him*
mata nanorasen	*speak his name again*

—SAIGYŌ

Refrigerator Pasta

SERVES 4

• •

A rather unglamorous title, I must admit, but a delicious, quick dish. The name refers to my own experience of walking into the kitchen and thinking, "What should we have for dinner?" only to find a few scraps of vegetables in the refrigerator. Rather than make an emergency run to the local supermarket, I usually opt for whatever is on hand. Since the major ingredients are items that are bottled and kept in the refrigerator, it is a pasta that can be prepared at a moment's notice.

2	cloves garlic, minced and peeled or put through a press
¼	cup olive oil or Roasted Garlic Oil, page 235
2 to 3	cups of any vegetables lying around—half a zucchini, some broccoli, fennel bulb, carrot, green beans, asparagus, fresh tomato, green or red bell pepper, mushrooms—whatever. Sliced or chop any way you desire.
¼	cup dry white wine or vermouth
1 to 2	teaspoons dried basil, oregano, or thyme, optional
½	cup diced, pitted Kalamata olives
½	cup diced, drained sun-dried tomatoes
¼	cup chopped pepperoncini (pickled Italian peppers) or green olives
½	cup toasted, chopped walnuts, pecans, almonds, or pignoli, optional
½	cup chopped fresh parsley
¾	cup grated Parmesan or Romano cheese, or a mixture
1	pound dry pasta—linguini, fusilli, penne rigate, or other
	Freshly ground black pepper
	Salt to taste

Sauté the garlic in 1 to 2 tablespoons of the olive oil in a large sauté pan over a moderate flame. After it has cooked through and is just beginning to toast lightly, add whatever vegetables you are using. Stir-fry the leftover vegetables until they are barely cooked, then add the wine and steam 30 seconds longer. Turn off the flame. Add the dried herb if desired.

Put a 3 to 5 quarts of salted water on to boil.

Meanwhile, dice the black olives, sun-dried tomatoes, pepperoncini or green olives, and nuts. Mix these ingredients together in a bowl and add the chopped parsley. Grate the cheese(s).

When the water is boiling, add the pasta and cook until it is just al dente. Drain in a colander, shaking off any excess water. Put the pasta back in the pot and add the remaining olive oil and cooked vegetables, tossing well. Garnish each serving with the chopped olive mixture and cheese(s). Serve immediately with freshly ground black pepper and salt to taste.

Aki fukami	So deep into autumn
narabu hana naki	their fellow flowers
kiku nareba	are all gone—
tokoro o shimo no	if the frost would only hold off,
oke to koso omoe	leave me the incomparable chrysanthemums!

—Saigyō

Three-Mushroom Pasta

SERVES 4

● ●

Portobello mushrooms, although delicious, are rather temperamental—they demand that everything they come in contact with be dyed a brownish hue. Portobellos are quite meaty, not only in appearance but in texture and taste; they have the consistency of the choicest part of a perfectly cooked filet mignon. This is, perhaps, a pasta dish to serve to hard-core carnivores.

The second method given for cooking the portobellos is preferable. Although (as usual) this is the more labor-intensive method, it also yields a more "outdoorsy" taste, a richer quality hinting at newly gathered mushrooms, open campfires, and fresh forest air.

4	large portobello mushrooms, large stems removed
¼	cup tamari
8	dried shiitakes
1	cup boiling water
2	white or crimini mushrooms, cut into cups ¼-inch to ½-inch chunks
2	tablespoons olive oil
1	cup finely minced onion
1	teaspoon thyme
¼	cup white wine or vermouth
¼ to ⅓	cup soaking liquid from the shiitakes
¼ to ½	cup cream cheese (regular or Neufchâtel)
½	cup milk, half-and-half, or cream
1	pound dried penne rigate
1	cup chopped fresh parsley
2	tablespoons chopped fresh tarragon, or a big pinch dried tarragon
½	cup freshly grated Parmesan cheese
	Salt and pepper to taste

Brush off any debris from the portobellos, then place them upside down on a plate. Dribble some tamari into the gills of the mushrooms, and allow them to stand for 30 minutes. (The tamari will bead up at first, but eventually the salt from the sauce will weaken the mushroom gills and it will enter the caps.)

Meanwhile, remove the tough stems from the dried shiitakes. Using a sharp knife, slice the dried mushrooms into ¹⁄₁₆-inch slices. Put the slices in a glass measuring cup and pour 1 cup of boiling water over them. Allow to soak for 30 minutes.

While the portobellos and shiitakes are soaking and marinating, clean and chop the white or crimini mushrooms, setting them aside. Place the olive oil and minced onion in a large sauté pan, setting it aside as well.

By now the portobellos should have marinated for 30 minutes. Either:

1) broil the portobellos, turning them often until they are cooked, about 8 to 10 minutes total, or

2) skewer a portobello mushroom with a kabob skewer and hold it over a medium high flame, turning often, open-roasting it until it is done, after around 7 to 9 minutes. Continue with the remaining portobellos in the same manner.

Place the cooked portobellos back on their plate and allow them to cool. Slice the portobellos into ½- to 2-inch chunks, tossing with any tamari that remains in the plate. Remove the soaked shiitakes from their liquid and add them to the pile of cooked, sliced portobellos. Reserve the soaking liquid.

Place the sauté pan containing the oil and onions over a moderate flame. Cook the onion until it is soft, about 5 minutes, then add the white mushrooms. Turn the flame to medium high and cook, stirring often, until the mushrooms begin to brown, another 5 minutes. Turn the flame to low and add the thyme, wine, some soaking liquid from the shiitakes, the cream cheese, and the milk or cream. Mix well, letting the cream cheese melt evenly. Add the portobellos and shiitakes (including any tamari on the plate), mixing the sauce well. It should be nut brown with dark chunks of mushrooms. Cover it and keep warm.

Bring a large pot of salted water to the boil. Add the pasta and cook until it is just done, around 12 to 14 minutes. Drain in a colander and return it to the large pot. Pour the sauce over the pasta and add the parsley and tarragon, stirring well.

Divide the sauced pasta among 4 warm plates, garnishing with Parmesan cheese. Add salt and pepper to taste. Serve immediately.

Cooling melon—
at a hint of footsteps,
you're a frog.
—Issa

Rapini Fusilli

Serves 4

● ●

If you've not tried rapini, please seek it out and make this recipe.

1   bunch rapini (see page 255)
2   tablespoons olive oil
3   cloves garlic, peeled and minced
1   teaspoon crushed red pepper flakes
1   teaspoon finely grated lemon zest
1   teaspoon dried basil
2   roasted red bell peppers (to roast peppers,
      see page 71)
1   pound dried penne rigate or fusilli
½   cup Vegetable Stock (page 26), water, or dry vermouth
1   cup freshly grated Parmesan cheese
½   cup grated smoked cheese, optional

Clean the rapini according to the directions on page 255 Cut into 2-inch pieces and set aside.

Combine the olive oil, garlic, red pepper flakes, lemon zest, and basil in a small bowl. Set aside.

Slice the roasted bell peppers into strips. Set aside.

Bring a large pot of lightly salted water to the boil. Add the pasta and cook, stirring often, until it is nearly done. Drain in a large sieve or colander (don't rinse).

Using the same pot in which you cooked the pasta, immediately return the pot to the flame and turn the heat to high. Add the olive oil mixture and sauté for 1 minute, until the garlic is cooked. Add the chopped rapini and stir for another minute; add the vegetable stock. Cover and let the rapini cook for 1 to 2 minutes more, until it is tender. Add the pasta and sliced bell peppers and toss thoroughly. Turn off the heat.

Place the pasta on warm plates and garnish with cheese. Serve immediately with freshly cracked pepper at the table.

Boil
mountains and rivers
in a two-quart pot!

Noodles Stroganoff

SERVES 4

● ●

A wonderful, creamy, rich side dish!

1 to 2	*tablespoons butter*
1	*tablespoon Roasted Garlic Oil (page 235)*
½	*cup peeled and minced onion*
8	*ounces sliced mushrooms*
	Big pinch of thyme
½	*cup half-and-half*
½ to 1	*teaspoon salt*
1	*tablespoon tamari*
	Freshly grated nutmeg
1½	*cups sour cream*
2	*cups dried egg noodles*
¼	*cup chopped fresh parsley*
	Cracked black pepper

Place the butter in a large sauté pan over medium heat; when it has melted, add the onion and cook, stirring once or twice, until the onion has begun to soften, about 2 to 5 minutes. Add the mushrooms and turn the heat to medium high; toss occasionally, allowing the mushrooms to brown, about 5 minutes. Add the thyme. In about 5 minutes the mushrooms will have released their juices and a wonderfully fragrant, woodsy smell will come from the pan. Reduce the heat to low and add the half-and-half, salt, tamari, a sprinkling of nutmeg, and the sour cream. Thoroughly stir and mix to a creamy, smooth blend. Cover and turn off the heat.

Bring a large pot of water to the boil and add salt if desired. Add the egg noodles and cook until just done. Drain in a sieve or colander and add to the mushroom mixture. Turn the flame to medium low and heat everything through; stir in the parsley. Serve immediately with a sprinkling of freshly cracked black pepper.

Brown leaf from a tree
unknown clings
to a strange
green-spotted mushroom
—Bashô

Classic Red Sauce

SERVES 4

● ●

There would be a great debate indeed to decide what constitutes a classic red sauce for pasta; one family would demand a bolognese sauce, another marinara, and yet another puttanesca—which is why I've made a very simple red sauce and you can add whatever options strike your fancy.

Please note that I've used canned tomatoes—this is strictly because they're easier and can be found year-round, unlike ripe, fresh tomatoes. Additionally, please note that the pasta will not be dripping with sauce: a frequent complaint from traditional Italian chefs is that Americans dump too much sauce on their pasta—the pasta should be coated, not swimming.

BASIC SAUCE:

1	tablespoon olive oil
1	teaspoon fennel seeds
1	medium onion, peeled and finely diced
4	cloves garlic, peeled and minced
½	cup dry red or white wine
1	28-ounce can crushed tomatoes (including juices)
1	18-ounce can whole Italian tomatoes, roughly chopped, excluding juice
1	bay leaf
1	teaspoon sugar
	Salt and pepper to taste

OPTIONS:

1	tablespoon chopped capers
1	teaspoon dried basil, oregano, or rosemary
1 to 3	tablespoons chopped fresh basil or oregano
1	tablespoon chopped fresh rosemary
¼ to ½	cup chopped green olives
¼ to ½	cup chopped Kalamata olives
1 to 2	tablespoons black or golden raisins
½ to 1	cup chopped roasted red bell pepper
1	cup grated carrot

Place a large, heavy pot over moderate heat; when it is hot, add the oil and fennel seeds. When they have sizzled for a few seconds, add the onion. Sauté until it has softened and begun to turn a bit brown, stirring often, for about 5 to 7 minutes. Add the garlic and cook for another minute. Add the wine (keeping your face averted, as it will splatter), and scrape off any browned bits from the bottom of the pot. Add the tomatoes, bay leaf, and sugar. Bring the mixture to the simmer and reduce the flame to very low.

Simmer the sauce with the cover ajar for 1 hour, stirring often. The sauce will turn from bright red to a deeper scarlet and will thicken.

Once the sauce has cooked for an hour, it is ready to be served with hot pasta and grated Parmesan cheese. However, you can add any combination of the options, simmering for another 15 to 30 minutes, then serve that special sauce with hot pasta.

Variation:
- If you happen to have some dried vegetable stock on hand (either bouillon or granulated), you can add a bit of this to the sauce while it is cooking to give a more complex taste. Be careful, though, as these products are usually quite high in salt.

Kyô no ohiru wa
mizu bakari.

Today's lunch:
Only water.
—SANTÔKA

MAIN COURSES

● ●

Moussaka

● ●

*This recipe looks terribly long and complicated, but it is quite simple really—
just four steps. First, the tempeh. Then the eggplants. Next the red sauce. Last
the white sauce. Assemble and bake. And since it can be made ahead of time,
the effort is well worth the ease of just popping it in the oven and relaxing with
a cocktail while it bakes.*

8	ounces tempeh (regular or whatever kind you wish—amaranth, quinoa, 5-grain, or other, if the tempeh is frozen, thaw it)
¼	cup tamari
1 to 2	cloves garlic, peeled and minced or put through a press
2	small to medium eggplants, peeled and sliced into ½-inch rounds
	Pam
1 to 3	tablespoons oil
1	teaspoon olive oil
1	teaspoon fennel seeds
2	cloves garlic, peeled and minced or put through a press
1	small onion, peeled and finely diced
½ to 1	teaspoon ground cinnamon
½	teaspoon oregano
½	teaspoon thyme

    1   *large 28-ounce can Italian tomatoes, whole*
          or crushed (if whole, cut into pieces),
          approximately 2 to 3 cups, drained of juice
    ½   *cup dry white or red wine*
       Salt to taste
    1   *tablespoon butter*
    1½ *tablespoons flour*
    1½ *cups hot milk (cow's milk or soy)*
    1   *teaspoon salt*
    ½   *teaspoon freshly grated nutmeg*
       Big pinch cayenne pepper
    1   *cup ricotta cheese (regular, light, or nonfat)*
    2   *egg yolks or 1 whole egg*
    ½   *cup freshly grated Parmesan cheese*
 ¼ to ⅓ *cup chopped fresh parsley*
       Parmesan or grated mozzarella cheese, optional

Slice the tempeh in half to make two equal squares, more or less. Slice each square of tempeh in half laterally to get two thin squares. You will now have four thin squares of tempeh. Pour the tamari into a deep, flat dish and add the garlic; lay the tempeh slices in the mixture, coating evenly on all sides. Allow the tempeh to marinate for 30 minutes while you prepare the eggplant. The tempeh should absorb all the liquid.

Preheat the broiler to high. Peel and slice the eggplant into ½-inch rounds. Lay them on a baking sheet and spray them evenly with Pam. Flip the rounds over and spray the other side as well. Broil the eggplant 4 to 6 inches under the heating element until it is reddish brown; turn the slices over and brown the other side. Repeat if necessary until all the eggplant slices are browned. Set aside.

Place a large sauté pan over a medium flame; when it is hot, add 1 tablespoon oil and spray with Pam. Lay the marinated tempeh slices in the pan; allow them to cook until they are browned. Flip them over and brown the other side, spraying the pan with Pam as necessary. When the tempeh has browned, remove it to paper towels to drain.

Add a teaspoon of olive oil to the same pan in which you cooked the tempeh and add the fennel seeds and garlic; stir-fry until the garlic is just cooked, about one minute. Add the onion and sauté for 5 minutes, scraping any accumulation from the bottom of the skillet. Add the cinnamon, oregano, thyme, tomatoes, and wine. Bring the mixture to the simmer, reduce the flame to low, and cook for 20 minutes, stirring occasionally. Add salt to taste. While the red sauce is simmering, prepare the white sauce.

Place a deep saucepan over a medium low flame and add the butter; when it has melted, add the flour. Cook and stir for 1 minute; then add the hot milk. Stir the mixture with a whisk vigorously over medium heat until it has thickened. Continue to stir and cook for 1 minute. Remove the white sauce from the flame and add the salt, nutmeg, cayenne, and ricotta, stirring well. Whisk in the egg yolks and Parmesan cheese. Cover and set aside.

Spray a 9 x 12 x 2-inch baking dish with Pam. Spread ¼ cup or so of tomato sauce in the bottom of the dish. Place a layer of browned eggplant slices over the sauce. Crumble or tear the tempeh pieces and scatter them on top of the eggplant, then cover the tempeh with any remaining eggplant slices. Pour on all of the red sauce, distributing it evenly. Sprinkle the fresh parsley on top. Pour on the white sauce, spreading it evenly with a spatula. If desired, sprinkle the top with a bit of extra parsley or a bit of Parmesan or mozzarella cheese. The moussaka may be covered and refrigerated now if desired. Allow it to come to room temperature before continuing.

Place the moussaka in the upper third of a preheated 375° oven for 50 to 60 minutes, until the mixture is bubbly and the top has browned. Allow to cool for 20 minutes before cutting and serving.

Rather than cutting them down
To spread out or gather up,
Let the wild flowers of autumn be
And enjoy the field
Just as it is
—RENGETSU

Spinach Crêpes

SERVES 4

● ●

This dish is simple, elegant, flavorful, and unexpected. It can be made ahead of time and baked at the last moment, so most of the work can be accomplished a day ahead. A lovely light dinner or brunch.

> At least 8 Crêpes, page 239
> 1½ to 2   cups Basic White Sauce, page 242
> 1   pound fresh spinach, blanched (or one 10-ounce package frozen chopped spinach, thawed)
> 1 to 2   cups chopped fresh sorrel
> Pam or 1 tablespoon butter
> 1   small onion, peeled and finely minced
> 2   cloves garlic, peeled and minced or put through a press
> Salt and pepper to taste
> ¼   teaspoon freshly grated nutmeg
> 1 to 1½   cups grated cheese, a mixture of Gruyère and Cheddar, or a mixture of cottage cheese and Gruyère (use low-fat cheese if desired)
> Finely chopped fresh tomato, optional
> Finely chopped parsley, optional

Prepare the crêpes and white sauce. Set aside.

Remove and discard the stems from the spinach and put the leaves in a large colander. Wash well several times to make sure there is no grit remaining. Bring a large kettle of water to the boil and pour the boiling water over the spinach leaves, turning the leaves with a spoon or knife once or twice as you pour. Let the spinach rest for 30 seconds, then rinse well under cold water. Take the wilted spinach between your hands and squeeze out as much liquid as possible. (If you're using thawed frozen spinach, squeeze out any excess liquid and continue.) Chop the spinach and set aside.

Wash the sorrel and dry. Thinly slice, then chop, adding the chopped sorrel to the spinach. Mix well.

Place a large sauté pan over a moderate to moderately low flame and add the butter. Add the onion and cook for 3 to 5 minutes, stirring often, until it is soft. Add the garlic and continue to cook for another minute. Turn the heat to low and add the spinach and sorrel; toss and cook just long enough to heat through, about 1 minute. Add salt and pepper to taste, then sprinkle in the nutmeg. Let the mixture cool somewhat.

Grate the cheese.

Spray a 9 x 12-inch baking dish with Pam. Assemble all components.

Lay a crêpe on a flat surface, and spread 1 to 2 tablespoons of the white sauce at one end, then a sprinkling of the cheese, then 2 to 3 tablespoons of the spinach mixture, then roll the crêpe up into a long roll like an enchilada. Lay the crêpe in the prepared baking dish.

Continue rolling crêpes until all of the spinach is used. Spoon the extra white sauce on top of the crêpes as well as any extra cheese. Cover the dish with foil. (Although the crêpes may be made ahead at this point and refrigerated for up to 24 hours, it would be a better idea to prepare all of the different ingredients separately and assemble the crêpes closer to the time you'll need them, as the crêpes will absorb some of the moisture from the white sauce and will become soggy.) The prepared dish should be at room temperature before you continue.

Bake the crêpes covered in a preheated 350° oven for 30 to 40 minutes until bubbling hot. Serve 2 crêpes per person, garnishing with some finely chopped tomato or finely chopped parsley if you wish.

Water birds!
Washing vegetables in a boat
there is a woman.
—BUSON

Garden Crêpes

SERVES 4

● ●

Brimming with fresh summer produce, these crêpes are like a sun-filled picnic for your mouth.

8	crêpes (page 239)
4	dried shiitake or black mushrooms
½	cup chopped green onion
1	large carrot
1	stalk celery
1	head broccoli
1	small or 1/2 large zucchini
2	tablespoons butter
½ to 1	cup peas (fresh or frozen)
1	teaspoon dried thyme
1	tablespoon tamari
¼	cup dry white wine
	Salt to taste
2	cups Basic white sauce (page 242)
⅓ to ½	cup sour cream (regular, light, or nonfat)
1½	cups grated cheese (a mixture of Cheddar, provolone, and/or Gruyère)
	Chopped parsley or thyme sprigs, for garnish, optional

Make the crêpes. Set aside.

Remove the stems from the dried shiitakes with a small sharp knife. Using a sharp chef's knife, slice the dried mushrooms into ¹⁄₁₆-inch slices. Put the mushroom slices in a cup or small bowl. Pour ½ cup boiling water over them and allow them to rehydrate for 30 minutes. Set aside.

Chop the green onion, peel the carrot, clean the celery, peel the broccoli stems, and trim the zucchini. Chop the onion, carrot, celery, broccoli, and zucchini uniformly into ¼-inch cubes.

Heat the butter in a large sauté pan over a moderate flame until it melts; add the green onion and cook for 1 minute. Add the carrot, celery, broccoli, zucchini, peas, and drained shiitake mushrooms, and cook and stir for 2 to 3 minutes, until the vegetables turn a bright, vivid color. Add the thyme, tamari, and white wine, stirring constantly until nearly all of the liquid in the bottom of the pan has evaporated. Turn off the heat and add salt to taste. Set aside and cool.

Prepare the white sauce. Add the sour cream, blending well. Remove 1 cup of the white sauce and add it to the vegetables, lightly coating everything with sauce. Sprinkle nearly all of the cheese into the cooled vegetables, reserving ¼ cup for the topping.

Fill the crêpes as directed for spinach crêpes, using ⅓ to ½ cup or so of the mixture per crêpe, laying the filled crêpes in a 9 x 12-inch baking dish sprayed with Pam. Spoon the remaining white sauce over the crêpes, then sprinkle the remaining cheese on top. For garnish, strew on a tablespoon of two of chopped parsley. Cover with foil. (Although the crêpes may be made ahead at this point and refrigerated for up to 24 hours, it would be a better idea to prepare all of the different ingredients separately and assemble the crêpes closer to the time you'll need them, as the crêpes will absorb some of the moisture from the white sauce and will become a soggy.) Either way, the filled crêpes should be at room temperature before baking.

Preheat the oven to 350°.

Bake the crêpes for 30 to 40 minutes, until they are bubbling hot. Serve 2 crêpes per person, garnishing with additional parsley or a sprig of fresh thyme.

Itadaite tarite
hitori no hashi
o oku.

I received them
And they served my needs;
my chopsticks.
—Santōka

Crêpes à l'Indienne

SERVES 4

● ●

*Since crêpes are French, I merely extended the theme of French cooking to
include an Indian flavor—this recipe isn't overwhelming with its spices or
tastes, but has a gentler, creamier, and subtler palate than what you'd expect
out of traditional Indian cuisine.*

8	crêpes (page 239)
1	cup cooked, drained chickpeas (canned are fine), roughly chopped
1	cup cauliflower florets, cut into ¼-inch pieces, steamed
1	red potato, cut into ¼-inch dice, steamed until tender
2	tablespoons oil or ghee
1	small to medium onion, peeled and finely chopped
2 to 3	teaspoons cumin seed
2 to 3	cloves garlic, peeled and minced or put through a press
1 to 2	finely minced fresh green chiles, or ¼ teaspoon cayenne pepper
¼	teaspoon turmeric
¼	cup green peas, fresh or frozen, optional
	Salt to taste
1 to 1¼	cups cottage cheese
2	cups Basic white sauce (page 242)
½	cup sour cream or plain yogurt
1	teaspoon finely minced gingerroot
¾ to 1	teaspoon garam masala
¾ to 1	teaspoon fragrant fresh curry powder
1	medium ripe tomato, peeled, seeded, and chopped into ¼-inch dice
¼	cup chopped cilantro or mint, for garnish

Make the crêpes. Set aside.

Place the drained chick-peas in a food processor or blender and
roughly chop them in two or three quick spurts until they are
about ¼-inch in size. Set aside.

Clean and chop the cauliflower into small florets. Steam until it tender, about 5 minutes. Set aside.

Clean, chop, and steam the potatoes, cooking for 5 to 8 minutes until they are tender. Set aside.

Heat the oil or ghee in a large sauté pan over medium high heat. Add the onion and cumin seed. Cook and stir for 5 minutes, until the onion is soft and may be beginning to brown lightly at the edges. Add the garlic, fresh green chilies, and turmeric, cooking for 1 minute. Remove the pan from the heat and add the peas (if you like), chopped chick-peas, cauliflower, and potatoes. Add salt to taste—probably ½ to 1 teaspoon will be needed. Allow the vegetables to cool, then add the cottage cheese and mix thoroughly.

Prepare the white sauce. Add the sour cream or yogurt, ginger-root, garam masala, and curry powder, blending well. Remove 1 cup of the white sauce and add it to the vegetables, lightly coating everything with the sauce.

Fill as directed for spinach crêpes, using ⅓ to ½ cup or so of the mixture per crêpe, and laying the filled crêpes into a 9 x 12-inch baking dish sprayed with Pam. Spoon the remaining white sauce over the crêpes, then sprinkle the chopped tomato on top. For garnish, strew on a tablespoon or two of chopped cilantro. Cover with foil. (Although the crêpes may be made ahead at this point and refrigerated for up to 24 hours, it would be a better idea to prepare all of the ingredients separately and assemble the crêpes closer to the time you'll need them, as they will absorb some of the moisture from the white sauce and will become a bit soggy.) Either way, the filled crêpes should be at room temperature before baking.

Preheat the oven to 350°.

Bake the crêpes for 30 to 40 minutes, until they are bubbling hot. Serve 2 crêpes per person, garnishing with additional cilantro or mint.

Variations:
- For a hotter version, increase the cayenne pepper to 1 teaspoon.
- For a spicier taste, increase the garam masala and curry powder to 2 teaspoons each.

Summer field—
thunder,
or my empty stomach
—Issa

Tarte aux Oignons
Onion and Mushroom Tart
on Puff Pastry

SERVES 4

● ●

This variation of a tart that contains onions and bacon is a delicious
substitute for those who don't eat pork or meat in general. If you have the
time to make your own puff pastry, by all means do so; otherwise store-
bought is fine.

2 to 3	**8-inch rounds or squares of puff pastry**
	pierced several times with a fork and placed
	on a baking sheet sprayed with Pam
½	**cup cottage cheese (regular, light, or nonfat)**
½ to ⅔	**cup crème fraîche, kefir cheese, cream cheese,**
	or sour cream
1 to 1½	**tablespoons flour**
1	**teaspoon salt**
½	**teaspoon pepper**
¼ to ⅓	**cup grated smoked cheese (such as smoked**
	Gruyère or smoked Gouda)
¼	**teaspoon freshly grated nutmeg**
1	**small onion, peeled, quartered, and thinly**
	sliced
2	**cups mushrooms**
1 to 2	**tablespoons butter or olive oil, or a**
	combination of oil and Pam

If using fresh puff pastry, roll the pastry to a ⅛- to ¾₆-inch thickness; if using store-bought pastry, simply thaw. Using a plate, cake
pan, or other mold as your guide, cut into rounds or squares, then
pierce the pastry with a fork. Place the pastry on the prepared baking sheet. Cover and refrigerate.

Place the cottage cheese in a food processor; purée until you
have a smooth cream. Add the crème fraîche, flour, salt, and pep-

per; blend briefly to mix thoroughly. Remove to a bowl and add the grated smoked cheese and nutmeg, mixing well. Cover and refrigerate.

Slice the onion into very thin quarters. Clean and thinly slice the mushrooms. Heat a sauté pan over a moderate flame; add butter or olive oil, then add the onions and mushrooms. Toss and cook until the onions have begun to soften (but aren't completely cooked) and the mushrooms have wilted and released some of their liquid, approximately 5 to 7 minutes. Remove from heat. (If the onion and mushrooms are very watery, drain them.)

Preheat oven to 425°.

Remove the puff pastry from the refrigerator; divide the cheese mixture between the rounds, and spread it evenly with a spatula or the back of a spoon to within ¾-inch of the edge of the pastry. Spread the onion mixture evenly on top.

Bake the tarts in the lower to middle portion of the preheated oven for 20 to 30 minutes. until the tops have browned lightly and the pastry has risen and is lightly browned around the edges. Remove and serve immediately.

Variations:
- Add a sprinkling of fresh thyme or herbes de Provence to the onion-mushroom mixture.
- Add 2 to 3 teaspoons Dijon mustard to the cooked onion mixture.
- Omit the mushrooms and increase the onions by ½ cup; proceed as usual.
- Add a few pitted, sliced Niçoise olives to the top of the tart before baking.

Aubergine Polenta Gratin

SERVES 4

● ●

This is not haute cuisine (more like hippie cuisine) but is enormously satisfying and tasty. If you like, feel free to cut the polenta into squares and layer it with the eggplant, tomato sauce, and the other ingredients. Polenta is loaded with complex carbohydrates, makes a nice alternative to pasta, potatoes, and rice, and is particularly soothing during the winter months.

1 cup cornmeal (or a mixture of cornmeal
     and corn grits)
2⅓ cups water
1 teaspoon salt or 1 tablespoon tamari
½ cup sour cream
   Basic tomato sauce (page 241)
2 smallish eggplants, peeled if desired*
   Pam
½ cup shredded Parmesan cheese
1 cup shredded Gruyère, regular or smoked
1 cup (or more) cottage cheese (regular, light,
     or nonfat)
½ cup chopped fresh basil, oregano, or parsley, or
3 teaspoons dried herbs

Place the cornmeal in a tall saucepan. Add the water gradually, whisking well until the cornmeal has no lumps. Add the salt or tamari. Place the pan over a medium to medium high flame, whisking constantly, until the mixture comes to the boil; once the boil has been reached, reduce the heat to medium low or low. The cornmeal will begin to thicken quite a bit. Add the sour cream and continue stirring the bubbling mixture for 2 to 3 minutes. The cornmeal will by now be quite thick, like porridge. Turn off the flame and pour the cornmeal mixture into a 9 x 12-inch baking dish sprayed with Pam, smoothing out the top with a spatula to make it as even as possible. Let it cool.

Prepare the tomato sauce. Set aside.

Preheat the broiler. Slice the tops and tails off the eggplant and peel them if desired. Slice the eggplant into ½-inch rounds and lay them on a baking sheet. Spray the slices with Pam. (For a lower-fat version, see Variations below.) Turn the slices over and spray the other sides. Place one baking sheet under the broiler and broil until the eggplant has turned reddish brown on top; turn the slices over and broil the other side. Continue until all of the eggplant slices have been cooked. Set aside.

Put a layer of cooked eggplant on top of the cooled polenta. Add a sprinkling of Parmesan cheese, ⅓ cup of Gruyère, and ½ cup

*Sometimes the peel on eggplant is like a piece of old shoe leather, other times it is not—I have no clue as to why one time it is edible and the next inedible. If you grow your own eggplant organically, I would suggest trying a few pieces first to see if the skin is tough; if not, leave it on. If you've purchased supermarket eggplant, it has been waxed, in which case I advise you to peel it.

cottage cheese. Sprinkle some herbs on top, then spoon about a third of the tomato sauce all over. Repeat the layering (eggplant, cheeses, herbs, and the remaining tomato sauce). Sprinkle on the remaining Parmesan and Gruyère cheeses, along with any leftover fresh herbs.

Cover the baking dish. If it is not to be baked immediately, it may be refrigerated now for future use. If the dish is prepared ahead of time and refrigerated, allow it to come to room temperature before continuing.

Bake, covered, in a preheated 350° oven for 45 to 50 minutes. Uncover and bake for another 10 to 20 minutes. Remove and allow to stand 10 to 15 minutes before slicing and serving.

Variations:
- For a subtler version, eliminate the herbs entirely or reduce their quantity by half.
- For a higher protein version, layer 1 cup of cooked beans, such as navy or white beans, to the baking dish along with the polenta.
- Increase the amount of cheese as desired, or substitute different types of cheese. Derby sage cheese, Asiago, mozzarella, Provolone, fontine, Monterey Jack, or port cheese all would be nice additions and/or substitutions.
- For a lower-fat version, steam the eggplant slices for 15 minutes until they are soft. This eliminates fat but also weakens the taste. Use reduced-fat cheeses if you prefer.

Bamboo shoot,
springing up
just anywhere.
—Issa

Phyllo Spinach Turnovers

MAKES ABOUT 20 TO 24 TURNOVERS,
SERVING 4 PER PERSON

● ●

These little turnovers are always a hit with guests, since they are so compact and unexpected. Although they could be considered finger food, I would hesitate to recommend them as cocktail munchies, since pieces of the flaky phyllo dough will undoubtedly (and unavoidably) wind up on your floor.

These are best eaten within 30 minutes of baking, yet they can be refrigerated and eaten another day as a snack. Leftover turnovers can be allowed to cool, then covered and refrigerated. The phyllo will moisten during refrigeration, but if you gently heat the turnovers uncovered at 300° for 15 to 20 minutes, they will crisp slightly; they will never be as flaky as when they've been freshly baked, alas.

10	ounces frozen chopped spinach, thawed and squeezed of excess water
1	cup cottage cheese
½	cup grated smoked cheese (such as Gouda) or regular Gruyère
2	green onions, finely chopped
¼	teaspoon freshly grated nutmeg
1	teaspoon finely grated fresh lemon zest
1	teaspoon dried thyme, oregano, or basil, optional but recommended
¼	cup chopped fresh parsley
¼	cup chopped almonds or walnuts
¼	cup bread crumbs
	Freshly grated black pepper
	Salt to taste
2	eggs, beaten
1	package frozen phyllo dough, thawed overnight in the refrigerator
2 to 3	tablespoons butter
⅓ to ½	cup olive oil

NOTE: If you've not made these before, I would recommend you make one by itself as a practice turnover before you get ahead of yourself; if you're an old hand at making these, buttering several sheets at once and stuffing the turnovers en masse saves you time.

THE SPINACH FILLING

Finely chop the spinach and put it in a medium bowl. Add the cottage cheese, grated cheese, green onions, nutmeg, lemon zest, optional herb, parsley, nuts, and bread crumbs. Mix thoroughly and taste for seasoning, adding salt and pepper as needed. Add the eggs and blend again. The mixture should hold together nicely and not be runny. Cover and refrigerate.

THE PHYLLO DOUGH

The most important thing to know about phyllo dough that you've never read in any cookbook until now: Phyllo dough never quite works the way you think it will. You'll often see pictures illustrating beautiful, clean, smooth sheets of dough being easily and effortlessly transformed into strudels and spanakopita, and when you open your own package of dough you'll see a wrinkled mess that most often sticks together at the edges and cracks somewhere in the center. The sheets never come apart as they should, and they tear, and you'll throw your hands up in dismay and feel like a complete and total incompetent. Never fear.

It's no big deal if the dough cracks or tears—all you have to do is put another layer on top of the torn one and get on with your life. Sometimes, for reasons only known to the phyllo dough, you can only separate double or triple sheets at a time; if this is the case, put down however many sheets you can separate and then some more. No problem. In this recipe, you need only 3 to 4 sheets of dough, and they needn't even be perfect pieces either. If one sheet is torn and has a ragged edge, don't worry about it. Once the thing is folded up you'll never know that you haven't even one good layer of dough!

Melt 2 to 3 tablespoons of butter in a saucepan and add the olive oil. Allow to cool somewhat.

Carefully unwrap the dough on your work surface and cover with a damp cloth so that it will not dry out. Most packaged phyllo dough is oblong in size (around 12 x 17 inches), so using a sharp knife and a ruler, cut off three 12 x 4-inch slices from the dough. Remember to keep the dough covered when you're not using it.

Place a single (or double) layer of dough in front of you on a smooth surface and brush it with some butter and oil. Place another layer of pastry on top, and brush it as well. Place one final layer down and brush it with oil. You now have 3 to 4 single layers of buttered dough.

STUFFING AND FOLDING

Take a heaping tablespoonful of the filling and place it at the lower left end of the dough (Illustration #1). Carefully fold over the dough to one side, forming a covered triangle (Illustration #2). Flip the triangle up (Illustration #3), then fold it over again (Illustration

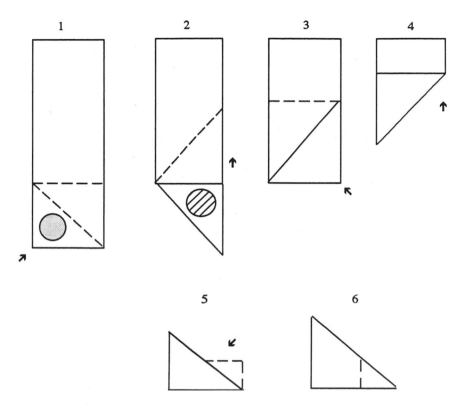

#4). You'll now have a stuffed triangle with a flap sticking out the end (Illustration #5). Fold the flap around the stuffed turnover, holding it in place (if necessary) with a bit more butter and oil (Illustration #6).

Continue making the little turnovers until you've used up all of the filling. Place the filled turnovers on a non-stick baking sheet and brush the tops with more butter.

Do-ahead note: phyllo turnovers can be made a day or two ahead of time and kept covered, refrigerated, until ready to bake. Allow them to warm to room temperature for 1 hour before baking.

Bake uncovered at 350° for 25 to 35 minutes until the turnovers have puffed slightly and are golden brown. Allow to cool for 10 to 15 minutes before serving.

Moon adrift in a cloud...
I have a mind
to borrow
a small ripe melon
—SHIKI

Garden Pot Pie

MAKES ONE LARGE POT PIE SERVING 4

● ●

This recipe looks quite daunting because of the long list of ingredients, but if you look carefully you'll notice it's quite simple—a white sauce, sautéed vegetables, and a crust. If you don't want to be bothered with a crust, take a look at the variations at the end.

Although I don't usually use bouillon cubes, in this particular recipe a cube gives a good flavor and is relatively low in fat, considering that the recipe will serve four people. If you have a very full-flavored vegetable stock, go ahead and use 1 or 2 cups of it, adjusting the milk accordingly.

1	recipe of Pie Crust, (page 244) or store-bought pie dough
1	cup water
1	vegetable bouillon cube
2	tablespoons butter
3	tablespoons flour
2	cups soy milk or milk
¼	cup sour cream, regular, light, or nonfat, optional
⅛ to ¼	teaspoon freshly grated nutmeg
1 to 2	tablespoons olive oil or a mixture of butter and oil
2	cups diced (¼-inch) mushrooms
1½	cups diced (¼-inch) potato
4 to 6	chopped green onions or ½ cup diced onion
1	cup diced (¼-inch) zucchini
1	large diced (¼-inch) carrot
2	cups diced (¼-inch) celery
1	cup frozen thawed peas
2	tablespoons chopped parsley
2	tablespoons dry white vermouth or dry white wine, optional
½	cup grated sharp Cheddar cheese
¼	cup shredded Parmesan cheese
¼	cup grated Monterey Jack or mozzarella cheese
	Flour for the dough

Prepare the pastry according to the directions and let it rest in the refrigerator. If using ready-made dough, make sure it is thawed.

Heat 1 cup of water in a small saucepan and add the vegetable bouillon cube, dissolving it thoroughly. Set aside.

Place the butter in a separate saucepan and melt over a moderate flame. Add the flour, stirring and cooking for 1 minute. Turn the heat to high and add the vegetable broth and milk, stirring constantly with a whisk until the mixture comes to a boil, thickens, and has no lumps. Reduce the flame to low and let cook for 2 minutes. Add the optional sour cream and the nutmeg. Taste for seasoning— the vegetable bouillon should have added enough salt, but if not, add as desired. Cover the pan and set it aside.

Place the olive oil in a large sauté pan over a moderate flame. Add the mushroom and potato pieces and turn the flame to high. Let them cook for 3 to 4 minutes, stirring occasionally, until the mushrooms begin to turn golden brown; the potatoes will probably stick to the pan somewhat. Reduce the flame to medium and add the green onions, zucchini, carrot, and celery. Cook the vegetables for 3 to 5 minutes, until they are barely tender. Add the peas, parsley, and optional wine. Heat everything through and then remove from the heat.

Pour the white sauce over the vegetables. Add the cheeses, stirring briefly.

Spray an 8-inch square baking dish with Pam. Pour in the vegetables and the sauce mixture. Set aside.

Lightly flour a flat surface and roll out half of the dough ⅛-inch thick. Gently position the dough over the baking dish, laying it on top of the vegetables. Cut off any excess dough, and feel free to decorate the top with a design if you wish. You can cut some slits in the dough, but this really isn't necessary, since the steam will escape from the sides.

Bake the pie in the center or upper middle of a preheated 350° oven for 50 to 60 minutes, until it is bubbly and the crust has browned. Let the pot pie cool for 10 minute before serving.

Variations:
- For a lower-fat version, eliminate the cheeses.
- Substitute cottage cheese for any of the cheeses.
- Add 1 cup of cooked navy beans to the vegetables.
- For a standard pot pie, completely line the baking dish with

dough using the entire recipe of Pie Crust; it with the vegetables and sauce, then cover the top with dough as well. Be
sure to cut several slits in the top crust for steam to escape.

- If you don't want to make a crust at all, make a Garden
  Pasta Pie as follows:

    1) Follow the directions above for the white sauce and veg-
       etables, omitting the potato.
    2) Boil 8 ounces of dry macaroni, fusilli, or penne rigate in
       plenty of water until it is nearly (but not quite) cooked.
       Drain and rinse in cool water.
    3) Combine the white sauce, vegetables, cheese, and pasta;
       pour the mixture into a baking dish (8-inches square or a
       10- to 12-inch round dish) that has been sprayed with
       Pam. Cover with foil until ready to bake.
    4) Bake, covered, at 350° for 60 minutes, until the pie is hot.

EGGS

● ●

Eggs have received much negative publicity in the last twenty years because of their cholesterol content, but eggs eaten in moderation are a versatile and delicious facet of vegetarian cookery. In fact, eggs have even been called the "perfect" food.

Some vegetarians don't eat eggs, and some eat neither eggs nor dairy products. These latter vegetarians (vegans by name) do not eat any animal products whatsoever, and subsist entirely from foods in the plant kingdom. For vegans who need something similar to an egg, however, there are vegetable-based egg substitutes available in some specialty markets. Unfortunately, vegan egg substitutes are exactly that, substitutes—eggs, for better or worse, are irreplaceable in their delicacy; they also whip to fluff and bind ingredients together. If you wish to experiment with vegan egg substitutes, feel free to do so, but when the whole point of the entrée is eggs (such as chawanmushi or curried eggs), a substitute will not work.

Health wise, eggs can contain bacteria, including salmonella, like chicken; but cooking, as always, kills any bacteria, making eggs completely safe. If you wish to cut down on your cholesterol intake, remove the yolk from the egg, for all of the fat (including all the cholesterol) is contained in the yolk.

Haru ga　　　　　　　　　　Spring is here —
kita watakushi no kuriya　　Even my kitchen
yutaka ni mo.　　　　　　　　Will be well stocked.
　　　　　　　　　　　　　　　—SANTÔKA

Two Vegan Egg Substitutes

● ●

These two recipes were given to me by a vegan friend. I pass them to you untested, making no claims as to their efficacy. Obviously they will not work with items such as soufflés or chawanmushi, but if you're very adventurous you could try them with quiches and desserts.

Egg Substitute #1:

All-Purpose Vegan Egg Substitute; the recipe equals 1 egg:

2	*tablespoons unbleached white flour*
1½	*teaspoons corn oil or canola oil*
½	*teaspoon baking powder*
2	*tablespoons water*

Mix the ingredients thoroughly and use immediately. Does not keep.

Egg Substitute #2:

For use in baked/pastry goods; ⅓ cup equals 1 egg:

¼	*cup flax seeds*
¾	*cup water*

Place the flax seeds in a clean coffee grinder and grind them as nearly as possible to a powder.

Put the ground seeds in a blender and add the water, mixing at high speed for 1 minute. Refrigerate the mixture, using it within 24 hours.

Ichiaku no kome A handful of rice,
o itadaki itakaite Received and eaten:
mainichi no tabi. My daily travel.
—SANTÔKA

Chawanmushi

SERVES 4

● ●

The first time I'd ever heard of chawanmushi (savory Japanese custard) was when I was glancing through Madhur Jaffrey's World Of The East Vegetarian Cooking. *I'd never thought of custards as a main course savory item, but I was willing to try anything once. Since I didn't have any chawanmushi cups, I ran to Pier I Imports and bought 4 delightful ceramic blue and white cups from Japan. Then I followed the directions in the cookbook and produced an extraordinarily light, subtle, and delicate custard that evening for dinner. I was hooked.*

A chawanmushi cup is a handleless ceramic cup about four inches tall and three inches in diameter with a lid that fits over the top. The cups can usually be found at import stores and are most frequently in blue and white Japanese designs. The cup is filled with the ingredients and then placed in a bain-marie, covered, and cooked until the custard has set. The lid is to prevent any accumulated water from entering the custard and thinning it out, but it is also to retain the heat inside the cup and ensure even cooking. If you don't have chawanmushi cups or can't find them, any ceramic mug will work as long as you put a piece of foil on top to keep the ingredients secure.

4	large shiitake mushrooms, fresh or dried (if dried, rehydrate by pouring boiling water over them and allowing them to soak for 30 minutes)
1	tablespoon sake
2	tablespoons tamari
2	teaspoons sugar
3	large eggs
2½ to 3	cups Japanese Broth (page 27)
1	teaspoon finely grated gingerroot
1	green onion, finely minced
1	sheet laver (nori seaweed), cut into four 1-inch squares
4	very thin slices of lemon

Slice the fresh or rehydrated shiitakes into ⅛-inch to ¼-inch strips.

Place the sake, tamari, and sugar in a small saucepan. Stir the liquid over a medium flame and dissolve the sugar. Add the mushroom pieces and stir, coating them with the mixture. Bring the mixture to the boil and let the mushrooms cook in the sauce, reducing until there is practically no liquid left, just the coated mushrooms. Turn off the heat and let the coated mushrooms cool. (If you like, you can remove the mushrooms from the pan and boil ½ cup of the Japanese stock in the same pan, scraping any accumulated tamari/sugar from the sides. Add this seasoned liquid to the mushrooms.)

Put the eggs in a large bowl and whisk vigorously. Add 1 cup of stock, beating well (but not so much that you form a froth), then add the remaining stock. Add the gingerroot and minced green onion and mix well.

Place the square of laver (nori) in the center of the lemon slices.

Divide the cooled mushrooms evenly among the chawanmushi cups. Pour in the egg/stock mixture so that it comes to within ½-inch of the top of the cups.

Very carefully, float 1 lemon slice (laver side up) on top of each portion of the custard mixture in each cup. Carefully put the cups in a large Dutch oven, then place the lids on the cups. Pour boiling water around the cups so that it comes half to two-thirds of the way up the sides. Cover the Dutch oven and place it over a flame just low enough so that the water is barely simmering but not boiling. Check the water temperature occasionally so that it does not boil. (Boiling water results in bubbles in the custard and a less delicate texture). Keep the water just simmering for 20 to 30 minutes, until the custards have set. They are done 1) if you remove the lid of the chawanmushi cup and the center has risen a bit, and 2) the custard does not appear liquidy but is firm and solid, and 3) if you slide a knife blade into the center and it comes out clean.

Carefully remove the cups from the hot water bath and place them on a small plate. Serve immediately with ceramic spoons. Be careful not to burn yourself.

Variations:
- Add different types of mushrooms as desired.
- Different types of stock result in vastly different tastes. Mushroom and onion stock would alter the custard enormously.
- Add diced water chestnuts, snow peas, or blanched spinach instead of, or in addition to, the shiitake mushrooms.

In stony moonlight
hills and fields
on every side
white and bald as eggs ...
—RANSETSU

Curried Eggs

SERVES 4

● ●

Curried eggs are a perfect brunch or light dinner choice, simply served with
plain basmati rice on the side, and a green salad. You may substitute hing for
the onion and garlic if you wish.

4 to 8	eggs (depending on whether you're serving one or two eggs per person)
1	small onion, peeled and roughly chopped
3	cloves garlic, peeled
1	2-inch piece of gingerroot, peeled and roughly chopped
1½	teaspoons whole cumin seed
1	tablespoon ground coriander
2 to 3	tablespoons ghee or oil
1	cup cream or half-and-half
½	cup sour cream (regular, light, or nonfat)
3	tablespoons almond butter or sesame butter
1	tablespoon tamarind paste
½	cup water
1	large tomato, peeled, seeded, and chopped
½ to 1	teaspoon garam masala
	Cilantro, for garnish

Bring a large pot of water to the boil and gently add the eggs
(in their shells). Once the water returns to the boil, gently boil the
eggs for 14 minutes. Drain the hot water off the eggs, then crack
the shells of each, leaving the eggs in the pot. Immediately fill the
pot with cold water and let the eggs cool for 30 to 60 seconds.
Gently crack them, peeling under cool, running water. Place the
cooked eggs in a bowl of cool water. You may refrigerate the eggs
at this point in an uncovered bowl, making sure they are completely immersed in water.

Place the peeled onion, garlic, and gingerroot in a food processor or blender. Process to a fine paste, pushing the mixture down with a spatula as necessary. Set aside.

Place a large sauté pan over a moderate flame and add the whole cumin seeds. Dry-roast them, stirring constantly, until they turn a bit darker and emit a lovely, deep, roasted aroma, after about 2 minutes. Add the coriander and ghee. Add the paste from the blender, keeping your face averted as you do so. Cook the spices and onion mixture for 10 to 15 minutes, until the onion has begun to brown and is completely cooked. The onion will stick to the pan and will become rather globby—this is normal. Add the cream, sour cream, almond butter, tamarind paste, and water. Bring the mixture to the simmer, stirring occasionally. Let the sauce simmer for 10 to 15 minutes over a low flame. Add the tomato, and cook for another 5 minutes.

Cut the hard-cooked eggs in half lengthwise. Add to the pan, basting with the sauce and heating through for 5 minutes. Just before serving, sprinkle the garam masala over the top.

Serve hot on a bed of basmati rice, spoon the sauce on top, and garnish with cilantro.

Samidare wa	*In fifth-month rains*
yukubeki michi no	*no trace of a path*
ate mo nashi	*where I can make my way*
ozasa ga hara mo	*meadows of bamboo grass*
uki ni nagrete	*awash in muddy water*
	—SAIGYŌ

Basic Cheese Soufflé

● ●

Egg whites should always be beaten at room temperature for maximum volume.

	Pam or softened butter
¼	cup Parmesan cheese
1	cup thick Basic White Sauce (page 242, consisting of 1 cup milk, 3 tablespoons flour, 3 tablespoons butter, milk, seasonings)
5 to 6	egg whites, at room temperature
	Big pinch of cream of tartar
	Pinch of salt
4	egg yolks
¾ to 1	cup shredded Gruyère, Jarlsberg, or Emmenthal cheese

Spray a 1- to 1½-quart soufflé dish with Pam or lightly grease it with softened butter. Coat the inside of the dish with grated Parmesan cheese by rolling the cheese around, getting as even a layer as possible. Set aside.

Set a 2-foot length of foil on a flat surface and fold it in half lengthwise. Lightly butter the upper two-thirds of the foil or spray it with Pam. With the ungreased side toward the bottom, carefully wrap the prepared foil around the soufflé dish, creating a collar. Using twine, tie the foil in place on the dish. If desired, insert a toothpick or a small metal skewer where the foil overlaps to create a stronger collar. If you don't have either of these, you may want to crimp the edges together.

Preheat the oven to 400°.

Separate the eggs, putting the yolks in a small bowl and the whites in a large copper bowl. (If you don't have a copper bowl, a large metal bowl will work.) Add the cream of tartar and salt to the egg whites and set aside.

Prepare the white sauce as directed on page 242. Beat the egg yolks into the hot sauce one at a time. Cover the pot and set aside.

Using a hand-held or countertop mixer, beat the whites to stiff peaks.

With a spatula, mix ¼ of the stiff egg whites into the warm white sauce. Pour the lightened white sauce into the bowl with the remaining egg whites. Begin folding the mixture with a rubber spatula, adding the cheese as you go. When you've folded everything together (being careful not to overmix), pour the soufflé mixture into the prepared dish. If there is some cheese remaining, sprinkle a tablespoon or so on top.

Put the soufflé in the lower third of the preheated oven. Reduce the temperature to 375°. After 35 minutes, carefully check to see whether the soufflé is done—it should have risen nearly to the top of the foil collar, and the very top should be golden brown. If you are in doubt, let it bake another 5 to 10 minutes. Remove the soufflé gently from the oven and put it on a trivet.

Take the soufflé (on the trivet) to the dining table, then remove the twine and foil. (This may not seem very glamorous, but the collar helps keep the soufflé from sinking en route.) Once the collar has been removed, serve the soufflé by plunging a large fork and spoon directly in the center, and scooping out the hot soufflé. Be prepared for admiration.

Words,
words, words:
> *fluttering drizzle and snow.*

Silence,
silence, silence:
> *a roaring thunderbolt.*

Spinach Soufflé

SERVES 4

● ●

This recipe is obviously a first cousin to cheese soufflé. If you have mastered
that recipe, this will be a snap.

¼	cup grated Parmesan cheese
8 to 10	ounces chopped fresh or frozen spinach
2	tablespoons butter
¼	cup finely minced onion or shallots
½ to 1	teaspoon thyme
¼ to ½	teaspoon salt
¼	teaspoon nutmeg
1	cup thick Basic White Sauce (page 242, consisting of 1 cup milk, 3 tablespoons flour, 3 tablespoons butter, milk, seasonings)
5 to 6	egg whites, at room temperature
	Big pinch of cream of tartar
	Pinch of salt
4	egg yolks
½ to ¾	cup roughly grated Gruyère cheese

Line the soufflé mold exactly as you would for a cheese souf-flé, using the foil, twine, and cheese. Set it aside.

Preheat the oven to 400°.

If you're using frozen chopped spinach, thaw it thoroughly and squeeze out any excess moisture. If you're using fresh spinach, wash it and remove the stems, and put the spinach in a colander. Pour a kettle of boiling water over the spinach leaves, allowing them to wilt for 30 seconds. Rinse them in cold water. Squeeze out any excess moisture and chop the greens roughly. Set aside.

Melt the butter in a large sauté pan over moderate heat. Add the onion, cooking until it is soft and translucent, about 3 to 4 minutes. Add the thyme, salt, nutmeg, and drained spinach. Heat everything through, tossing together and skimming any excess liquid from the spinach, for about 1 minute. Set aside.

Separate the eggs. Put the yolks in a small bowl and the egg whites in a large copper or metal bowl. Add the cream of tartar and salt to the whites and set aside.

Prepare the white sauce as directed, using 3 tablespoons flour per cup of milk. Beat the egg yolks one at a time into the hot white sauce. Put in the spinach mixture and stir thoroughly. Cover and set aside.

Using a hand-held or countertop mixer, beat the egg whites to stiff peaks.

With a spatula, gently mix ¼ of the stiff egg whites into the warm sauce and spinach mixture. Pour this lightened sauce into the bowl with the egg whites. Sprinkle the cheese on top, folding with a rubber spatula. When you've completely folded everything together (being careful not to overmix), pour the soufflé into the prepared dish.

Put the soufflé in the lower third of the preheated oven. Reduce the temperature to 375°. After 35 minutes, carefully check to see whether the soufflé is done—it should have risen nearly to the top of the foil collar, and the very top should be golden brown. If you are in doubt, let it bake another 5 to 10 minutes. Remove the soufflé gently from the oven and put it on a trivet.

Take the soufflé (on the trivet) to the dining table, then remove the twine and foil. (This may not seem very glamorous, but the collar helps keep the soufflé from sinking en route.) Once the collar has been removed, serve the soufflé by plunging a large fork and spoon directly in the center, and scooping out the hot soufflé.

Nani to naku   No reason,
ura kanashiki wa   yet it makes me sad—
waga kado no   by my door
inaba soyogasu   the first fall winds
hatsuaki no kaze   rustling through rice stalks
                             —RYŌKAN

Quiche Printemps

SERVES 4 - 6

● ●

Although this quiche uses vegetables available all year, it has a bright, fresh spring taste, hence its name. It would make a stellar luncheon or dinner entrée accompanied with new potatoes and bright green sugar snap peas.

2	tablespoons butter
⅓ to ½	cup minced shallots or onion
1	stalk celery, cut into ¼-inch dice
1	large carrot, cut into ¼-inch dice
1½ to 2	cups sliced mushrooms
1	cup zucchini, sliced into ¼-inch rounds
2	tablespoons vermouth or white wine
1	teaspoon herbes de Provence
½ to 1	teaspoon salt
4	eggs
½	cup milk
½	cup half-and-half or cream
¼	teaspoon cayenne pepper
¼	teaspoon nutmeg
⅓	cup shredded Gruyère
⅓	cup shredded smoked Gruyère
⅓	cup shredded (not grated) Parmesan cheese
1	partially baked 9- to 10-inch pie shell (page 244), or a partially baked store-bought pie shell

Preheat the oven to 350°.

Melt the butter in a large sauté pan over moderate heat. Add the shallots, cooking and stirring for 2 minutes, until they have softened. Add the celery, carrot, mushrooms, and zucchini; sauté for another minute. Add the wine, herbs, and salt; cook for another 2 minutes. Remove the pan from the heat.

Put the eggs, milk, half-and-half, cayenne, and nutmeg in a bowl and mix thoroughly with a whisk.

Place ⅓ of the cheeses on the bottom of the partially baked pie shell. Add the cooled vegetables, then sprinkle the remaining cheeses on top. Pour the egg mixture into the shell. Immediately put the filled quiche in the upper third of the oven and bake for about 35 to 45 minutes, until done. (The quiche will puff slightly in the center when it is done, and a small knife inserted into the center will come out clean.)

Remove the quiche and let it cool 20 minutes before slicing and serving.

Nanigoto ni
tomaru kokoro no
arikereba
sara ni shimo mata
yo no itowashiki

Is it because my mind
keeps dwelling
on every worldly thing
that the world seems
more hateful to me than ever?
—Saigyô

Mushroom Quiche

One 8- or 9-inch quiche

● ●

2   tablespoons butter or olive oil
½   cup minced onion
1   clove garlic, peeled and minced or put through
       a press
3   cups sliced mushrooms
¼   cup port
1   teaspoon thyme or marjoram
1   tablespoon fresh lemon juice
2   tablespoons chopped fresh parsley
3   eggs
1   cup milk, cream, half-and-half, or a combination
1   teaspoon salt
¼   teaspoon black pepper or cayenne pepper
¼   teaspoon nutmeg
1   cup grated Gruyère cheese or a combination of
       Gruyère and Cheddar
1   8- to 9-inch partially baked pie shell (page 244),
       or a store-bought pie shell, baked

Preheat the oven to 350°.

Melt the butter in a large sauté pan over moderate heat. Add the onion and garlic, and stir and cook for 2 to 3 minutes. Add the mushrooms, sautéing them until they have softened. Turn the flame to high, and cook the mushrooms for 2 to 3 minutes, until they begin to brown. Reduce the flame to medium, and add the port (keeping your face averted), the thyme, and lemon juice. Cook for 1 minute, until the liquid has evaporated. Remove the pan from the heat and add the parsley, tossing once.

Mix the eggs, milk or cream, salt, pepper, and nutmeg in a bowl or blender until smooth. Set aside.

Sprinkle ⅓ of the cheese in the bottom of the prebaked pie shell. Spread all the mushroom mixture over the cheese, then top with the remaining cheese. Carefully pour in the egg mixture, making sure that everything is covered. If you use all of the egg mixture and the quiche still looks a bit in need of more liquid, carefully dribble some additional cream on the top, mixing it in with a knife or fork.

Immediately put the quiche in the upper third of the preheated oven for 35 to 45 minutes, until it has risen in the middle and is lightly browned on top.

Remove the quiche and allow it to cool for 20 minutes before serving.

> *Taberu mono mo naku*   Nothing left to eat;
> *natta kyô no asayake.*   Today's sunrise.
>   —SANTÔKA

Broccoli Quiche
ONE 8- TO 9-INCH QUICHE

• •

1	8- to 9-inch partially baked pie shell (page 244), or a store-bought pie shell
1	roasted red bell pepper (see page 71)
2	tablespoons butter or olive oil
1½	cup minced onion
1 to 2	cloves garlic, peeled and minced or put through a press
2	cups ¼-inch to ½-inch broccoli florets
¼	cup dry white wine or vermouth
¼	cup freshly chopped parsley
3	eggs
1	cup milk, cream, half-and-half, or a combination
1	teaspoon salt
¼	teaspoon black pepper or cayenne pepper
¼	teaspoon nutmeg
1	cup grated Gruyère cheese
1	teaspoon dried basil, or 10 to 12 large fresh basil leaves, torn into bits

Roast the bell pepper (or use store-bought roasted pepper) and slice into thin lengths. Set aside.

Preheat the oven to 350°.

Melt the butter in a large sauté pan over moderate heat. Add the onion and garlic, and stir and cook for 2 to 3 minutes. Add the broccoli, stirring for 1 minute until it is just beginning to turn bright green. Add the wine, and turn the flame to high until the liquid has cooked off and the broccoli is just done. Remove from the heat. Add the parsley and toss.

Mix the eggs, milk or cream, salt, pepper, and nutmeg in a bowl or blender until smooth. Set aside.

Scatter ⅓ of the cheese in the bottom of the prebaked pie shell. Spread all the broccoli mixture over the cheese, then top with the remaining cheese. Carefully place the basil leaves in a nice pattern across the top (or sprinkle on the dried basil), then arrange the red bell pepper slices attractively on top. Carefully pour in the egg mixture, making sure that everything is coated. If you use all of the egg mixture and the quiche still looks a bit in need of more liquid, carefully dribble some additional cream on the top, mixing it in with a knife or fork.

Immediately bake the quiche in the upper third of the preheated oven for 35 to 45 minutes, until it has risen in the middle and is lightly browned on top. Remove the quiche immediately and allow it to cool for 20 minutes before serving.

Variation:
- Use 2 cups broccoli rabe (rapini) instead of broccoli.

Fresh start—
New Year's dinner,
on my own.
　　　—Issa

Onion Quiche

ONE 8- TO 9-INCH QUICHE

● ●

Onion quiches are savory, delicious, and don't overpower you with onion taste, despite the large quantity of onion they contain. The inherent sweetness of the onion is brought out by the extended sautéing.

1　8- to 9-inch partially baked pie shell (page 244),
　　or a store-bought pie shell
3　tablespoons butter
2　large onions, very thinly slices and finely chopped
¼　cup port or dry vermouth
1　teaspoon thyme
¼　cup chopped fresh parsley
3　eggs

> 1 cup milk, cream, half-and-half, or a combination
> 1 teaspoon salt
> ¼ teaspoon black pepper or cayenne pepper
> ¼ teaspoon nutmeg
> 1 cup grated Gruyère cheese, or a mixture of
>   smoked and regular Gruyère

Preheat the oven to 350°.

Heat the butter in a large sauté pan over moderate heat. Add the onion, cover, and stir and cook for 15 minutes, until it is soft and translucent. Toss and continue to cook for an additional 10 minutes over medium low heat; the onion may have begun to brown lightly. Add the wine and thyme, turning the flame up a bit, until the liquid has cooked off. Remove the pan from the heat. Add the parsley and toss.

Mix the eggs, milk or cream, salt, pepper, and nutmeg in a bowl or blender until smooth. Set aside.

Put ⅓ of the cheese in the bottom of the prebaked pie shell. Spread all of the onion mixture over the cheese, then top with the remaining cheese. Carefully pour in the egg mixture, making sure that everything is coated. If you use all the egg mixture and the quiche still looks a bit in need of more liquid, carefully dribble some additional cream on the top, mixing it in with a knife or fork.

Immediately bake the quiche in the upper third of the preheated oven for 35 to 45 minutes, until it has risen in the middle and lightly browned on top. Remove immediately and allow it to cool for 20 minutes before serving.

Yume samuru	In rhythm with
kane no hibiki ni	the tolling of the bell
uchisoete	that wakens us from dreams
totabi no mina o	ten times I intone
tonaetsuru kana	the sacred name
	—SAIGYŌ

Swiss Chard Tart

SERVES 6

● ●

This dense, flavorful quiche is quite rich, so it easily serves six. Be sure to use a tall, false-bottomed tart pan if you have one, so you can remove the baked tart after cooking for an impressive presentation.

1   partially-baked Savory tart crust shell
        (page 246), about 9 to 10 inches in diameter
1   bunch Swiss red or green chard
1 to 2 tablespoons olive oil or butter
1   small onion, peeled and chopped into ¼-inch dice
2 to 3 tablespoons port, Madeira, or sweet vermouth
1   tablespoon chopped fresh thyme
2   teaspoons chopped fresh lemon thyme
    Salt and pepper
1   8-ounce package cream cheese (regular,
        Neufchâtel, light), softened
4   eggs
½   cup milk or half-and-half
½   teaspoon salt
    Large pinch nutmeg
1   cup grated smoked cheese

Partially-bake the tart shell. Set aside.

Wash the chard and cut away the leafy parts from the stalks. Bring a large pot of water to the boil and put the chard greens in, stirring once. Let the greens blanch for 20 seconds, then drain in the colander. Rinse thoroughly with cold water. Squeeze to remove excess water, then roughly chop the greens. Set aside.

Place a large sauté pan over moderate heat; when hot, add the olive oil and onion, sautéing for 10 minutes until the onion is soft and tender. Add the chopped chard, breaking apart the greens, and heat well to remove any excess liquid. When the mixture is hot, add the port and both regular and lemon thyme. Stir and let the wine cook off for 2 minutes, then remove from heat. Add salt and pepper to taste.

Place the softened cream cheese, eggs, milk, ½ teaspoon salt, nutmeg, and a grind or two of fresh pepper in a food processor or blender. Blend until you have a smooth mixture. Set aside or refrigerate until ready to proceed. (The tart can be made ahead of time to this stage and assembled later.)

Preheat the oven to 375°.

Sprinkle one quarter of the grated cheese in the bottom of the partially-baked tart shell. Add the onion mixture, then sprinkle in the remaining cheese. Gently mix the cheese with the chard so that it is evenly distributed. Pour in the egg mixture.

Place the filled tart in the upper center of the preheated oven and bake for 45 to 60 minutes until it has set and is lightly browned on top. Remove from the oven and allow to cool somewhat (or completely) before serving. (The tart may also be reheated at 250° for 30 minutes until it is warmed through.)

If you use a false-bottomed pan, the cooled tart may be removed from the mold for an attractive presentation.

Variation:
- Substitute fresh spinach for the chard, or a mixture of spinach and sorrel.

> *Only the shoots*
> *of new green leaves, white water,*
> *and yellow barley.*
> —BUSON

Timbales

SERVES 4

● ●

Timbales are custards to which you add fresh, well-seasonal vegetables and herbs, complimenting them with simple sauces or serving them by themselves. They can be used as a brunch dish, or if you "beef them up" with a grand assortment of other vegetables as side dishes, timbales make a first-rate main course. Anytime you would serve a quiche or soufflé, think about timbales instead.

As you will see, all of the following timbales are variations on the same custard theme. With any of the variations below, you can either use 4 to 6 small (1 cup) ramekins or one large dish, such as a charlotte or soufflé mold.

The sauces listed at the end are suggestions only—feel free to experiment. A corn timbale tastes quite different served with a tomato sauce than with a sour cream and herb sauce.

THE CUSTARD BASE:

4	*eggs*
1	*cup cream, milk, or half-and-half*
½	*cup fresh bread crumbs*
⅛	*teaspoon cayenne pepper*
⅛	*teaspoon nutmeg*
1	*teaspoon salt*
2 to 3	*tablespoons Parmesan cheese*
⅔ to ¾	*cup grated Gruyère, Cheddar, or a mixture*

Mix the above ingredients in a large bowl. Add the vegetables of your choice.

For Corn Timbales

These are also delicious served cold or at room temperature—a perfect do-ahead brunch. Serve with Basic Tomato Sauce (page 241) or perhaps Basic White Sauce (page 242) with an enrichment of sour cream and fresh chives or marjoram, or a teaspoon of cumin for a more Southwestern flavor.

2 to 2½ cups fresh yellow or white corn kernels
¼ to ½ cup grated onion
    ¼ cup chopped parsley
    ¼ cup finely diced red bell pepper

Combine the corn, onion, parsley, and bell pepper with the custard base and cook as directed below.

For Broccoli Timbales

    2 cups blanched broccoli florets
    ¼ cup finely minced onion
    1 clove garlic, peeled and minced or put through
        a press
    1 teaspoon dried basil or 1 tablespoon chopped
        fresh basil

Blanch the broccoli and dice into ¼-inch pieces. Add the broccoli along with the onion, garlic, and basil to the custard base and cook as directed below.

For Carrot Timbales

Although they are quite tasty, carrot timbales seem to be more suitable as a side dish rather than a main course—I don't know why exactly, but there you are!

2 to 2½ cups shredded carrots
1 to 2 tablespoons butter
    ¼ cup chopped fresh dill

Lightly sauté the carrots in the butter over a moderate flame until the carrots turn bright orange and are slightly soft. Remove from the heat and allow to cool. Add the carrots and dill to the custard base, cooking as directed below.

FOR SPINACH OR SORREL TIMBALES

Although spinach keeps its color better than sorrel during cooking, sorrel is more of a delicacy. If you don't have enough sorrel, combine it with spinach to make the necessary amount. Serve this with Basic White Sauce (page 242) enriched with sour cream, the Mushroom Duxelles (page 238) or a Yeast Brown Gravy (page 243).

> 2 to 2½ **cups blanched, chopped spinach or sorrel**
> **(about 2 pounds raw)**
> ¼ to ½ **cup finely minced onion**
> 1 **teaspoon thyme**

Blanch the spinach, squeezing out any excess liquid; chop fine. Add the spinach, onion, and thyme to the custard base and cook as directed below.

FOR MUSHROOM TIMBALES
(Two Versions)

VERSION I:

> 2 **tablespoons butter**
> 2 **cups sliced mushrooms**
> 1 **cup Mushroom Duxelles (page 238)**
> ¼ **cup chopped chives**

Heat the butter in a sauté pan over a moderate flame, then add the mushrooms. Raise the flame to high and sauté briskly, stirring, until the mushrooms are cooked and may have begun to brown lightly. Remove the pan from the flame and mix in the duxelles. Add the chives, mix everything into the custard base, and cook as directed below.

VERSION II:

This is quite delicate, strangely like a veal quenelle in appearance and taste. I recommend using a subtle sauce with it, as anything terribly strong will overpower it.

Important note: for this version, it will be necessary to increase the amount of bread crumbs in the custard base from ½ cup to ¾ cup.

4   cups finely chopped mushrooms
        (approximately one 8-ounce package)
2   tablespoons butter
1   clove garlic, peeled and minced or put through
        a press
3   tablespoons finely minced onion
1   teaspoon herbes de Provence
1   tablespoon tamari

Chop the mushrooms by hand or in a food processor (in short, quick spurts). Heat the butter in a sauté pan over a moderate flame, add the garlic and onion, and cook for about 2 minutes, then add the mushrooms and herbes de Provence. Raise the flame to high and continue cooking, stirring, until the natural liquid from the mushrooms has evaporated and the mushroom bits have begun to brown lightly. Add the tamari and for another minute. Allow the mushrooms to cool somewhat, then mix it into the custard base and cook as directed below.

FOR SWEET PEA TIMBALES

1   tablespoon butter
½   teaspoon salt
1   tablespoon sugar
2 to 2½ cups peas, thawed if frozen (don't use
            canned peas)
¼ to ⅓ cup torn fresh spearmint leaves

Place the butter in a sauté pan over a moderate flame. Add the salt and sugar, cook for 30 seconds, then add the peas. Toss and stir the peas until they are coated with the sweet butter, about 30 seconds. Remove them to a bowl and allow to cool. Add the peas and mint to the custard mixture and cook as directed below.

TO COOK THE TIMBALE

Preheat the oven to 325°. Prepare a bain-marie (see page 251).

Pour the timbale mixture into individual molds or one large mold buttered or sprayed with Pam. Place the molds in a bain-marie.

Put the pan in the center of a preheated 325° oven and bake until the timbale has puffed and a small knife inserted into the timbale comes out clean. Cook small individual timbales for 30 to 45 minutes, and one large timbale for 1 hour and 15 to 30 minutes. If you're prepared all of the ingredients ahead of time and have refrigerated them until needed, add 15 to 20 minutes to the total cooking time.

When done, remove from the oven and allow to stand for 10 minutes in the hot water before removing and serving.

To serve, run a knife around the edge of the mold to loosen the timbale. Put a lightly warmed plate over the timbale and flip both the plate and timbale over simultaneously. Remove the mold and serve the timbale immediately with a sauce, if desired.

SAUCES TO CONSIDER FOR TIMBALES:

- Light Basic White Sauce (page 242) enriched with some sour cream and 2 teaspoons fresh thyme and parsley
- Light Basic White Sauce enriched with ¼ cup Mushroom Duxelles (page 238) and 2 tablespoons fresh parsley
- Basic White mixed with ¼ to ⅓ cup Pesto Cream Sauce (page 64)
- Basic Tomato Sauce (page 241)
- Yeast Brown Gravy (page 243)

Variations:
- As with any egg-cheese dish, feel free to substitute cheeses that you have on hand or that you particularly like for the ones suggested. Try adding a bit of smoked cheese, or some Derby sage, or port cheese, or perhaps some fresh goat cheese, or crumbled feta. Be careful with blue cheese, though, as a little bit goes a long way.
- As long as you start with the custard base, you can experiment with practically anything you have in the refrigerator—half a zucchini, some green onions, an ancho chile. You're only limited by what you have around and your imagination!
- Since the custard base stays the same for all but one of the above timbales, you can make two, three, or four timbales at once. For example, if you're making two timbales—the spinach and the sweet pea—just cut the recipe amounts for the vegetables in half and put them in different baking dishes. Prepare the full amount of the custard base, then mix half of the custard base into each vegetable dish. Place both dishes in the bain-marie and bake accordingly. This is an easy way to add variety to a meal.
- For a creamier custard, add 4 ounces of cream cheese to the custard base.

*Asa na tsumu
shizuga kadota no
ta no aze ni
chikiri naku nari
haru ni wa narinu*

*Picking morning greens
in skimpy rows
of my kitchen garden
I hear a wagtail singing—
spring's really here!*
—RYŌKAN

Winter Puff

● ●

A vegetable puff is delightful—light, cheesy, and delicately flavored. It's a soufflé really, but not as dramatic as the soufflés given previously. And since it has eggs in it, it is a perfect complete protein.

2	russet potatoes, scrubbed and chopped into 1-inch cubes
2	carrots, peeled and chopped into ½-inch cubes
½	tablespoon butter
½	cup diced onion
½	teaspoon thyme
½	teaspoon basil
½	teaspoon marjoram
1 to 1½	cups milk (cow, goat, soy)
	Salt and pepper to taste
4	eggs, separated
1	cup grated cheese (a mixture of Gruyère, smoked Gouda, sharp Cheddar, and/or Parmesan)
	Chopped parsley for garnish, optional
	Dollops of sour cream, optional

Place the scrubbed, diced potatoes in a vegetable steamer and steam until they are tender, about 20 minutes. Place them in a large bowl.

Put the carrots in the same steamer and cook 10 to 12 minutes. When they are soft, place them in the bowl with the potatoes.

Place a small sauté pan over a moderate flame and add the butter. When the butter has melted, add the onion and cook for 5 to 8 minutes, until it is soft and translucent. Add to the bowl and toss the herbs with the vegetables.

Using a fork or potato masher, mash the potatoes, carrots, and onions to a fairly smooth mixture—it's fine if there are some lumps left. Add the milk, stirring well, then salt and pepper to taste. Let the vegetable mixture cool to room temperature before proceeding.

Meanwhile, separate the eggs, placing the yolks in a small bowl and the whites in a large bowl.

Once the vegetable mixture is cool, add the egg yolks and beat well. Fold in the cheeses.

Preheat the oven to 350°.

Using a hand-held or countertop mixer, beat the whites until they nearly reach firm peaks. Add ¼ of the beaten whites to the vegetable mixture, mixing well. (At this point you're just lightening the potatoes.) Fold in the remaining whites, deflating them as little as possible. Pour the mixture into an 8-inch square baking dish sprayed with Pam.

Place the dish in the upper third of the preheated oven and bake for 45 to 60 minutes, until it has puffed slightly and browned on top. Remove from the oven and serve immediately, garnishing with some freshly chopped parsley and a dollop of sour cream on the side, if you like.

Variations:
- The list here could be endless. If you think of the potato, milk, and eggs as being the base.

YOU MIGHT SUBSTITUTE STEAMED:
> acorn squash for the carrot
> sweet potato for the russet potatoes
> cottage cheese for the mixed cheeses

YOU COULD ADD:
> *1   cup finely diced and lightly steamed broccoli*
> *½   cup sour cream, plain yogurt, or softened*
> *   cream cheese for ½ cup of the milk*
> *1   cup chopped steamed spinach*
> *½   cup additional onion, for a total of 1 cup*
> *   More herbs to taste*

YOU COULD OMIT:
> the cheeses
> the herbs
> the onion

Sake wa nai   No sake;
tsuki shimijimi mite ori. *I stare at the moon.*
—SANTŌKA

RICE

●●●●●●●●●●●●●●●●●●●●●●●●●●●●

INTRODUCTION

From very early on I adored rice. I believe in using the appropriate grain for the job, so I don't have just one kind of rice in my pantry. I may keep on hand long- and short-grain (brown and white) rices, brown and white basmati rices, wild rice, glutinous rice, and arborio rice. Because of the differences in taste, texture, and appearance, I would never use arborio rice for an Indian pilaf, just as I wouldn't think to use brown basmati rice for risotto. As with any craft, you must use the right materials for the job.

SHORT- AND LONG-GRAIN RICE:

These are different varieties of rice altogether, and have different characteristics. All rice can be classified under one of these two headings; the many varieties are all subsets of these two types.

Long- and short-grain rices contain starch. Specifically, rice has two types of starch in differing quantities—amylose starch and amylopectin starch. Interestingly, the characteristic of the starch makes the difference in the grains. Long-grain rices contain a greater amount of amylose starch, which is why long-grain rice stays separate in the pot and doesn't clump together. Short-grain rice, on the other hand, contains more amylopectin starch, so it does clump together. (A device for remembering the difference between the two: standard old pectin causes liquids to gel and become thick, hence, amylopectin starch causes short grain rice to stick together.)

Other differences:

SHORT-GRAIN RICE	LONG-GRAIN RICE
plump	thin
gummier/stickier	does not stick together (unless improperly cooked)
warming (winter food)	cooling (summer food)
great for Asian dishes	great for European and Middle Eastern/Indian dishes
easy to eat with chopsticks	difficult to eat with chopsticks

BROWN RICE VERSUS WHITE RICE

Brown rice, whether it be basmati or regular, is rice that retains its outer husk. It takes longer to cook than white rice, and is sweeter, chewier, and nuttier in flavor. Brown rice is as different in texture and appearance from white rice as an artichoke leaf is from an artichoke heart; neither should be regarded as superior to the other, they're just different.

The choice is up to you. Brown rice has additional nutrients that white rice has had polished away with the husking process, but they're really so different in taste and use that it's best to judge for yourself which you prefer in what dish.

WHITE BASMATI VERSUS JASMINE RICE

Basmati rice is originally from the highlands of India. Jasmine rice is from Southeast Asia and Indonesia. Regular long-grain rice is from anywhere there's standing water.

For most purposes, I prefer white basmati rice to jasmine or long-grain rice. Admittedly, there's not a huge difference between jasmine rice and basmati rice, but the difference between basmati/jasmine and long-grain rice is huge. White basmati is not difficult to find, as it is surfacing all over the country in grocery stores (sometimes at outlandish prices), but the best place to get it is at an Indian market. There you'll see

5-, 10-, and 20-kilo bags full of fragrant, aged basmati at bargain prices.

Jasmine rice can be found at Thai, Vietnamese, and/or Indonesian markets, and now is popping up in supermarkets. Despite its name, jasmine rice has no jasmine in it (unlike jasmine tea); the fragrance of the rice, however, carries heavy flowery overtones, sometimes quite strong, hence the name. It is about twice the girth of basmati rice and can be used anywhere you would use white long-grain rice. I tend to think of jasmine rice as being "long-grain glutinous rice," since it has a stickier, more glutinous quality than regular long-grain rice. Jasmine rice is perfect for Southeast Asian cuisine.

GLUTINOUS ("STICKY" OR "SWEET") RICE

I love glutinous rice and it's practically unknown to most Americans. It is simplicity itself to prepare, since there are no measurements needed! Glutinous rice is the quintessential "sticky" rice; it is perfect for chopstick-food and is not the slightest bit gummy. "Sweet" or "sticky" rice sticks together in neat little clumps without being mushy or porridgelike, yet every grain is separate and maintains its texture and lovely shine. Contrary to its name, this variety of rice is not sweet, nor does it contain gluten.

WILD RICE

Wild rice isn't rice at all—it's the seed of an aquatic grass plant. The long, deep brown kernels look quite exotic, and they possess an earthy, warm, comforting taste. For years, the exorbitant cost of wild rice relegated it to use on special occasions or merely as an adjunct to brown rice (the notorious "brown and wild rice blends" that contain 99 percent brown rice and 1 percent wild rice). Wild rice does have a powerful, woodsy taste that some people may not find appealing, but it's much like a mushroom, with its foresty, natural flavor. It may be hard to find recipes using 100 percent wild rice, but I've included a lovely one that is delicately herbed and tasty.

"PARBOILED" RICE

"Parboiled" (sometimes referred to as "converted") rice has undergone a steaming process that hardens the grains to keep them from sticking together. Parboiled rice is minimally more nutritious than regular white rice, but I dislike its plastic texture and thus never use it.

As she washes rice,
her smiling face
is briefly
lit by firefly
                    —ANON.

Basic Rice Recipes

● ●

Sometimes it's nice to have plain, no-nonsense rice side dish to accompany an entrée; no fuss, no worry, just plain rice. Plain rice is delicious and very simple to make, so don't feel you're not treating yourself to the best rice has to offer by having it au naturel.

With all rices, one of the most important components is a good rice pot; this doesn't have to be anything special, just a good solid, heavy pot with a tight-fitting lid. I use an enamel-coated cast-iron pot (Le Creuset)—both the pot and lid are quite heavy, and the iron retains and distributes heat evenly.

I've used and seen electric rice cookers from Asia, which are unquestionably fine products, but for me it always comes back to the same issue: why buy a separate electric gadget to do what a simple pot will do?

White Basmati Rice

SERVES 4

● ●

Sometimes the best accompaniment to a spicy dinner is snow white, delicate basmati rice.

1	cup white basmati rice
1 to 3	teaspoons butter or ghee
1⅓	cups water
1	teaspoon salt

Place the rice in a bowl and add water to cover. Swish the rice around with your fingers until the water is milky in appearance. Rinse the rice several times in cool running water until the water is clear. Cover the rice with cool, clean water and allow it to soak for 30 to 60 minutes.

After soaking, drain the rice in a colander and allow it to stand and dry for 20 minutes.

Place a small, heavy pot over a moderate flame and add the butter. When it is hot, add the rice and sauté for 30 to 60 seconds, coating all the grains with the butter. Be careful to stir the rice gently and break as few grains as possible. The rice will change slightly in appearance and will be opaque and glistening. Add the water and salt; bring the mixture to the boil. Cover the pot with a tight-fitting lid and turn the flame to low. Cook the rice for 15 minutes. Once the rice has absorbed all of the liquid, allow it to stand, covered, for another 15 minutes. Serve.

Sabae toru	*In paddies among the mountains*
yamada no oda no	*girls transplant*
otomego ga	*rice seedlings—*
uchiaguru uta no	*the sound of their singing*
koe no harukesa	*rifts up from far away*
	—RYÔKAN

Brown Basmati Rice

SERVES 4

● ●

Brown basmati has a wonderful, popcornlike aroma when it is cooking. It is much fluffier than plain long-grain brown rice and the taste is exquisite.

1   cup brown basmati rice
2   cups water
1   teaspoon salt
1 to 3   teaspoons butter or ghee, optional

Place the rice in a heavy pot and wash under cool water to remove any dirt and/or floating debris. Drain the rice. Add the water, salt, and butter. Place over a medium high flame and bring to a boil. Cover the pot and turn the heat to low. Cook for 30 to 40 minutes, checking occasionally near the end of the cooking period to be sure the rice has absorbed all the liquid.

Once the water has been absorbed, replace the lid and turn the heat to high for 30 seconds. Remove the pot from the flame and allow to stand, undisturbed and covered, for 15 minutes before serving.

Short-grain White Rice and Sushi Rice

SERVES 4

●●●●●●●●●●●●●●●●●●●●●●●●●●●●●●

In some health food stores you can find a version of sushi rice that is partially husked; it is nearly white with a few tan speckles. This variety of rice is marketed as being the "true, original sushi rice" because it isn't completely husked, the theory being that hundreds of years ago in Japan this would have more closely approximated what would have been available. I once served this type of rice to my dear friend Shozo Sato; he wasn't amused. "Sushi rice should be snow white," he instructed. To procure this "neotraditional" sushi rice, visit a health food store; for the real thing, visit your Japanese market .

The soaking period for sushi rice is debatable; some cooks suggest soaking the rice overnight, but some say that an hour is sufficient. Since I frequently don't know if I'm making sushi until a few hours before dinner, I use the latter method.

For plain short-grain white rice:

1   cup white short-grain rice
1   cup water

Place the rice in a bowl and wash it several times in cool water, swishing the grains around gently with your fingers until the milkiness disappears. Drain and place it in a small, heavy pot with a tight-fitting lid. Add water to cover and let the rice soak for 60 to 90 minutes.

After soaking, drain the rice and add one cup of water. Bring the rice to a vigorous boil over a medium high flame; cover and turn the heat to low. Let the rice cook for 15 minutes, then turn the heat to high and cook for 30 seconds. Immediately remove the rice from the heat and allow it to stand, covered and undisturbed, for 15 minutes before serving.

TO MAKE SUSHI (VINEGARED) RICE

While the rice is cooking, mix these ingredients in a small bowl, dissolving the sugar well:

2 to 2½   tablespoons rice wine vinegar
2 to 3   tablespoons sugar
1 to 1½   teaspoons salt

Once the rice has cooked and sat for 15 minutes, spread it on a platter. Pour the vinegar mixture over the rice, mixing it gently with a wooden paddle. While you are tossing the rice with the vinegar mixture, cool it by fanning it with a hand-held fan (obviously) or a folded newspaper. When the rice is at room temperature, place a slightly dampened cloth over it to keep it from drying out. The rice is now ready to use for sushi (nigiri sushi or sushi-maki), but many people enjoy the taste of vinegared rice by itself, so perhaps you may want to serve the rice in a bowl along with some thinly sliced shiso leaves or chopped chives.

NOTE: I've tasted preseasoned vinegar that can be used to make sushi rice, but in all honesty I find it unduly sweet and sometimes salty. I prefer to season sushi rice myself and know that I will be in control of the taste.

Short-Grain Brown Rice

SERVES 4

● ●

Most macrobiotic enthusiasts believe that short-grain brown rice is a grain best eaten in the winter to stimulate the digestive system. I find short-grain brown rice to be tastier than long-grain brown rice, but it is sometimes gummy if the rice has been cooked in too much water.

1   cup brown short-grain rice
2   cups water
1   teaspoon salt, optional

Place the rice in a small, heavy pot with a tight-fitting lid. Rinse it in cool water, removing any floating debris and dirt. Drain the rice and add the 2 cups water and the salt. Bring to the boil over a medium high flame, then cover the pot and reduce the flame to low. Cook for 40 minutes, or until the water has been absorbed. Allow the rice to stand for 15 minutes, covered and off the heat, before serving.

Jasmine Rice

SERVES 4

• •

Jasmine rice is great for fried rice and stir-fries.

> 1   cup jasmine rice
> 1   cup water
> 1   teaspoon salt, optional

Pick over the rice, removing any grains that are not hulled or appear darker than the others.

Place the rice in a small, heavy pot with a tight-fitting lid and wash it once, swishing it around with your fingers until the water is milky. Drain the rice and briefly rinse it once again with clean water. Drain, then add the cup of water to cover, and let the rice soak for 30 to 60 minutes.

After soaking, drain the rice and add the cup of water. Add the salt (if desired). Bring the water to the boil, cover the pot, then turn the flame to low. Cook the rice for 12 to 15 minutes, or until it has absorbed the liquid. (It's fine to remove the lid and check the rice.) Once all the liquid is absorbed, cover and turn the heat to high for 30 seconds. Remove the pan from the heat and allow it to stand, undisturbed, for at least 15 minutes.

Glutinous (sweet) Rice
(o-mochi-gome)

Although you will need no proportions here, approximately 1 cup of rice will serve 4 or less, depending on how much you like rice and how important the rice is to your meal. If the rice is not merely a side dish but the basis of a dinner (like a Thai stir-fry with sticky rice), then you'd probably increase the amount to 2 cups of rice for 4 people. This is steamed, not boiled, so you can make as little or as much rice as you desire; the process remains the same.

Place your rice in a bowl and cover it with water. Using your hand, swish around the rice and the water. After 20 seconds or so, the water will become cloudy and milky. Pour off this water and refill the bowl, rinsing with clean water two or three times until the water runs clear. Fill the bowl with water and allow the rice to soak, uncovered and unrefrigerated, for 4 to 12 hours. (This is easy to do first thing in the morning—then your rice is sufficiently soaked for dinner.)

When the rice has soaked, get a steamer contraption ready. (I have a big, heavy Dutch oven with a tight-fitting lid in which I put a couple inches of water and an aluminum steamer lined with a layer of cheesecloth, but any similar arrangement will do as long as you have the rice above the water and set up for steaming.) Make sure you have one to two inches of water in the bottom of the pot.

After soaking, drain the rice. Place the soaked rice on the cheesecloth (which is on the aluminum steamer), then put the steamer into the pot. Bring the water to the boil and cover; reduce the heat to medium low so the water is at a steady (but not vigorous) boil.

Depending on how much rice you're cooking, it may take anywhere from 15 to 30 minutes to steam. The best way to check for doneness is to open the steamer after 15 minutes, remove a bit of the rice with a fork, and taste it; if it still has a slightly starchy center, replace the cover and steam for 5 to 10 more minutes. If it has changed from dull and opaque in appearance to smooth, glossy, and slightly transparent, then it is probably done. You can either serve it immediately, or replace the cover and turn off the heat, allowing the rice to sit for 10 to 30 minutes or so until you're ready to serve.

As soon as you try to spoon the rice out of the steamer you'll know why it's called "sticky" rice.

Wild Rice

● ●

Wild rice is not exactly the kind of thing one frequently eats by itself, though there's no reason why one shouldn't. It is a luscious treat. Since it cooks longer than regular white rice, you cannot put raw wild and white rices in a pot and expect them both to come out perfectly. Brown rice, however, does mix well with wild rice, hence the common brown-wild blends you see in most markets. If you want to make your own mix, go ahead—half and half of each is a good starting point, but some prefer a lesser amount of wild rice, in which case ¾ brown to ¼ wild rice would be better.

Here's a way to make basic wild rice. I find plain wild rice boiled in nothing but water to be rather Spartan and daunting—hence the herbs and stock.

1	cup wild rice
1	tablespoon butter, ghee, or oil
1	cup finely diced onions or shallots
1	carrot, peeled and diced into 1/8-inch cubes
1½ to 2	cups strong mushroom stock
1	teaspoon herbes de Provence, optional
	Salt or tamari to taste

Pour 4 to 5 cups of water into a saucepan and bring to the boil. Add the wild rice and boil, uncovered, for 5 to 8 minutes. Drain the rice in a sieve.

Place a heavy 6-cup pot with a tight-fitting lid over medium heat; add the butter and onion. Sauté the onion for 3 to 5 minutes, until it is soft and translucent. Add the carrot pieces, the stock, and the optional herbs. Bring to the boil; take a small spoon and taste the liquid for salt, keeping in mind that the mixture will reduce and whatever salt is in the stock will become more concentrated by the time you're finished. Add the drained rice and cover, cooking over a low flame for 30 to 45 minutes, until the liquid is absorbed.

Allow the pot to stand, covered, for another 15 minutes before serving. Note: This is really an easy item to make ahead of time, reheating at the last moment. The longer the rice sits, the fluffier and "drier" it will be.

Kaze no naka kome   Walking in the wind
morai ni iku.   To receive some rice.
                                    —SANTŌKA

Basmati Rice with Lemongrass

SERVES 4

● ●

Lemongrass has a distinct, intense lemon flavor similar to lemon peel—yet not quite. Its taste is bright and refreshing.

1	cup white basmati rice, washed
1 to 2	tablespoons ghee or butter
1	cup thickly sliced mushrooms
¼	cup finely chopped fresh lemongrass*
1 to 2	teaspoons sugar
1	teaspoon salt
½	teaspoon turmeric
1⅓	cup water

Wash and drain the basmati rice according to the directions on page 125. Melt the ghee in a heavy pot with a tight-fitting lid over a moderate heat; add the mushrooms and turn the heat to medium high. Sauté, browning the mushrooms slightly, for 2 to 3 minutes.

Reduce the flame to medium and add the drained rice. Coat the rice with the ghee for about 30 seconds as you stir it in with the mushrooms. Add the lemongrass, sugar, salt, turmeric, and water; bring the mixture to a boil. Cover the pot, turn the heat to low, and cook for 15 minutes. Remove the pot from the heat and allow it to stand, undisturbed and covered, for 15 minutes. Fluff the rice gently with a fork or rice paddle before serving.

*available in Asian markets and the specialty section of large supermarkets

Winter fields—
garden sparrows
begging rice.
—ISSA

Basmati Royale

SERVES 4

● ●

There's something exquisite about the combination of rice, nuts, and dried
fruit. Sweet, salty, savory, crunchy, moist, toothsome—wonderful!

1	cup white basmati rice, washed and dried in a sieve
	Big pinch of saffron
2 to 4	tablespoons ghee
1	2-inch cinnamon stick
4	whole cloves
¼	teaspoon freshly ground cardamom, or 6 green cardamom pods
1½	teaspoon salt
1⅓	cup boiling water
⅓ to ½	cup raw cashew or almond pieces
¼ to ⅓	cup currants
½ to 1	teaspoon garam masala

Wash the rice in a bowl until the water runs clear; allow it to soak in clear water for 20 to 30 minutes. Drain the rice in a sieve and allow to air-dry for 20 minutes.

Place the saffron in a 2-cup measuring cup and add ¼ cup boiling water. Set aside until needed.

Have a kettle of boiling water ready.

Heat 2 tablespoons of the ghee in a heavy pot; add cinnamon stick, cloves, cardamom, and 1 teaspoon salt. Sauté for 30 to 45 seconds over medium heat until the spices give off a lovely aroma; add the drained, dry rice and sauté for 1 to 2 minutes, until each grain of rice has absorbed some of the ghee and has become opaque. Fill the measuring cup (with the steeped saffron) to the 1⅓ cup mark with boiling water; pour this into the pot with the rice. Make sure the rice is boiling, then stir once and cover. Turn the heat to very low and cook for 12 minutes.

While the rice is cooking, heat 1 to 2 tablespoons of ghee in a small skillet over medium heat. Add the cashews or almonds, stirring constantly until they are a light tan color; add the currants and continue stirring until the currants have puffed up a bit and the cashews are medium brown. Drain on several layers of paper towels and sprinkle with ½ teaspoon of the salt and the garam masala on top. Set aside.

When the rice is done, remove it from the heat and allow to stand covered and undisturbed, for 10 minutes. Remove lid and add the nut and fruit mixture; fluff the rice gently and serve immediately.

> *Gathering mist,*
> *eternal mornings—*
> *how good the tea.*
> —Issa

Risotto with Sun-Dried Tomatoes

SERVES 4 AS A SIDE DISH

● ●

The only trick with arborio rice is knowing when it is done. Unfortunately, since all rice differs in age and cooking time, there is no exact time measurement to follow. You'll have to test it by tasting it; when ready, it will be creamy and possess the texture of pasta cooked al dente. After you've added 2 cups of liquid, begin tasting for doneness. You may need to add more stock, depending on the age of the rice and weather conditions. But don't worry about it—it's quite simple; just keep stirring and adding liquid until it's done.

1 to 2	tablespoons olive oil (perhaps the oil the sun-dried tomatoes were packed in)
¼	cup finely chopped onion
1	cup arborio rice
3½	cups Vegetable, Mushroom, or Onion Stock*, heated
½	teaspoon dried basil or 3 tablespoons chopped fresh basil
¼	cup chopped parsley
½	cup sliced sun-dried tomatoes packed in oil
½ to ⅔	cup Parmesan cheese
	Salt and freshly ground black pepper

*mushroom or onion stock will make the risotto a deep tan color.

Place a heavy pot with a tight-fitting lid over moderate heat. Add the olive oil; when it is hot (about 1 minute), add the onion. Sauté for 4 minutes, until soft and translucent. Add the rice, stirring and sautéing, until some of the olive oil is absorbed and each grain of rice is shiny. Reduce the heat to low.

Add the hot (or boiling) stock ½ cup at a time, stirring constantly. As soon as nearly all of the stock has been absorbed, add another ½ cup, stirring as before. Continue stirring the rice gently and adding stock until the rice is almost done. At this stage the rice should have a tiny amount of liquid left to be absorbed.

Remove the pot from the heat and add the dried basil, chopped parsley, sun-dried tomatoes, and Parmesan cheese, stirring quickly but thoroughly. Add salt and pepper as needed. Serve immediately.

Kore de cha wa	*So this is what*
tariru	*He calls his tea grove —*
to iu cha no ki.	*A single bush!*
	—SANTŌKA

Mock Risotto

SERVES 4

● ●

What do you do with 2-plus cups of leftover rice? You could use it to stuff some peppers, or make this quick side dish. It's not true risotto like the preceding recipe, but it's so easy, who cares?

2	tablespoons olive oil
2 to 3	cloves garlic, peeled and minced or put through a press
¼	cup finely minced onion
2 to 3	cups leftover cooked white rice (long- or short-grain)
½	cup half-and-half or water
1	cup halved or whole cherry tomatoes or ¼ cup sliced sun-dried tomatoes
1	cup chopped fresh basil, or ½ cup chopped fresh oregano
½	cup freshly grated Parmesan cheese
	Freshly ground black pepper
	Salt to taste

Place the olive oil in a sauté pan over moderate heat. Add the garlic and onion, stirring and cooking until the garlic is tender and the onion is translucent but thoroughly done. Add the rice, breaking it up with the back of a spoon; add the half-and-half. Reduce the heat to low and cover the pan. Allow the rice to steam and heat through for 2 to 5 minutes, stirring occasionally.

Add the tomatoes and cover again; just heat them through. Remove from the heat and add the basil, stirring well. Sprinkle in the Parmesan cheese and add a grating of black pepper, stirring quickly. Taste for seasoning; add salt as necessary. Serve immediately.

Variation:

- The options are many. Experiment with what you have on hand. Add mushrooms, carrots, celery, olives, capers, substitute herbs when available, reduce the amount of Parmesan cheese and add some smoked cheese, or try other ideas.

> *"How am I doing?"*
> *Sponge cucumber*
> *hanging on cactus.*
> —Issa

Risotto con Funghi
Mushroom Risotto

SERVES 4

● ●

Mushroom risotto is one of the oldest and heartiest of risottos. The deep, rich flavor of the mushrooms is intensified during cooking, particularly when you use a variety of mushrooms rather than just the plain, run-of-the-mill white button type. This side dish would go well with any Mediterranean or French menu.

1 to 2 *tablespoons olive oil or butter, or a*
            combination
    ½   *cup finely diced white or yellow onion*
    1   *cup sliced white mushrooms, or a mixture of white*
            and other mushrooms (crimini, shiitake, oyster,
            chanterelle, morel or the like)
    1   *cup arborio rice*
    ½   *teaspoon thyme*

¼ cup rehydrated dried wild mushrooms* (morel, porcini, shiitake, black or others), drained and cut up
3 cups hot Mushroom Stock, page 28
½ cup white wine
Freshly ground black pepper
Salt to taste
Fresh parsley or thyme, for garnish
Parmesan cheese to taste, optional

Place the oil in a heavy pot over a moderate flame. Add the onion and sauté for 3 to 5 minutes, until it is soft and translucent. Add the fresh mushrooms and continue sautéing. Once the mushrooms have begun to soften slightly, turn the flame to medium high; continue stirring and sautéing until the mushrooms begin to brown and exude juices, 2 to 3 minutes.

Reduce the flame to low and add the rice, stirring well with the mushrooms and making sure all the grains are coated with some of the oil. Add the thyme, rehydrated mushroom pieces, and ½ cup of the hot stock, stirring. As soon as nearly all of the stock has been absorbed, add another ½ cup, stirring as before. Continue adding stock and stirring the rice until the rice is done. Add pepper, salt, and Parmesan cheese as desired. Garnish with parsley and serve immediately.

Below the mountains
a noise of rice being hulled—
and wisteria.
—BUSON

Risotto with Broccoli Rabe
SERVES 4

● ●

Broccoli rabe (rapini) may be found in the gourmet or specialty sections of many supermarkets, and its popularity has caused some markets to carry it as a regular item in the produce section. Sold in bunches, it looks like a cross between broccoli and turnip greens, with pencil-thick stems, lush leaves, and tiny knobs of broccoli florets at the top. Rabe is what I would call an "adult" food, for it has a complex taste of greens combined with a slight bitterness.

*To rehydrate mushrooms: place the dried mushrooms in a bowl or measuring cup. Pour on enough boiling water to cover them by ½-inch. Allow to soak for 30 minutes. After soaking, remove any tough stems (reserving them for soup stock) and slice the mushroom tops for the recipe. Save the rehydrating liquid for soup stock as well.

½ cup white wine or dry vermouth
3 cups flavorful vegetable stock
1 teaspoon thyme
1 to 2 tablespoons butter or olive oil, or a
    combination
1 small onion, finely diced
1 cup arborio rice
2 cups broccoli rabe (rapini), cleaned, chopped,
    and blanched*
1 cup freshly grated Parmesan cheese
   Freshly cracked black pepper

Place the wine, stock, and thyme in a pot and bring to a simmer.

Put the butter in a heavy pot over moderate heat. When it is hot, add the onion and sauté for 3 to 5 minutes until soft and translucent. Add the rice, stirring well to make sure all of the grains are coated with some of the butter. Reduce the flame to low. Add ½ cup of the hot stock mixture, stirring well. As soon as nearly all of the stock has been absorbed, add another ½ cup, stirring as before. Continue stirring every 30 seconds or so and adding stock until the rice is nearly done. When there still is a bit of liquid left, add the broccoli rabe and any remaining stock. Cover the pot and cook for 1 minute undisturbed. Turn off the heat and let the pot stand for 5 minutes.

When the rice is done and the broccoli rabe tender, add the Parmesan cheese and stir. Serve immediately, garnishing with freshly cracked black pepper.

---

*To clean broccoli rabe, wash the stems thoroughly under cool water. Since the lower stems will be tough, cut off the bottom ½-inch or so and peel the stalk upward. If the bottom is particularly tough, this will be simple, as the cellulose in the outer skin will pull effortlessly up the stalk, leaving you with a pale green center stem. If the stem breaks easily as you peel, then you will need a minimal amount of peeling, because the stalk is tender. Use all of the rabe, chopping the stem, leaves, and florets. Blanch for 1 minute in boiling water; drain in a colander and rinse with cold water. Squeeze out excess liquid.

Hinata mabushiku   Shining brightly
meshi bakari   In the sunshine:
no meishi o.   My meal of boiled rice.
                                    —Santôka

Nori Rolls

MAKES ABOUT 3 ROLLS,
SERVING 4 PEOPLE GENEROUSLY

● ●

The sushi lunch box,
while washing it in the shallows,
playful drifting fish!
                                    —Buson

Contrary to popular opinion, all sushi does not contain raw fish.

In the world of sushi, nori rolls fall into the category of sushi-maki (also called zushi-maki or nori-maki), translated as "rolled sushi." A piece of laver or nori (seaweed) is laid out, then vinegared rice is patted down, then a layer of whatever you want to put in the center of the nori roll. (Here is a perfect opportunity for you to experiment with different ingredients, with the only criterion being that the pieces must fit nicely into a nori roll; thus pencil-shaped objects, such as carrot or cucumber strips, avocados, or very thin leafy fillings like chives, sorrel, or shiso leaves, cut and layered in, are perfect.) Last, you roll up the packet and slice it into pieces, and voilá! You have your own sushi.

The art of proper, authentic sushi-making is complex and difficult; in Japan it requires years of study and practice. I have not attempted to give a recipe intended to rival the best sushi houses of Kyoto or Tokyo, but merely a recipe that you can use for your own purposes. I have not gone into detail about tossing and cooling the vinegared rice, for example, nor have I given a full description of all the possibilities for different kinds of sushi-maki. For the true, authentic sushi (as well as other Japanese specialties), consult the myriad of excellent Japanese cookbooks on the market, the foremost being Shizuo Tsuji's Japanese Cooking, A Simple Art *(Kodansha Publications). However, if you just want to try your hand at making your own nori-maki, here's how. The directions are long, not because there is anything particularly difficult, but because there are several steps that must be followed.*

Itadakemasu!

1	cup sushi rice (short-grain white)
3	tablespoons rice wine vinegar, or to taste
3	tablespoons sugar, or to taste
½ to 1	teaspoon salt
3 to 4	sheets nori (laver)

STUFFED WITH:
> Toasted sesame seeds (see Ingredients page 256)
> Hot mustard (see Ingredients page 253)
> Wasabi (see Ingredients page 256)
> Fresh chives
> Blanched, peeled carrot pieces, approximately
>   4 x ⅛ x ⅛-inches
> Peeled, seeded, sliced cucumber sticks, about
>   4 x ¼ x ¼-inches
> Tofu, sliced into 4 x ¼ x ¼-inch pieces
> Sorrel leaves or shiso leaves, thinly sliced
> Braised sliced shiitake mushrooms
>   (see end of recipe)
> Store-bought pickled gingerroot

Pick over the rice, discarding any grains that are not pure white. Place the rice in a small, heavy pot with a tight-fitting lid. Rinse under cool water, swishing it around with your fingers, rinsing and draining a couple of times, until the milkiness disappears. Drain the rice as completely as you can. Pour in water to cover and let the rice soak for 1 to 4 hours.

While the rice is soaking, combine the rice wine vinegar, sugar, and salt in a small bowl, stirring until the sugar and salt are completely dissolved. Set aside. Next prepare whatever stuffing you choose, peeling cucumbers, blanching carrots, braising mushrooms, and the like. Set aside.

Once the rice has soaked, drain and add 1 cup of water. Place it over a moderate flame and bring it to a boil. Cover the pot, turn the flame to low, and cook the rice for 15 minutes undisturbed. At the end of 15 minutes, peek in and check the rice—there should be little if any liquid left in the pot. Replace the cover and turn the heat to high for 30 seconds; immediately turn off the flame and let the rice steam, covered, for 15 more minutes.

Assemble your ingredients before you, including the sudare mat (see Footnote next page).

Once the rice has steamed, remove the lid, pour in the vinegar mixture, and blend quickly with a rice paddle or wooden spoon, turning the rice over and letting it cool. If you have a hand-held fan, you can fan the rice to speed the cooling process. (This is considered vital to proper sushi rice preparation, but if you don't feel like fanning the rice, just let it cool gradually, turning and tossing as you go.) When the rice is cool to the touch, begin forming the nori rolls.

Place a piece of nori at the bottom of the sudare mat*, shiny side down. Using your wet fingers, a rice paddle, or a spoon, scoop about a third of the rice out of the pot and place it along the bottom ⅔ of the nori sheet. Wet your hand with cool water (or, more traditionally, with rice wine vinegar) and press the rice down (the rice will be quite sticky), trying to get as even a layer as possible, including the edges. It will be necessary to wet your hand a couple of times. Fill the center of the nori roll. If you're using wasabi, smear a thin layer horizontally in the center of the rice layer. Next add cucumbers/ carrots/ mushrooms/ tofu, or other choices. Sprinkle chives or toasted sesame seeds on top.

Just before you're ready to roll the nori, wet your fingers again and moisten the upper third of the nori sheet, the part that has nothing on it.

Holding the center "stuffing" as well as you can, and using the sudare mat for support, fold the bottom edge toward the center, pressing gently, rolling as you go. Theoretically you should have a firm roll of rice and stuffing, but chances are you'll have a fairly loose roll the first few times. Nori rolling takes a bit of practice and patience, believe me. Set this roll aside. Follow the same procedure for the remaining rolls, filling them with whatever you wish.

Starting with the first roll made and using a very sharp knife, cut the roll into 1-inch lengths, cleaning your knife under cool water with each cut. Arrange the nori pieces attractively on a small plate, accompanied with a small mound of pickled gingerroot, a dollop of wasabi, and perhaps a small bit of hot mustard as well. Serve with a small bowl or plate of soy sauce, mixing the wasabi/mustard in a tablespoon or so of soy before dipping an edge of the nori into the soy mixture, then popping the whole thing in your mouth.

PLEASE NOTE: sushi in any form is not meant to be dunked into and drenched with soy sauce; at most you should dip a small side of the nori into the soy mixture for piquancy, not to mask the taste of the nori roll itself. And if you're out at a Japanese restaurant and are served some nigiri-zushi with fish on top, once again, don't dip the rice into the soy sauce. Instead, holding the entire piece of sushi with chopsticks, turn it upside down and dip only the fish into the soy/wasabi mixture.

---

*A sudare mat can be found in Japanese and health food stores. It is made of smooth, thin pieces of bamboo that are tied together with twine, resulting in a mat that is flexible yet firm. Although you could substitute a sturdy cloth towel for the mat (or use nothing at all), these mats are not expensive and are an integral part of nori-maki making.

To braise fresh shiitakes: take 3 shiitake mushrooms and remove the stem and any clinging debris. Slice them into ¼-inch strips. Pour 3 tablespoons of soy sauce, 2 tablespoons of sake, and 1 table-spoon of sugar into a small saucepan; bring the mixture to the boil. Add the mushrooms and cook them for 10 minutes over low heat, until the mushrooms are tender and almost all of the liquid has reduced. Cool and use.

Alternatively, you may roast the mushrooms by placing the cleaned, stemmed shiitakes on a skewer and marinating them with a bit of soy sauce for 30 minutes. Then hold the mushrooms over an open flame until they are soft and have some black specks on them, turning as you cook, for about 5 minutes. Cool, slice and use.

Chimubaso ni
sake ni wasabi ni
tamawaru wa
haru wa sabishiku
araseji to nari

Dulse and wine
and wasabi—
with such gifts
my spring
can never be lonely!
—Ryōkan

Piláfi Lahaniká

Serves 4

● ●

I don't know how popular brown rice is in Greece, but its nuttiness lends yet another layer to the complex assortment of tastes. If you prefer, you can use white rice instead, reducing the amount of vegetable stock to 1⅓ cups and the cooking time from 30 minutes to 15.

1	cup brown basmati rice
2	cups vegetable stock or water
1	tablespoon olive oil
1	small onion, peeled and chopped
	Big pinch saffron, optional
½	zucchini, sliced into thin half-moons
1	carrot, peeled and chopped into ¼-inch dice
1	broccoli spear, stem cut into ½-inch dice and the head into florets (about 1½ to 2 cups total)
2 to 4	green onions, chopped
	Finely grated zest of 1 lemon
⅓	cup chopped fresh dill
¼	cup chopped fresh spearmint
⅓	cup chopped fresh Italian parsley
½ to ¾	cup crumbled feta cheese
	Salt and pepper

Place the rice in a heavy pot with a tight-fitting lid; add the stock and bring to a boil. Cover the pot and reduce the heat to low, cooking for 30 to 35 minutes until the rice is done. Set aside.

Place a sauté pan over a moderate flame and add the olive oil, onion, and optional saffron. Cook until the onion has begun to soften, about 2 minutes, stirring occasionally. Add the zucchini, carrot, and broccoli, sautéing for another minute. Add the green onions and lemon zest, tossing a couple of times to warm through. Place this mixture in a large bowl.

Add the chopped herbs to the cooled vegetables; toss. Add the feta cheese and cooked rice; toss again and taste for seasoning.

Spread the mixture evenly into a baking dish sprayed with Pam and cover with a lid or with foil. The pilaf may be made ahead and refrigerated at this point. Bring back to room temperature before baking.

Bake the covered pilaf into a preheated 350° oven for 30 to 40 minutes or until it is hot. Serve immediately. (A cold pilaf may take 10 to 15 additional minutes to heat through.)

Variations:
- Substitute broccoli rabe for broccoli.
- For more color, add a chopped, ripe tomato to the cooled vegetables.

A bad tempered priest
spilling from the bag as he walks,
the rice donation!
—BUSON

Basic Rice Pilaf

SERVES 4

● ●

1 to 2	*tablespoons butter*
1	*small onion, peeled and minced*
1	*clove garlic, peeled and minced*
1	*cup long-grain white or brown rice, washed and drained*
	*Vegetable stock**

*If using white rice, use 1½ cups stock; for brown rice, use 2 cups stock.

3   *green onions, sliced into 1-inch lengths*
½   *red bell pepper, cut into ¼-inch dice*
1   *cup broccoli florets*
1   *carrot, cut into matchsticks*
½   *cup peas, thawed frozen or fresh*
    Salt to taste

Place a heavy-bottomed pot with a tight-fitting lid over medium heat. When it is hot, melt the butter, add the onion, and cook, stirring often, until soft and translucent, about 5 to 8 minutes. When the onion has begun to brown, add the garlic and cook for another 2 minutes. Add the rice and vegetable stock and bring the mixture to the simmer. Cover, reduce the flame to low, and cook until all the liquid has been absorbed (white rice: 15 minutes; brown rice: 35 minutes). Let the rice stand 10 minutes before proceeding.

Place the green onions, bell pepper, broccoli, carrot, and peas in a large bowl. Add the hot cooked rice and gently mix everything together. Pour into a 1½-quart baking dish sprayed with Pam and cover with foil. The pilaf may be made ahead of time and refrigerated at this point.

Bake at 350° until heated through: if you make the pilaf immediately, bake for about 20 to 30 minutes. For a refrigerated pilaf, bake for 40 to 50 minutes.

Variations:
- Add 2 teaspoons thyme, basil, or herbes de Provence to the rice while it is cooking.
- Add 1 tablespoon fragrant curry powder or 2 teaspoons garam masala to the onion while it is cooking.
- Add 2 teaspoons cumin seed to the onion while it is cooking, and sprinkle 1 teaspoon chili powder in with the vegetables before tossing with the rice.
- Add ½ to 1 cup grated, shredded, or cubed cheese(s) to the rice mixture before baking. (Options: ½ cup Parmesan cheese, 1 cup cubed Cheddar cheese, a mixture of Italian cheeses, or whatever appeals to you.)

Haru wa utsuro na ikbukuro
o mochiaruku.

Spring—with an empty stomach
I walk along.
—Santôka

Onion Rice

SERVES 4

● ●

2 tablespoons butter or olive oil, or
    a combination
1 large onion, peeled and chopped into
    ¼-inch dice
1 teaspoon salt (depending on the salt in
    the stock), optional
1 teaspoon tarragon or thyme
2 tablespoons brandy
¼ cup dry vermouth or dry white wine
1⅓ cups vegetable stock
1 cup white rice*, washed and drained
½ cup chopped parsley

Place a heavy-bottomed pot with a tight-fitting lid over medium heat. When it is hot, melt the butter and add the onion and optional salt. Cook, stirring often, until the onion begins to brown—this may take up to 15 minutes or so. When the onion has browned, add the tarragon, brandy, wine, vegetable stock, and rice. Bring the mixture to the simmer, cover, and cook over low heat until the liquid has been absorbed, about 15 to 18 minutes. Remove from the heat and allow to stand for 10 minutes, covered.

Carefully mix the parsley into the rice. Serve immediately.

Variation:
- After the rice has cooked and cooled a bit, mix in 1 cup grated smoked cheese or 1 cup crumbled feta cheese.

If you prefer to use brown basmati rice, increase the vegetable stock to 2 cups and cook the rice for 30 minutes, or until the liquid has been absorbed.

Wild geese have eaten
all of my barley
alas,
they are flying on!
—Yasui

Riz au Gratin

Serves 4

● ●

Not diet food. A cheesy, hearty side dish, and a good way to use up those bits of cheese in your refrigerator.

1	*tablespoon butter, or olive oil, or a combination*
1	*medium onion, peeled and finely chopped*
1	*cup short- or long-grain brown rice*
2	*cups clear vegetable stock or water*
1	*teaspoon thyme, savory, or herbes de Provence, optional*
½	*cup freshly grated Parmesan cheese*
1½	*cups grated cheeses, a mixture of Cheddar, mozzarella, Gruyère, pepper Jack, goat cheese, feta, or others, reserving a tablespoon or two for the end*
1	*cup half-and-half, cream, buttermilk, or a very liquid mixture of sour cream and milk*
1	*teaspoon fresh, bright paprika*
2	*tablespoons chopped parsley for garnish, if desired*

Place a heavy 1½ quart pot over moderate heat. Melt the butter and add the onion, sautéing for 3 to 5 minutes, or until it is soft and translucent. Add the rice, stirring so all the grains are coated with a bit of butter. Add the vegetable stock and optional herbs, and bring the mixture to a boil. Cover the pot and turn the flame to low. Cook for 30 minutes, or until the liquid has been absorbed. Let the rice stand, covered and off the flame, for another 15 minutes before using.

While the rice is cooling, place the Parmesan cheese, mixed cheeses, and half-and-half in a large bowl. Mix well. Once the rice has cooled for 15 minutes, add it to the cheese mixture, stirring quickly and thoroughly. Spread the rice mixture in a 1-quart gratin dish sprayed with Pam. Sprinkle on a tablespoon or so of extra cheese and a sprinkling of paprika. Cover the dish with foil.

Bake the gratin in a preheated 350° oven for 30 to 40 minutes until hot throughout, removing the foil at the end and allowing the top to brown a bit if desired, another 10 minutes. Garnish with chopped parsley.

Variation:
- Use white rice instead of brown. Proportions: 1 cup basmati/jasmine rice and 1⅓ cups vegetable stock.

> *While cutting down the rice,*
> *the little weeds with autumn*
> *sunlight on them.*
> —BUSON

Spanish Rice

SERVES 4

• •

Simple, hearty, and nutty. Browning the rice adds an outdoorsy element to what would ordinarily be a pretty standard side dish.

1 to 2	tablespoons canola oil, or olive oil
1	cup medium- or short-grain white rice
1	tablespoon olive oil
1	large onion, peeled and chopped into ¼-inch dice
2	cloves garlic, peeled and minced
1	18-ounce can Italian tomatoes, chopped, including ½ cup of the juice
1	cup vegetable stock* or water
1	teaspoon salt (if using bouillon cubes, omit the salt)

Place a large sauté pan over a medium high flame. Add the oil and rice. Reduce the flame to medium and stir the rice constantly until it becomes a uniform golden color, about 15 to 18 minutes. (The browning process takes a bit longer than you'd think—just about the time you're wondering if the rice will ever turn brown, it does.) When the rice is a lovely golden brown, remove it to a large metal or ceramic bowl.

Put the hot sauté pan back on the flame and add the olive oil, onion, and garlic. Sauté the onion until it is soft, about 3 to 5 min-

*This is a dish in which vegetable bouillon cubes work well—use 1 cube per cup of water.

utes. (If you wish, you can continue cooking it until it has browned a bit.) Return the browned rice to the pan and add the tomatoes and juice, the vegetable stock, and optional salt. (Be careful when you're adding liquid to a hot pan as it will splatter.) Bring the mixture to a simmer, cover, and turn the heat to low. Let the rice cook undisturbed for 20 minutes.

After 20 minutes check to see if there is any liquid left in the pan; if there is, replace the lid and continue cooking until it is all absorbed. If there is no liquid remaining, remove the covered pan from the heat and allow it to cool for 10 minutes before serving.

Variations:
- Add 1 to 2 teaspoons whole cumin seed to the onions as they cook.
- Sprinkle 1 teaspoon chili powder over the rice after it has finished cooking.
- Add 1 teaspoon dried oregano with the tomatoes.

> *Rain bamboos,*
> *Wind pines:*
> *All preach Zen.*

Verdant Rice

SERVES 4

● ●

White rice speckled with flecks of green, this colorful side dish counts as both a vegetable and a grain. Its mild taste goes with practically anything and thus is quite versatile. If you don't have any vegetable stock on hand, you can use plain water for the cooking liquid, but the taste will be milder.

> 1 cup white rice*, rinsed and drained
> 1⅓ cups vegetable stock or water
> 1 tablespoon butter or olive oil
> ½ cup onion
> 1 clove garlic, minced, optional
> ¼ teaspoon freshly grated nutmeg or ground cinnamon
> 1 to 2 teaspoons thyme or oregano

Brown rice may be used instead. Increase the vegetable stock to 2 cups and boil for 30 minutes for the preliminary cooking. The finished dish won't be quite as green, but just as tasty in a more "whole foods" way.

> 1½ cups chopped blanched spinach, fresh or frozen
> (approximately one 10-ounce package frozen
> chopped spinach or 16-ounces fresh spinach,
> blanched)
> ⅔ to 1 cup ricotta cheese (whole milk, light, or nonfat)
> ⅔ cup freshly grated Parmesan cheese
> ½ cup milk, soy milk, half-and-half, cream, or water
> Salt and pepper to taste

Place the rice and vegetable stock in a heavy pot with a tight-fitting lid. Bring the liquid to the simmer, reduce the flame to low, and cover the pot. Cook the rice for 15 minutes, until all the water has been absorbed. Let the cooked rice stand, covered, for 10 minutes before proceeding.

Place a small sauté pan over moderate heat. When it is hot, melt the butter and then add the onion and optional garlic. Sauté the onion until it is soft and translucent, about 5 minutes. Remove from the heat and place in a large bowl. Sprinkle the nutmeg and thyme over the onion, tossing once.

Squeeze any excess water out of the blanched spinach. Place the spinach in a food processor with the ricotta cheese and process the mixture to a nearly smooth paste. Add the spinach mixture to the bowl with the onion mixture and stir. Add the Parmesan cheese and milk, stirring well. Add the cooked rice, stirring again. Taste for seasoning, adding salt and pepper as desired.

Spread the rice in a 1-quart baking dish sprayed with Pam and cover with foil. Bake in a preheated 350° oven for 30 to 40 minutes, until hot. Serve immediately.

Variations:
- Add 2 tablespoons of raisins (golden or regular) or currants to the bowl as you're mixing in the cheese.
- To turn this into more of a main course, add two whole eggs to the ricotta/spinach mixture when it is being puréed; bake as usual. The rice mixture will set and be firmer, similar to a soufflé.

Mrs. Leonowens's Rice Curry

SERVES 4

● ●

Mrs. Leonowens was the character (and real Englishwoman) who traveled to Siam in the mid-1800s to teach King Mongkut's (Rama IV) children, including Prince Chulalongkorn. Mrs. Leonowens was the "Anna" in Margaret Landon's book and the film Anna and the King of Siam, *or as Rodgers and Hammerstein renamed the work when they turned it into a musical,* The King and I.

This dish is rich, a bit saucy (in the best sense), and gives you the feeling of Anglo-Thai cooking. Since it's not overpowering, it could work well with many different accompaniments and is a perfect introduction for those not initiated into Thai cuisine.

1	cup white jasmine or basmati rice, washed and drained
2	tablespoons canola oil
1	small onion, peeled and very thinly sliced into half-moons
3	cloves garlic, peeled and thinly sliced
2	teaspoons fragrant curry powder
1	teaspoon salt
1⅓	cups water
1½	cups unsweetened coconut milk (regular or light)
1	tablespoon finely grated gingerroot
2 to 4	teaspoons chili paste with garlic (depending on how hot you like it)
2	tablespoons soy sauce
2	tablespoons brown sugar
1 to 2	tablespoons lime juice
1	cup drained pineapple chunks
1	cup fresh tomato chunks
1	green onion, minced, for garnish
¼	cup chopped cilantro, mint, or a mixture

Wash the rice in a bowl, rinsing a few times. Drain in a colander or sieve for 20 minutes.

Heat the oil in a heavy-bottomed pot over moderately high heat; add the onion and fry until it has begun to turn brown. Add the garlic and continue cooking until both the onion and garlic have browned. Remove the pan from the heat and add the curry powder, stirring once or twice. Add the salt, drained rice, and water. Return the pot to the heat and bring to the simmer, then lower the flame to low, cover, and cook for 15 minutes, until the water has been absorbed. Let the rice stand while you continue.

Combine the coconut milk, gingerroot, chili paste, soy sauce, brown sugar, and lime juice in a saucepan and bring to the boil. Cook for 15 minutes. Set aside.

Empty the rice into a large bowl, adding the pineapple and tomato chunks. Toss quickly, then add the hot coconut milk mixture. Stir again. Serve immediately, garnishing with green onion and cilantro.

Mokumoku	*Sitting alone,*
kaya no uchi hitori	*Silently, in the mosquito net,*
meshi kû.	*Eating my rice.*

—SANTÔKA

BEANS, TOFU, AND TEMPEH

●●●●●●●●●●●●●●●●●●●●●●●●●●●●

INTRODUCTION

I adore beans. They're homey, earthy, and give comfort as few other foods can. They're flexible in their use, offer an enormous amount of variety of taste and texture, and are loaded with nutrients.

A Brief Note On Mixing Types of Beans

Many times I've seen "gourmet bean soup" packages in specialty stores that appear to contain every type of bean known to man—a pretty idea and an attractive package, but how practical is it? As I look at the split yellow peas, the chick-peas, black beans, red beans, or lentils, I think, "But they all have different cooking times." Even if properly soaked, lentils cook in a fraction of the time that a chick-pea does, so what kind of soup could possibly come out of such a package? No soup that *I'd* serve, is the answer. Combine only beans that are approximately the same size and require the same cooking time and you'll have a "proper" mix!

SORTING

Before soaking dried beans, you must measure and sort through them, picking out any debris that may have inadvertently gotten into the package. Sometimes this debris can be a pebble or stone, a small nugget of dirt, or a piece of stem or husk from the bean plant. Sorting through the beans also gives you a good opportunity to examine each bean, removing any that are drastically discolored or simply don't look good. This sorting process isn't time-consuming—it should take no more than a minute or two. I usually spread the beans on a countertop and pick through them, as spreading the beans out helps separate them from any debris. After sorting your beans, wash them in cool water, swishing them gently to remove any dirt that may have stuck to them during processing. Rinse a couple of times until you're satisfied that they're clean and ready to soak. I think it's best not to mix beans you have just bought with beans you've had sitting around for a couple of months, even if they're the same type of bean, since beans are affected by age. Mixing older beans with newer beans causes a cooking nightmare; you could wind up with a pot full of half-cooked and overcooked beans simultaneously.

SOAKING TECHNIQUES

Soaking beans seems to be self-explanatory, without much room for variety, but there are different methods, with the following being only a few.

THE BEST OLD-FASHIONED METHOD

This method entails soaking beans overnight in a large bowl filled with cool water. The only problem is that you must be foresighted enough to plan ahead for the extended soaking period. Although I have no scientific proof that this is the *best* method, it is æsthetically my favorite. It makes me feel as if I'm continuing an age-old tradition in the kitchen.

THE SECOND BEST OLD-FASHIONED METHOD

This involves putting your beans on to soak first thing in the morning in hot water and keeping the beans warm for several hours either by: 1) placing the bowl of beans over a pilot light, or 2) periodically changing the cooled bean water to hot water to keep the beans warm. Soak them for 2 to 4 hours until the beans have rehydrated and doubled in size.

BOIL AND SOAK

Place the washed beans in a large pot and cover with plenty of water (three to ten times the amount of water to beans). Put the pot over high heat and bring to the boil; allow to boil for 1 minute. Turn off the heat and cover. Allow the beans to soak in the water for 3 hours before cooking.

RINSING BEANS

This is a very important step. Scientists have discovered that up to 80 percent of the components of beans that cause flatulence are water-soluble and can be removed by discarding the soaking water. Thoroughly drain and rinse the soaked beans. This is a good opportunity to look through the beans again and discard any that still look dry, discolored, shriveled, or otherwise out of place.

COOKING BEANS

Once again, there are many methods for cooking the soaked beans. Both stove-top and slow cookers are ideal for all types of beans, but a pressure cooker can make mush of more tender beans, so be warned. You can also add some seasoning to the stove-top and slow-cooked beans, such as carrots, celery, or herbs.

You will notice that as soon as many beans have come to a boil they will form a scum on the top of the water. Remove this with a spoon before continuing. (Removing the scum is particularly important when using a pressure cooker, as it can clog the pressure vent.)

Alternatively, instead of removing the scum with a spoon you could completely drain and rinse the beans and fill the pot with water again. This seems like an unnecessary added step, but considering the fact that the flatulence component of beans is water-soluble, suddenly the extra effort begins to make a bit more sense! I don't know if completely changing the cooking liquid radically alters the flatulence level, but it certainly can't hurt—and it gets rid of the scum in one easy step.

Stove-top cooking

This method works for all kinds of beans. Place the beans in a large, heavy pot and cover with at least 3 times as much water as beans. Bring to the boil, reduce the heat to low, and simmer, covered, until done, adding water if necessary. The beans will differ in cooking time depending on their size and age. Figure at least one to two hours of cooking time.

Slow cookers (Crock-Pots)

This method is best for maintaining the shape of beans, and (best of all) does all the work while you're doing something else. It also cooks any type of bean. The only problem is that you must be foresighted enough to have your meal planned ahead of time to allow for the slow-cooking process.

The method is simple: place soaked beans with fresh liquid in the cooker along with any seasonings, cover, and turn on. Six to twelve hours later you will have perfectly cooked beans. Slow cookers also come with small recipe books to help you explore the world of Crock-Pots.

Pressure cookers

A pressure cooker doesn't work perfectly for all types of beans (it will frequently make mush out of more delicate and smaller beans such as lentils or sometimes navy beans.) But if you want a bean purée for creamy bean soups or for vegetarian pâtés, it does a great job of reducing small, soaked beans/peas into mush in no time flat. I use this method more than any other because of time considerations. Instead of cooking the beans for upwards of 1½ hours, you can have cooked beans in 15 minutes.

Each cooker is slightly different, but the basic process is: bring the beans to a boil and remove any scum on the surface (or drain and rinse the beans, then bring the beans with fresh liquid back to the boil). Cover and bring under pressure, cooking for 15 or more minutes, depending on the amount of beans and type of cooker. (Follow the instructions for your pressure cooker.) The cooker I use, for example, doesn't have a "pounds of pressure" gauge—it's either under pressure or it's not.

When are the beans done?

Beans cook at their own pace. The cooking time will vary depending on the age of the bean, whether they've been properly soaked, how large they are, the altitude—beans cannot be gauged by "cook for x amount of time," since they are affected by weather and age. The only way to tell if they're done is to taste one or mash one between your fingers; if it is soft and cooked through, it is done; if not, continue cooking until it is. It's that simple.

Can I use stock instead of water to cook the beans?

Well, perhaps. It's up to you, really. Most commercial stocks contain a high amount of salt, and some people insist that adding salt to the cooking liquid makes the beans tough, so salt should be added only after the beans are done. I've prepared beans without adding salt to the water and found them quite tasteless—and personally I've never noticed that the beans were tougher because I did add salt. I think that a small amount of salt (mildly salted stock or a dash of tamari) works perfectly for cooking the beans, particularly if you're using a slow cooker to which you could also add some vegetables and herbs. Another method (a compromise) would be to simmer the beans until they are nearly done, then add salt or tamari and finish the cooking. This way you aren't cooking the beans entirely in a salted broth, but by the same token you give them a little bit of salt during the cooking process.

ER....TOOTING

Many people dislike beans not because of their taste but because they can cause flatulence. The biological reason is that beans (and other vegetables, such as cauliflower, broccoli, cabbage) contain complex sugars that can't be digested, and subsequently ferment in the intestines, causing a gas build-up. But there are a few things you can do to attempt to reduce this "social" problem.

1. Be sure to drain and rinse the beans thoroughly after soaking. Do not cook beans in the soaking water.

2. Be sure to soak the beans thoroughly and cook them completely. Undercooked and undersoaked beans can cause enormous gastrointestinal distress. Thoroughly cooked beans will solve 95 percent of your gas problems.

3. See if you have a sensitivity to certain types of beans. Some people may be able to digest certain varieties better than others. Once you've discovered which beans cause a problem, avoid them.

4. Eat a smaller portion of beans. Beans are powerhouses of nutrition; it isn't necessary to eat a big bowlful of them to get their nutritional benefits. Try using smaller amounts mixed with grains and vegetables instead of having a vat of beans by themselves.

5. There is a product on the market called Beano. This is a food enzyme that you take immediately prior to eating your first bite of

beans, and it supposedly breaks down the complex sugars that cause gas in the first place. I've used it numerous times with differing results, but even the Beano package reads: "Experience will tell you how many drops will be needed for specific foods."

6. Some people find that adding a strip of kombu (a seaweed from kelp) to the beans while cooking may reduce the flatulence level. It is also thought to reduce the cooking time and keep the beans tender. Kombu contains a natural form of MSG, glutamic acid, so use it at your discretion.

7. I've noticed sometimes that if I inadvertently overcook beans (usually in my pressure cooker) their flatulence level is drastically reduced. Perhaps you may find a pressure cooker helpful; perhaps not.

8. When beginning a vegetarian diet, some people's systems aren't used to beans; in other words, sometimes flatulence is merely a matter of allowing your body to adjust to a new type of food. After a couple of weeks your body should have accustomed itself to beans and there won't be a noticeable problem, if any.

> *Sora takaku*   *The sky above,*
> *bentô itadaku*   *The bentô in my hands,*
> *hikari amaneku*   *Sunlight all around,*
> *gohan shiroku.*   *The rice's whiteness.*
> —SANTÔKA

TYPES OF DRIED BEANS AND PEAS

Here is a quick list of commonly found beans and their characteristics. Although I've not included recipes for all the various beans listed below, you may wish to experiment with the recipes and form new favorites of your own.

Anasazi beans—These beans are the size of kidney beans and are mottled cream and burgundy in color. They look rather like kidney beans that have been splattered with white paint. They are attractive dried, but like all beans, they lose their color upon soaking and cooking, turning a dirty-salmon color. They are tasty, quite nutritious, and are slightly sweeter than other beans, and their texture is a bit mealy. Not terribly different from kidney, pinto, or red beans, they could easily be used in chili, enchiladas, or any type of soup.

Azuki beans (aduki, adzuki)—These are very small, dark red beans that are mostly used in Asian cooking and are thought to be one of the most digestible of beans. Traditionally used as the base for Asian desserts like bean cakes, azuki beans are much sweeter than other beans (but that's not to say that they are actually *sweet*). One of the best ways to cook azukis is to soak the beans overnight as usual; drain, rinse, and bring them to boil in a large pot with fresh water; drain, rinse, and bring the beans to boil *again* in the pot with fresh water; simmer until done, adding 1 cup of ice cold water once or twice during the cooking process (known in Japanese as "surprise water"). This addition of cold water to the boiling beans drastically reduces the cooking time. I haven't got any idea why, but it does. I find azuki beans to have a distinctly pointed taste that I'm not sure everyone would like.

Black beans (turtle beans)—Black beans are a very familiar item. In their dried state they're like medium-sized black pebbles; cooked, they're the size of kidney beans and are still black, or sometimes dull brown. If you cook black beans at home, you'll be surprised at the purplish inky water that results from soaking the beans, and how easily that water will stain towels if you're not careful. Black beans are ideal for Crock-Pots or pressure cookers because they maintain their shape quite well during cooking. They're mildly flavored and make an interesting contrast to a bright colored rice pilaf.

Black chick-peas (small, brown chick-peas)—These can be found in Middle Eastern markets; they look exactly like the regular yellow chickpea except that they're half the size and are dark brown. They have a tough skin that doesn't change after cooking (even in a pressure cooker), and up to now I've yet to find a decent, edible use for them. They are great to use as weights when you're prebaking pie shells—just put a piece of waxed paper in the uncooked pie shell, spread the brown chick-peas in, and bake away.

Black-eyed peas—These beans are dull grey, medium-sized, with a brown "eye" at one side; in the South they are traditionally prepared and eaten on New Year's Day in a ritual thought to ensure good luck during the upcoming year. They are an acquired taste.

Butter Beans (see Lima beans)

Cannellini beans—An Italian white kidney bean. They're the same size as kidney beans except they're a creamy color, and they have a slightly bitter aftertaste.

Chick-peas (garbanzos, ceci beans)—Chick-peas have a nice, firm texture, keep their shape well during cooking, and are a necessity in Middle Eastern and Indian cookery. They are cooked exactly like any other bean.

Dahls—Dahl (dal) is technically the Indian word for split beans or peas, though sometimes you'll see the word coupled with whole legumes as well. Dahls are available in any Indian market, either whole or split, sometimes raw or roasted, skinned or unskinned, sometimes covered with an edible oil. You will see bag upon bag of split and whole beans of seemingly infinite varieties, but the five named below are the most commonly used. As with all beans, the split variety cooks faster than the whole version. All dahls have an earthy taste, some more so than others.

Chana dahl (Indian chick-pea)—This resembles a small chick-pea. It is yellow and looks rather like a standard yellow split pea.

Masoor (masur) dahl—A small, salmon-colored split pea that is quite pretty in its raw state, but turns from its attractive salmon color to dull yellow upon cooking. It is sometimes sold as "red lentil," but it is in fact not a red lentil, as red lentils are larger. It is among the mildest of the dahls.

Moong (mung) dahl—Also called "green gram." This is available either skinned or unskinned (the skinned variety is easier to deal with). This is none other than the split, skinned green moong (mung) bean. The split moong dahl is pale yellow in appearance and rather small, and has a stronger flavor than masoor dahl. These beans are probably better known for their sprouts—the large, white bean sprouts you find in Chinese and other Asian cuisines.

Toovar (arhar, toor) dahl—Toovar dahl is a medium-sized split pea (much like chana dahl) and is excellent for soups. Toovar dahl can also be found as "oily toovar dahl" or "oily toor dahl"; this means it has a fine film of castor oil over the bean to act as a preservative and to deter bugs that like to munch on it. Toor dahl has a warm, mellow taste and is one of my favorites.

Urad dahl (split black grams)—The whole urad dahl is a small bean the size of a mung bean and is black, hence one of its names. This bean is available whole, split with the skin on, and split without the skin (this variety is the most commonly used). The split, skinned bean is a very pale yellow color (antique white, if you will), and has a mild flavor. It is also used as a seasoning in some Indian recipes.

Fava beans—These beans are larger than lima beans and are bright green when fresh. They can be found in season as a fresh produce item in long, wrinkled pods, or dried in the bean section of your health food store, or even bottled and pickled in some Italian markets. They're used from Italy to Japan and are a staple in the Middle East. Fava beans have a tough exterior skin that must be removed before being eaten. As beans go, fava beans are pretty close to the bottom of my list of beans I'd choose to eat, as I find they have a bitter quality and mealy texture.

Great Northern beans—These large, white beans taste and look very like navy beans except for their size. They are mild in taste and are prepared exactly like other beans.

Kidney beans— Kidney beans are aptly named because not only are they kidney-shaped, but they have a dull, red kidney color as well. They're great in salads, in chili, in Mexican dishes, and are easily prepared. They're slightly larger than their near-twin, the red bean, and are mild in flavor.

Lentils (green, brown)—Even people who don't like beans usually like lentils. They're the quintessential "home cooking" type of bean; they can be made into a creamy soup, a vegetarian pâté, or used in summer salads. They can go from dried to cooked in as little as 30 minutes. Green lentils are the normal, run-of-the-mill grocery store variety, about ¼-inch in diameter; they aren't green at all, but a light brown. Brown lentils, on the other hand, are tiny reddish brown beans about ⅛-inch in diameter. I've found that brown lentils must be soaked before boiling (unlike green lentils), but they maintain their shape through cooking. The brown lentils have a richer taste than their "green" counterparts, but they also seem to create more intestinal gas.

Lentils (red)—I've seen masoor dahl listed as red lentils (masoor dahl being ⅓ the size of a regular lentil), but I've also seen red lentils that are exactly the same size as a regular green lentil. In either case, masoor dahl and red lentils are both a light salmon color in their raw state, but become dull yellow upon cooking. They are mild and slightly grainy. They don't keep their shape well, so they're probably best used for soups and pâtés.

Lima beans (small and large, butter beans)—Baby lima beans are quite creamy in texture and delicate in taste (much like navy beans), and the large lima beans (butter beans) are just a bit stronger in taste, but as creamy as their smaller cousins. I think it is an unjustly neglected bean that is flavorful and great for stews. Once soaked, they cook in no time and practically disintegrate, yielding a delicious, soppy, mushy concoction that is easy to digest and homey. Buttery soft, smooth, and luscious.

Mung beans—(See moong dahl, previously discussed)—Very small, dark green, round beans that have a unique fresh taste. Mung beans aren't for everyone, but they do have a "springtime" quality that invites their use after a long, cold winter. I think most people would prefer split moong dahl to the whole bean, but there's certainly nothing wrong with using the whole mung.

Navy beans—I think navy beans are fabulous. They are mellow, mild, nutritious, and can be used in practically anything. When people you know say they don't like beans, they should be introduced to navy bean soup, since it's one of the mildest and creamiest.

Pinto beans—The typical South of the Border bean, pintos are a speckled brown bean of medium to small size, and have a distinct, earthy taste that is extremely popular. Pintos take a bit more time to cook than other beans their size, but maintain their shape well.

Red beans—Well, red beans are small, red beans. After soaking they are nearly identical in size and appearance to kidney beans. They are mild and can be used in chili and enchiladas. They are great in summer salads.

Soybeans (see also Tofu and Tempeh below)—Many people don't think of soybeans as a bean you would eat whole; they think of them as being made into tofu, tempeh, soymilk, or used as a food additive. Cooked soybeans are about the same size and color as navy beans, have a mellow texture, and possess a bit stronger taste than navy beans. They are loaded with nutrition so you don't need to eat a big bowlful of them. Dry soybeans are round, small, almost white beans that nearly triple in size when soaked. I recommend trying them if you like navy beans.

Split peas (green and yellow)—Split peas have their own special quality; many people adore split pea soup while others detest it. They're almost exclusively puréed in recipes, so their cooking time is quite flexible—if you overcook them, you'll wind up with mush, which is exactly that you want anyway. I find the green split peas have a brighter, more "green" taste (not surprisingly), and that the yellow split peas are a bit milder and mellower.

White beans—Recently I was in a market and saw on the shelf four packages of beans: navy beans, Great Northern beans, white beans, and small white beans. The navy beans and the small white beans looked identical, as did the Great Northerns and the regular white beans. I was at a loss to guess the difference between them; I still don't know. The only explanation I can come up with is one of marketing. Perhaps some people prefer the term *white bean* to *navy bean*. At any rate, I'd guess they're exactly the same as navy beans and Great Northerns.

Tofu, Tempeh, and Miso

● ●

Although most of the world knows what tofu is, its alter ego, tempeh, has yet to acquire the same fame. For the sake of clarification, here are descriptions of both.

TOFU AND DRIED BEANCURD

> *Tea bush flowers.*
> *Coming out of a back gate,*
> *a tofu peddler.*
> —BUSON

Tofu is known as soybean curd, soy curd, dofu (dôfu), or simply "bean curd." Tofu is made by soaking whole soybeans in water, puréeing them, cooking the puréed beans with hot water, straining the mixture through cheesecloth to render a rich soy milk, then subsequently cooking the leftover liquid (soy milk) and adding a thickener, usually a derivative of minerals from sea salt called nigari. The nigari causes curds to form in the heated milk and it is then strained through cheesecloth and pressed to form a block. Presto—you have tofu.

Tofu has very little taste in and of itself, which is why many people object to it. It acts as a sponge to absorb the flavors surrounding it, so it is very versatile. Tofu that has been cubed and deep-fried changes from white squares into golden little nuggets with a crunchy, nutty taste, and are a good way to introduce tofu to those who claim to dislike it.

Many criticisms of tofu, though, come from its texture. There are many different kinds of tofu, all with different textures and purposes. Firm-curd tofu (usually known as Chinese tofu, or the first kind of tofu easily found in the United States) is great for deep-frying and for stir-fries; the silken and delicate Japanese tofus are excellent for serving in hot stock with a garnish of green onion and ginger. The point is that the plain, white tofu most Americans think of isn't the only kind of tofu that exists; there are various types of tofu just as there are various types of cheese.

TEMPEH

Tempeh is a soybean product found in 4 x 6 x 1-inch cakes, usually in the frozen or refrigerated section of your natural food store. It is of Indonesian origin, and unlike tofu, has a distinct texture that can be substituted for beef or chicken in many recipes.

Tempeh is made by partially cooking hulled soybeans and then inoculating them with a starter culture (not unlike a starter for sourdough or yogurt). Then the beans are placed in wrappers where the culture is allowed to grow. A day or two later, a partially fermented cake of soybeans with a mushroomish fragrance is the result.

Tempeh is a vegetable-based protein product that has extraordinarily high protein, about as much as chicken or beef. Tempeh, like its counterpart tofu, doesn't have a great deal of taste until you've seasoned and cooked it, but herein lies the great divide between the two. Seasoned and lightly fried tempeh is delicious by itself; it has texture, taste, and a reddish brown appearance. It is perfect for stir-fries and as a substitute for meat in such dishes as lasagne, chili, or hamburgers.

There are many different types of tempeh available in your natural foods store, from plain soy tempeh to soy and amaranth, soy and quinoa, soy and seaweed, or even a 5-grain tempeh.

MISO

Miso is a Japanese fermented bean paste, usually made from soybeans but sometimes made from chick-peas or other beans. It is normally found in the refrigerated section of a natural foods store and can be used as a major flavoring ingredient in soups or as a subtle seasoning for soup stocks. Because it can be made from different beans, it has different tastes, from dark and salty (rather like an intense soy sauce) to pale yellow and slightly sweet, but still salty. It is extraordinarily nutritious. In addition to soybeans and chick-peas, it may be made from azuki beans, barley, or rice. The pastes are categorized as sweet, mellow, red, or other types.

Since miso is a fermented "live" paste (just as yogurt contains live bacteria), some people eschew the packaged miso commonly found unrefrigerated on the store shelf, as they claim that the aseptic packaging process kills the beneficial bacteria of the miso. Beneficial bacteria aside, the tastes of aseptically sealed misos and refrigerated misos are practically identical.

CANNED BEANS

Do I use canned beans? Of course. Many a time I've been too rushed even to think about dinner, let alone having thought about soaking and cooking beans, and a can of beans in the pantry is an easy short cut to a fast and nutritious meal. Since there are so many kinds of beans now available in cans, you needn't be reduced to just pinto or black beans in your cupboard.

The canned beans you'll find in health food stores are usually in lined aluminum cans and contain no preservatives or col-oratives. Many standard supermarket varieties, however, do con-tain sugar, disodium EDTA, and calcium carbonate, among other things, not to mention lots of salt. All you need to do is look at the ingredients list—if it reads "beans, water, salt," it's fine.

Chick-peas in a Creamy Almond Sauce
SERVES 4

● ●

Hinduism is responsible for the tradition of vegetarianism across India, a balanced vegetarianism that has kept Indians alive and healthy for thousands of years. Obviously, with all that practice, India possesses a rich, varied vege-tarian cuisine. There are many books devoted to vegetarian Indian cooking, two of which are Yamuna Devi's Lord Krishna's Cuisine, The Art of Indian Vegetarian Cooking *(Bala Books, Dutton), and Julie Sahni's* Classic Indian Vegetarian and Grain Cooking *(Morrow), but you shouldn't overlook Madhur Jaffrey's* World of the East Vegetarian Cooking *(Knopf), a book that contains not only Indian recipes, but other delicious recipes from all over Asia—China, Japan, Korea, and the Philippines, for example.*

2	*teaspoons black mustard seeds*
1	*teaspoon cumin seeds*
1	*3-inch cinnamon stick*
2	*teaspoons whole coriander seeds*
1	*large onion, peeled*
2 to 3	*cloves garlic, peeled*
1	*1-inch piece of gingerroot*
1	*tablespoon oil or ghee*
2	*cups cooked chick-peas (about one 18-ounce can)*

•

½   teaspoon turmeric
⅛ to ½   teaspoon cayenne pepper, to taste
¼   cup finely ground almonds, or 3 tablespoons
     almond butter
½   cup water
½   cup sour cream (regular, light, or nonfat,
     or unsweetened coconut milk for a
     nondairy version)
½   cup milk, half-and-half, or cream,
     or coconut milk
   Salt to taste
½   teaspoon garam masala

Put the black mustard seeds, cumin seeds, cinnamon stick, and coriander seeds in a small skillet over medium heat. Stir and dry-roast the spices until they emit a lovely, roasted aroma, about 2 minutes. Place the roasted spices in a clean coffee/spice grinder and grind them into a powder. Set aside.

Put the onion, garlic, and gingerroot into a food processor or blender and process to a smooth paste. It will be necessary to push the mixture down from the sides occasionally with a rubber spatula to ensure thorough blending. Set aside.

Place a large skillet or a deep pot over medium heat; when it is hot, add the oil or ghee and swirl to coat the bottom of the pan. Carefully add the onion mixture, keeping your face averted, as it will splatter and sizzle. Stir and fry the onion purée for 5 to 10 minutes, or until it is cooked and may be lightly browned. (The mixture will probably stick to the bottom of the pan, so scrape it with a wooden spatula as you go.) Add the ground, roasted spices; stir-fry for 30 seconds with the onion mixture. Add the chick-peas, turmeric, cayenne, and almonds; mix well. Add the water and bring the mixture to a simmer, cooking over low heat for 20 to 30 minutes. Occasionally scrape the bottom of the pan to remove any stuck-on bits. Remove from the heat. (The dish can be made ahead of time and refrigerated at this point; merely bring the mixture to the simmering point for 10 minutes before continuing.)

Add the sour cream and milk, mixing well. Add salt to taste, then sprinkle in the garam masala. Taste for seasoning. You should have a lovely, delicately seasoned, creamy, golden sauce enrobing the chick-peas. Serve the dish with basmati rice, garnishing with chopped cilantro or mint if desired.

*A snowy morning
and smoke from the kitchen roof—
it is good.*
—Buson

Black Bean Enchiladas

SERVES 4

● ●

These provide a complete vegetarian protein and are an easy do-ahead meal.

1	ancho chile, roasted, chopped, and rehydrated
1	teaspoon oil
	Pam
½	medium onion, peeled and finely chopped
2	cloves garlic, minced or put through a garlic press
3	cups cooked black beans, half puréed and half whole, (or two 16-ounce cans of black beans, one drained and rinsed, the other puréed in a blender or food processor)
1	small (4- to 6-ounce) can diced green chiles
1	tablespoon soy sauce or tamari
1	tablespoon Worcestershire sauce, optional
1	tablespoon ground coriander
2	teaspoons ground cumin
1	teaspoon chili powder
½	teaspoon curry powder
¼	teaspoon cayenne pepper or ½ teaspoon crushed red pepper flakes

CHEESE FILLING:

½	cup sour cream (regular, light, or nonfat)
1	cup cilantro leaves, washed thoroughly, drained, and chopped
1 to 2	cups grated Cheddar cheese, or a store-bought Mexican cheese blend
12	corn tortillas
	Picante sauce—red salsa, fresh or store-bought; salsa verde; pico de gallo; or a combination

Hold the ancho chile by the stem with metal tongs and roast over an open flame (or, if using an electric range, over a burner that has been preheated to high) until blackened; it will smoke and might expand to the original size of the pepper. This process may take as little as 30 seconds or as long as 1 to 2 minutes, depending on the freshness of the chile and the heat from the flame. After roasting, quickly remove the stem and seeds (careful—it will be hot). Fold the chile as tightly as possible and slice into thin strips, then chop the strips into smaller bits. Place into a small bowl and pour in ⅓ cup of hot water. Set aside until needed.

Place a large sauté pan over medium heat; add the oil and spray the pan with Pam. Immediately add the chopped onion and cook until it is translucent and soft, about 5 minutes. Add the garlic and cook another 30 seconds or so; then add the ancho chile with its soaking liquid, being careful since the liquid will splatter. Stir and cook for a minute. Add the whole and puréed black beans, the green chilies, soy sauce, Worcestershire, coriander, cumin, chili powder, curry powder, and cayenne. Bring the mixture to a simmer. Reduce the heat to low and cook for 30 to 50 minutes or so, stirring occasionally. The beans will stick to the bottom, but this is normal. At this point you are just getting rid of excess liquid; eventually the beans will begin to thicken. Continue cooking and scraping the bottom until the mixture starts to become quite thick, and heavy enough to hold together easily. Remove the pan from the heat, keeping in mind that as the beans cool they will thicken a bit more. When the mixture is cool, you should have a brownish, very thick paste. Taste for seasoning, adding soy sauce or more cayenne for spiciness. While the beans are cooking, prepare the cheese filling.

Place the sour cream, chopped cilantro, and grated Cheddar cheese in a bowl and mix thoroughly. Set aside for the cheese filling.

Spray a 9 x 12-inch baking dish with Pam.

Heat the tortillas. Roast each tortilla over an open flame, turning frequently with metal tongs, until it has changed from dull yellow to an opaque yellow; it may puff up, or may have some black specks from the flame. (If you're using an electric stove, turn the burner to medium high.) Place the tortillas on a plate and cover with a piece of foil or a lid to retain the heat and seal in the moisture.

Assemble the cooled bean mixture, the cheese mixture, salsa(s), warm tortillas, and the baking dish within easy reach. Take a warm tortilla in your hand, spoon on 2 to 3 tablespoons or so of the bean mixture, spreading the beans around the upper third of the tortilla, then add 2 to 3 tablespoons of the cheese filling. Starting from the end of the tortilla with the filling, roll the tortilla toward the plain side, creating a cylinder with the filling in the center, and place the filled enchilada in the prepared baking dish. Continue until the beans and tortillas are used up. Garnish the top with any leftover cheese filling. Spoon a bit of salsa over the tops of the enchiladas. Cover the baking dish with foil. (You can refrigerate the enchiladas now and eat them at a later time—they'll keep for a couple of days without any harm, but extended storage in the refrigerator will make them soggy.)

Bake, covered, at 350° for 40 to 55 minutes until hot. Serve immediately, with extra salsa and a large salad.

Summer stove,
winter fan.

Country Butter Beans

SERVES 4

● ●

If this were really made in the country, it would undoubtedly have a couple of slices of bacon or perhaps a ham hock in it, but I've substituted a bit of smoked cheese for the bacon.

I love the way the lima beans practically disintegrate into a thick, creamy stew, great to sop up with hot, fresh bread.

1	cup dried lima (butter) beans, soaked overnight
2	teaspoons butter or oil
2	onions, peeled and diced
2	cloves garlic, peeled and minced or put through a press
2	carrots, peeled and chopped
2	potatoes, washed and cut into ½-inch squares
2	stalks celery, cut into ¼ to ½-inch dice
	Big pinch thyme
	Big pinch ground cumin
	Big pinch allspice
1	bay leaf
1	cup vermouth or white wine
3	cups water or vegetable stock
	Salt or tamari to taste
¼	cup chopped fresh parsley
	Smoked cheese to taste, or a teaspoon of smoked yeast if you don't eat dairy products

Place the lima beans in a large bowl and cover them with plenty of water, allowing them to soak at room temperature for 8 to 14 hours (overnight is usually easiest). Drain the soaked beans, rinsing well in several changes of cool water. Set aside.

Place a large soup pot over a medium flame. Add the butter; when it is hot, add the onions, garlic, carrots, potatoes, and celery; sauté the vegetables for 2 minutes. Add the drained beans, herbs, and spices. Add the water and wine and bring the mixture to a simmer. Reduce the flame to low, cover the pot with the lid ajar, and cook the beans and vegetables for 50 to 60 minutes, or more, depending on the freshness of the beans.

Once the beans have cooked and are soft, taste the broth for seasoning. Add salt or tamari as needed. The beans should be practically dissolving in the pot and the broth should be slightly thickened from the disintegrating beans. This can be made completely ahead of time, refrigerated for several days, and reheated gently before serving.

Serve hot with fresh parsley and smoked cheese on top.

Falafel Loaf

SERVES 4

● ●

I love falafel, but I'm not crazy about all that deep-frying, since the smell of hot oil seems to linger in the kitchen for days. This loaf version, in addition to being much lower in fat, is served in slices and is ideal for sandwiches.

½	cup dried chick-peas
¼	cup dried soybeans
¾	cup water
¼	cup tamari (or 2 tablespoons tamari and 2 tablespoons water)
2	cloves garlic, peeled and roughly chopped
2	green onions, roughly chopped
1	teaspoon salt
½	teaspoon cayenne pepper
½	teaspoon black pepper
1	teaspoon roasted cumin seeds
1	teaspoon ground coriander
1	teaspoon garam masala
2	tablespoons chopped parsley

2   *tablespoons chopped cilantro or mint*
⅓   *cup tahini (sesame seed butter)*
¼   *cup wheat germ or wheat bran*
½   *cup whole wheat flour*
½   *cup leftover cooked brown rice (or 1/4 cup*
      additional wheat germ, or ½ cup whole
      wheat bread crumbs)
      Pam
      Fresh lemon juice

Place the chick-peas and soybeans in a large bowl; add enough water to submerge them 3 inches under water. Soak the beans overnight (or about 8 to 12 hours).

After soaking, rinse the beans in cool water, discarding any that haven't plumped up or are discolored. Be sure to wash the beans thoroughly in several changes of clear, cool water before proceeding.

Preheat the oven to 400°.

Put the soaked, washed beans in a food processor and process them briefly to begin breaking them up. Add the water, tamari, garlic, green onions, salt, cayenne pepper, black pepper, cumin, coriander, garam masala, parsley, cilantro, and tahini. Purée until smooth. Using a spatula, remove the bean mixture from the processor and put in a large bowl. Add the wheat germ, flour, and cooked rice, mixing well with a spoon or spatula.

Spray a 10 x 3 x 3½-inch loaf pan heavily with Pam. Spoon the bean mixture into the prepared pan, forming a nice loaf. Cover with foil. Place the covered loaf in the middle of the preheated oven and bake for 1 hour. Remove the foil and continue baking for another 15 to 25 minutes, until the loaf is nicely browned on top. Remove from the oven and allow to cool for 20 minutes before cutting into ½-inch slices. Squirt the falafel slices with a bit of fresh lemon juice just before serving, or serve lemon wedges on the side.

Serve with a cucumber-yogurt or peanut sauce if you wish.

Variation:
- Substitute 2 eggs for ¼ cup of the water.

Fukamigusa   *Woody peonies*
ima wo sakari to   *now just at the*
saki ni keri   *best of their bloom—*
taoru mo oshishi   *too beautiful to pick*
taoranu mo oshi   *too beautiful not to pick*
                       —RYŌKAN

White Bean Pâté

MAKES ABOUT 2 CUPS

● ●

This spread is delicate and savory, ideal for crackers, crudité, or flat breads like pita or Indian naans.

2	**tablespoons olive oil or Roasted Garlic Oil (page 235)**
1	**small onion, peeled and diced**
1½	**cups sliced mushrooms**
½	**cup fresh bread crumbs or cracker crumbs**
1 to 1½	**cups cooked, drained navy or white beans**
½ to 1	**teaspoon salt, to taste**
1	**teaspoon lemon juice**
¼	**cup ground almonds or walnuts**
1	**tablespoon fresh parsley, optional**
2	**teaspoons chopped fresh thyme, or ½ teaspoon dried thyme**
1 to 2	**teaspoons chopped fresh tarragon, or ¼ teaspoon dried tarragon**
⅛ to ¼	**teaspoon ground allspice**

In a sauté pan, heat the oil over a moderate flame and add the onion. Sauté for 2 minutes or so, until the onion just begins to soften, then add the mushrooms. Stir and cook for 3 to 5 minutes, until the onion and mushrooms are soft and cooked (if you like, you can turn the flame up to medium high and lightly brown the vegetables). Set aside.

Place the bread crumbs in a food processor; add the cooked beans and the onion mixture, and purée well. Add some salt, the lemon juice, nuts, herbs, and spice; blend again. Taste for seasoning, adding more salt to taste.

Put the pâté in a small bowl and cover; refrigerate for at least an hour. Serve cold or at room temperature with croûtes, crackers, toast, or fresh bread slices.

NOTE: if you're using dried herbs, the flavor will be improved if the pâté sits for 2 to 3 hours before serving to blend the tastes well.

Tempeh Burgers

● ●

Tempeh burgers are a natural vegetarian alternative for cookouts, picnics, or for a simple meal at home. Tempeh doesn't taste like meat but has a burgerlike texture, enabling it to slip easily into a hamburger bun.

2	8-ounce pieces of tempeh, thawed if frozen
½	cup tamari
¼	cup dry white wine or vermouth
3 to 4	large cloves garlic, minced or put through a garlic press
1	teaspoon curry powder
1	teaspoon thyme
1	teaspoon basil
1	teaspoon oregano
	About 3 to 4 tablespoons oil for frying
	Hamburger buns (or slices of bread)

TOPPINGS:

> Mustard
> Pickles
> Lettuce
> Onion slices
> Tomato slices
> Ketchup

Place the thawed tempeh flat in front of you so that it is wider than it is tall. Cut the tempeh in half down the center, forming it into as much of a square as you can.

Combine the tamari, wine, garlic, curry, and herbs, and pour the mixture on a platter. Lay the tempeh pieces on the platter, turning to get equal coverage from the marinade and allowing them to sit and soak for at least 30 minutes.

Place a large sauté pan over a moderate flame. Add enough oil to coat the bottom lightly. Lay the tempeh pieces in the pan and sauté for 5 to 8 minutes, until reddish brown in color. Using a metal spatula, scrape the tempeh up and flip them over, adding a small amount of oil if necessary. Cook the other side the same way. Lay the tempeh pieces on paper towels to absorb any excess oil; keep them quite warm in an oven.

Slice and toast the hamburger buns (or use slices of sourdough bread). Serve 1 piece of tempeh per person: guests may add mustard, pickles, lettuce, onion slices, tomato slices, or ketchup as they wish.

Variation:
- Broil or grill the cooked and browned tempeh briefly to get a slightly charred "outdoors" taste.

London Broil

SERVES 2

● ●

So it's not a real London broil. Think of the cow you just saved.

½	teaspoon oregano
	Juice of 1 lemon
¼	cup tamari
1 to 2	cloves garlic, peeled and minced or put through a press
2	teaspoons Dijon mustard
1	8-ounce piece of tempeh, thawed if frozen
	Oil for frying
2	cups sliced mushrooms
⅓	cup dry white wine
3	tablespoons chopped fresh parsley, plus additional for garnish
	Lemon wedges, for garnish

Combine the oregano, lemon juice, tamari, garlic, and mustard, and pour the mixture on a plate.

Place the tempeh flat in front of you so that it is wider than it is tall. Cut it in half down the center. Now stand each half up on its end, and carefully slice the tempeh down the middle into two, thin squares (for four squares total). Lay the tempeh pieces on the plate, turning to get equal coverage from the marinade, and leave them for at least 30 minutes.

Place a large sauté pan over a moderate flame. Add enough oil to coat the bottom lightly. Lay the tempeh pieces in the pan, sautéing for 5 to 8 minutes until they are reddish brown. Using a metal spatula, scrape the tempeh up and flip them over, adding a small amount of oil if necessary. Cook the other sides the same way. Lay the tempeh pieces on paper towels to absorb any excess oil, keeping them quite warm in an oven.

Add the mushrooms to the sauté pan and cook for 4 to 5 minutes, until cooked through. (The pan will probably look a complete mess by now.) Add the wine, keeping your face averted as you do, since it will splatter. Scrape any brown bits from the bottom of the sauté pan, creating a sauce. Add the parsley and turn off the flame.

Serve 1 or 2 tempeh pieces per person, pouring on the sauce just before serving. Garnish with some additional parsley and wedges of lemon.

Variations:
- Add ½ cup sour cream to the mushroom mixture.
- Add ¼ cup (½ stick) butter to the mushroom mixture, and bring the sauce to a boil just before serving.

> *Hoping to recapture my youth;*
> *My old body, however, has piled up*
> *More years than this*
> *Growing mound of flowers!*
> —RENGETSU

Cold Tofu for a Summer's Night

SERVES 4

● ●

The key to success here is the tofu—the firm, spongelike Chinese type will not do. Mori-nu tofu from Japan is easily found in many supermarkets; it's easy to spot because it's in an aseptically sealed box, sometimes in the produce section and sometimes with Asian ingredients. Mori-nu has six types of basic tofu, all of which are termed "silken," which describes the texture perfectly. The types are: silken-soft, silken-firm, silken-extra-firm, silken-lite-soft, silken-lite-firm, and silken-lite-extra-firm. For this recipe I would recommend silken soft.

1 to 2	blocks (depending on how much you like tofu) silken tofu (such as Mori-nu silken soft), refrigerated
4 to 6	fresh shiso (perilla) leaves, or 4 curly lettuce leaves
2 to 4	tablespoons finely sliced green onion tops
2 to 4	tablespoons gingerroot
	About 4 teaspoons wasabi and/or hot mustard
	Tamari, to serve at the table

Open the tofu box(es) and carefully remove the tofu. Be careful, as silken soft tofu breaks quite easily. Slice the tofu into 4 equal, neat portions. Lay a shiso leaf on each of 4 small plates, and attractively arrange one or more pieces of tofu near its edge, so the shiso is sticking out from underneath. Place a teaspoon of the green onion rings directly in the center of the tofu. Off to the side, place a dollop of freshly grated gingerroot and a dollop of wasabi or hot mustard. If you have extra shiso leaves, you may wish to slice some of these very fine and scatter them over the top of the tofu as well.

Serve the tofu immediately. Each guest pours 1 to 2 tablespoons of tamari into a small bowl and mixes in the seasonings (gingerroot, wasabi, mustard) as desired. The pieces of cold tofu are dipped into the tamari mixture with chopsticks.

Serve with any cool, cooked vegetable and perhaps some nori rolls.

Variation:
- This recipe is limited only by your imagination. Try adding some toasted sesame seeds, pickled ginger, finely grated lemon zest, ketchup, or, if you eat fish, some dried bonito flakes. You may wish to use some teriyaki sauce instead of tamari.

Kyô mo mata	Today again
matsu no kaze fuku	I'll go to the hill
oka e yukan	where pine winds blow—
kinô suzumishi	perhaps to meet my friend
tomo ni au ya to	who was cooling himself there yesterday
	—Saigyô

Hot Tofu in Japanese Broth
SERVES 4

● ●

Hot tofu is subtle, delicate, and an ideal seasonal treat. The same rules apply for using Japanese silken tofu rather than regular tofu.

2   cups Japanese Broth (page 27)
1   tablespoon mirin (sweet rice wine)
        or 2 teaspoons sugar
2   tablespoons tamari

2 to 4   *shiitakes (dried and rehydrated, or fresh),*
           thinly sliced
   2   *tablespoons sake*
   1   *green onion, very finely minced, plus additional*
           for garnish
1 to 2   *blocks (depending on how much you like tofu)*
           silken tofu (such as Mori-nu silken soft
           or silken firm)
   ¼   *cup grated daikon*
   4   *teaspoons grated gingerroot*
   1   *sheet nori (laver), sliced into very fine strips*
           2 x ¹⁄₁₆-inch) (this can be bought sliced at
           the market, or you can slice it yourself)

Combine the broth, mirin, tamari, shiitakes, sake, and half of the minced green onion in a skillet deep and wide enough to hold the tofu. Bring the mixture to the simmer, and cook gently for 10 minutes. Cover the pan and allow to stand for 30 minutes before proceeding.

Carefully slice the tofu blocks into four to eight 2 x 2 x 1-inch pieces. Set aside.

Return the broth at the simmer, then carefully add the tofu. Cover the pan and allow the tofu to simmer very gently for 10 minutes, or until it is thoroughly heated.

While the tofu is heating, peel and grate the daikon on a ginger grater, to get daikon paste. Set aside. (The daikon will exude liquid as it sits; pour off any liquid before serving.)

Peel and grate the ginger on the ginger grater. Place equal amounts of grated ginger and grated daikon on 4 condiment plates in attractive mounds, being sure that they are not touching.

Using a spatula, carefully remove the hot tofu (which will be even more delicate now that it is warm), and gently place it in the 4 wide, shallow bowls. Divide the hot broth equally among the bowls. Sprinkle the sliced nori over the tofu, and add a sprinkling of fresh green onion. Serve immediately.

NOTE: The daikon and ginger are used as seasonings for the tofu instead of dipping sauce; place a small amount of one or both on a bite of tofu before eating it.

A fierce tiger paints
coquettish eyebrows.

Tofu-Yung

SERVES 4

● ●

Firm tofu is an excellent base for sautéed vegetable patties, as the tofu and egg combination is quite nutritious. This is humble, simple fare for the family—nothing fancy or fussy.

1	block firm (Chinese style) tofu, drained
2 to 3	eggs, beaten
2	tablespoons tamari, plus more for serving
1	teaspoon sugar, optional
1	tablespoon flour
½	cup finely chopped onion
1 to 2	cloves garlic, peeled and minced or put through a press
1	cup finely diced green and/or red pepper
½	cup finely diced celery
1	cup bean sprouts
¼	cup chopped cilantro
½	teaspoon sesame oil
	Oil for frying or Pam

Slice the tofu into ½-inch pieces. Lay the pieces on several layers of paper towels (or clean tea towels), then cover with another layer of towels. Place a weight (such as a wooden cutting board) on top, pressing to remove excess water. Allow the tofu to drain for as long as possible—anywhere from 30 minutes to several hours. Change the towels as necessary; some tofu is very wet, some quite dry. After draining the tofu, crumble the pieces in a large bowl. Smash the tofu with a fork until no piece of tofu is larger than a ¼-inch chunk. Add the eggs and mix well. Add the tamari, optional sugar, and flour, stirring once or twice. Add the remaining ingredients, blending well. Set aside.

Place a large sauté pan over moderate heat. When it is quite hot, add a thin layer of oil or spray with Pam. Spoon in about ½ cup of the tofu mixture, forming a patty of sorts. Spoon in as many ½-cup measures as will comfortably fit in the pan (usually no more than 3). Using your spatula, tamp down the patties a bit.

Cook the patties over a moderate to moderate low flame until they have set and are nicely brown on the first side, then carefully flip them over using a spatula. (This can sometimes be difficult.) Cook the other side until it, too, is brown. Remove the patties to a warming oven or a warm toaster oven when finished. Continue until all of the tofu mixture is used.

Serve 2 patties per person with extra tamari or teriyaki sauce as seasoning.

Everything is true
Just as it is:
Why dislike it?
Why hate?

Tofu "Egg" Salad

ABOUT 1½ CUPS

● ●

There are probably hundreds of recipes for tofu "egg" salad, each with differing degrees of success—some look like eggs but taste like tofu, while others merely look like a lumpy mayonnaise salad. This one, however, utilizes black salt (available in Indian markets) to give a true "eggy" taste. Black salt contains trace minerals that have iron as well as small amounts of sulfur, resulting in the "egginess." Too much black salt would be unbearable—all you need is a small pinch.

1	package firm tofu (Chinese style)
	Pinch of black salt (see Ingredients, page 251)
2 to 3	tablespoons tamari
1	rib celery, diced into very small cubes
½	red bell pepper cut into small cubes, optional
3 to 4	tablespoons chopped sweet pickles or sweet pickle relish
1 to 2	teaspoons curry powder, to taste
½	teaspoon garam masala
¼	teaspoon cayenne pepper
⅓	cup mayonnaise, regular or light
⅓	cup sour cream or yogurt, regular or light
1 to 2	teaspoons Dijon mustard
2 to 3	tablespoons chopped parsley or cilantro

Slice the tofu into 3 or 4 pieces and place it on several layers of paper towels. Cover it with more paper towels and lay a cutting board and a weight on top, forcing the excess water from the tofu to drain off. Allow to drain for 20 minutes. It may be necessary to repeat this procedure if the tofu is very wet.

Place the drained tofu in a large bowl, breaking it up with a fork. Add a pinch of black salt (just a pinch!), and the remaining ingredients. Taste for seasoning and serve cold as a sandwich spread, or in the center of a hollowed-out tomato for lunch.

> *Yesterday,*
> *I shattered the ice*
> *To draw water—*
> *No matter, this morning*
> *Frozen just as solid.*
> *—RENGETSU*

Tempeh Lasagne

SERVES 4

● ●

Sautéed tempeh is a great addition to vegetarian lasagnes because it has texture, a robust taste, and is loaded with nutrition. If time is short, feel free to substitute your favorite pasta sauce for one of the specified sauces. As with all lasagnes, this can be prepared a day or two ahead of time and baked on the day you want to serve it, making it ideal for parties. In fact, you could freeze the prepared, uncooked lasagne, thawing it in the refrigerator for two days before cooking.

2 to 3	*cups Basic Tomato Sauce (page 241), or your favorite bottled pasta sauce*
1 to 1½	*cups Basic White Sauce (page 242)*
2	*cloves garlic, peeled and minced or put through a press*
3	*tablespoons tamari*
2 to 3	*tablespoons canola oil*
1	*block tempeh, thawed and cut into 4 thin pieces*
1	*cup finely chopped onion*
1	*10- to 16-ounce package frozen, thawed spinach or 16-ounces fresh spinach, cleaned, blanched and chopped*
¼	*cup currants or raisins, optional*
	Lasagne noodles
	Parmesan cheese as desired
1½	*cups shredded mozzarella (regular, part skim, or low-fat)*

½ to ¾ cup shredded smoked Gouda or smoked
              Provolone
  ½ cup pitted, chopped Kalamata olives
       Herbs (if desired or necessary) such fresh or
              dried basil, oregano, fennel seed*
  ¼ cup chopped pepperoncini (pickled Italian
              peppers), optional
2 to 3 tablespoons chopped fresh parsley

Prepare the sauce(s) according to the directions. Set aside.

Place the garlic and tamari in an 8-inch square pan; add the thawed, sliced tempeh, coating both sides with the mixture. Allow the tempeh to marinate for 15 minutes or more.

Place the oil in a large sauté pan over moderate heat. When it is hot, add the tempeh slices. Sauté until they turn reddish brown on one side, then turn over and cook the other side. Remove the slices to paper towels to drain off any excess oil. Once the tempeh has cooled a bit, cut it into 1 x 2 x ½-inch chunks.

Put the chopped onion in the same sauté pan. (The moisture from the onion will remove the cooked-on tempeh pieces.) When the onion has softened, about 3 minutes, add the spinach and currants and heat everything through for 1 more minute. Let cool somewhat.

Assemble all the ingredients in front of you.

Spread about ¼ cup of the tomato sauce in the bottom of a 9 x 12-inch baking dish sprayed with Pam (the sauce will not completely cover the bottom). Place a layer of uncooked lasagne noodles in the dish; break the noodles to fit and make them cover the sauce as neatly as you can. Spoon a layer of white sauce over the noodles, spreading evenly. Arrange about half of the tempeh on top of the white sauce, and layer about half of the spinach mixture on top. Sprinkle with a bit of the Parmesan cheese, about ½ cup of the mozzarella cheese, and a few tablespoons of the smoked Gouda. Sprinkle on a tablespoon or so of the chopped Kalamata olives, herbs if you wish, and pepperoncini. Spoon on about ½ to ⅔ cup of the tomato sauce. Repeat the layering. Now place a final layer of lasagne noodles on top, spread on 1 cup of the tomato

*If you're using a bottled pasta sauce, the addition of more herbs may be unnecessary. If you've made the Basic Tomato Sauce, you may wish to include some herbs, but if you prefer less spiced meals, feel free not to include any herbs at all. I would recommend that you to experiment a bit—although I love herbs, sometimes just having the simple tastes of tomato, cheese, and vegetables is a welcome relief from their complex overtones.

sauce, and add a layer of cheese. Garnish with a sprinkling of chopped parsley or fresh chopped herbs. Cover the casserole with foil. (You may refrigerate it at this point for up to 2 days.)

Bake the lasagne in a preheated 375° oven for 40 to 50 minutes, then remove the foil and bake for another 20 minutes, or until the top has browned nicely and the dish is bubbly and hot throughout. (Depending on the pan and oven temperature, lasagne may bake in less time, or require more. Check it to ensure it has cooked thoroughly.) Remove from the oven and allow to cool for 15 minutes before cutting and serving.

If you've prepared the lasagne ahead of time, bring it to room temperature, then bake it, covered, for 60 to 70 minutes, then 20 minutes uncovered. Cool as above.

> *Pity! This*
> *vessel*
> *Needs*
> *no one to fill it.*

Tempeh à la Bourguignonne
SERVES 4

● ●

A vegetable version of that French classic, bœuf Bourguignonne, which marries beef with red wine, mushrooms, onions, and bacon. Here the bacon and beef are eliminated, but the taste is still robust.

1	8-ounce block of tempeh (thawed if frozen)
3	cloves garlic, peeled and minced or put through a press
¼	cup tamari or soy sauce
2	tablespoons plus 1 cup dry red wine
1 to 3	tablespoons olive oil
2 to 2½	cups ¼-inch chunks of mushrooms
1	medium onion, chopped
½ to 1	cup diced green bell pepper, optional
1½	cups Vegetable Stock (or 1½ cups water and one vegetable bouillon cube)
3	tablespoons tomato paste
1	teaspoon thyme
1	tablespoon Worcestershire sauce
1½	teaspoons Dijon mustard
1 to 3	tablespoons canola oil

1 to 2   *teaspoons cornstarch or arrowroot, mixed with*
     2 tablespoons water
     Chopped fresh parsley or basil, for garnish

Slice the tempeh in half down the middle so you have 2 pieces exactly the same size. Slice the pieces down the center to make 4 thin, nearly square blocks. Combine the garlic, tamari, and 2 tablespoons of red wine in a platter or large plate, and marinate the tempeh in the mixture for 30 minutes.

While the tempeh is marinating, place a deep, heavy pot over moderately high heat; when it is hot, add the olive oil. Immediately add the mushrooms, tossing in the oil. Turn the heat to high; stir the mushrooms in the very hot pan until they begin to brown, in 5 to 7 minutes. Reduce the heat to medium and add the onion. Toss and sauté until it is soft, about 5 minutes. Add the optional green pepper, sautéing for 1 minute. Add the remaining red wine, the stock, tomato paste, thyme, Worcestershire sauce, Dijon mustard, bringing the mixture to the boil. Reduce the heat to low and simmer the sauce, partially covered, for 20 minutes.

Once the tempeh has marinated, place a large sauté pan over moderately high heat; add the canola oil. Carefully lay the tempeh in the pan, sautéing on each side until it has turned reddish brown. Remove the tempeh and place on folded paper towels to drain excess oil. Set aside. While the sauté pan is still hot, add 3 to 4 tablespoons water or wine to deglaze the pan, scraping off any stuck-on bits from the bottom. Add this liquid to the simmering sauce.

Slice the tempeh into bite-sized pieces. Set aside.

When the sauce has simmered sufficiently, taste for seasoning. Add just enough of the cornstarch mixture to thicken the sauce slightly. Add the sliced tempeh and heat everything through, another 5 minutes. Garnish with chopped parsley or basil. Serve with hot French bread (to sop up the sauce) and a green vegetable.

Variation:

- To make Tempeh Stroganoff: Follow the directions above and add 1 cup of sour cream (regular or nonfat) to the sauce before serving. Serve with rice or egg noodles instead of bread.

Dare mo	*No one has come;*
konai tôgarashi	*The cayenne peppers*
akô naru.	*Have turned bright red.*
	—SANTÔKA

Tofu Scramble

SERVES 4

● ●

Tofu scramble looks amazingly on the surface like scrambled eggs but is lighter and quite tasty, a nice brunch with freshly toasted sourdough bread.

1	block firm tofu (Chinese style)
1 to 2	tablespoons canola oil
½	cup finely diced onion
1	cup diced mushrooms
2 to 3	stalks celery, finely diced
2	green onions, sliced into 1-inch lengths
1	clove garlic, peeled and minced or put through a press
½	cup finely diced red bell pepper, optional
	Pinch of black salt (Ingredients page 251)
	Pinch of curry powder or turmeric or ½ teaspoon herbes de Provence
	Tamari to taste

Slice the tofu into ½-inch pieces, then lay these piece between triple layers of paper towels; put a weight on top (such as a cutting board with a pot on top). Let the paper towels absorb any excess water from the tofu for 20 minutes. Occasionally, if the tofu is for some reason quite moist, it may be necessary to remove the weight and replace the wet paper towels with fresh, dry ones.

Drain the tofu and break it up with a fork or between your fingers into small pieces. Set aside.

Heat the oil in a large sauté pan over a moderate flame; add the onion, and stir-fry for 3 minutes, until it is soft and translucent. Add the mushrooms, celery, green onions, garlic, and optional red bell pepper; stir-fry for another 2 minutes until the vegetables are nearly cooked. Sprinkle in the black salt, the spices or herbs, and the tofu. Continue cooking for another 2 minutes until the tofu is hot; it may be necessary to reduce the flame somewhat to prevent overcooking. When everything is hot, sprinkle the tamari over everything to taste—you'll probably use 2 to 3 tablespoons or so. Serve at once.

> Tou to ka ya
> nani yue moyuru
> homura zo to
> kimi o takigi no
> tsumi no hi zo kashi
>
> Did I hear you ask
> what the fires of hell
> are burning for?
> They burn away evil
> and the firewood is you!
> —SAIGYŌ

Lentil-Stuffed Tomatoes
SERVES 2 TO 4

● ●

You can serve a large or small stuffed tomato, depending on whether you're serving it as a side dish or as a main course. If you're using it as the latter, you'll probably want to include additional vegetables for color. What follows is the basic recipe. You're invited to make any additions you wish.

1	cup green lentils
2	cups water
1	vegetable bouillon cube from a health food store
1	bay leaf
4	large or small tomatoes
⅓ to ½	cup grated Cheddar or smoked Gouda cheese
2	tablespoons chopped fresh parsley, thyme, or oregano

Sort through the lentils and remove any debris. Wash them once in cool water, drain, and put them in a pot. Add the water, vegetable bouillon cube, and bay leaf. Place the pot over moderate heat and bring the mixture to the boil; as soon as the water boils, turn the heat off and cover the pot with a lid. Let the lentils soak for 45 to 60 minutes before continuing.

After the lentils have soaked, bring them back to the boil. Reduce the flame to low and cook, covered, for 15 to 20 minutes, or until they are soft and tender, but still retain their shape. Remove them from the heat and let cool.

In the meantime, wash and core the tomatoes. Gently scoop out the inner portion of each (reserving for soup stock or something else).

Using a slotted spoon, place the cooked lentils in a bowl, draining off the excess liquid. Mix the grated cheese and herbs with the cooled lentils; spoon as much of the mixture as will fit into the tomatoes.

Bake the tomatoes uncovered at 350° for 20 to 25 minutes until the cheese has melted and everything is hot. (The tomatoes need not cook completely, since the firmer texture and fresh taste is a nice contrast to the lentil mixture.) Serve immediately.

Variations:

- If you're serving whole stuffed tomatoes as the center of attraction, you'll want to add more vegetables. Finely mince and lightly sauté whatever you have on hand and add the cooked vegetable bits to the cooked, cooled lentils. Suggestions could be any combination of onion, celery, mushroom, carrot, fennel, chard, spinach, diced Kalamata olives, toasted walnut pieces, or garlic.
- If you like, you may toss 2 to 4 tablespoons of pesto into the cooked lentils before stuffing the tomatoes.

> *Tomato o tanagokoro ni*
> *Mihotoke no mae ni*
> *chichi haha no mae ni.*

> *Holding a tomato as an offering,*
> *I place it before Buddha,*
> *Before my mother and father.*
> —SANTÔKA

Potato and Navy Bean Curry

SERVES 4

● ●

Don't be daunted by the long list of ingredients—most of them are spices that are toasted and ground at the beginning, then added near the end. This recipe is another do-ahead type of dish, perfect for buffets or pot-luck dinners. If you use oil instead of ghee, you will have a very creamy vegan dish.

2	red or yellow Finn potatoes, about 3- to 4-inches in diameter
1	2-inch cinnamon stick
1	teaspoon whole cloves
1½	teaspoons whole cumin
½	teaspoon cardamom seeds (not pods)
1	tablespoon whole coriander seeds

1   teaspoon whole black peppercorns
¼   teaspoon whole fenugreek seeds
¼   teaspoon whole fennel seeds
1   dried red chile pepper
1   tablespoon ghee or canola oil
8   fresh curry leaves
1½ teaspoons cumin seed
    Big pinch hing
½   teaspoon turmeric
2   cups canned, unsweetened coconut milk
1½ cups cooked navy beans (canned if desired)
2 to 3 teaspoons finely grated gingerroot
1   tablespoon lemon juice
    Salt to taste
1   tablespoon tamari
2 to 3 tablespoons toasted sesame butter (tahini)
1   large, ripe tomato, peeled, seeded, and chopped
        into ¼-inch cubes, for garnish
    Chopped fresh cilantro or parsley, for garnish

Wash and scrub the potatoes; cut them into 1½-inch cubes. Put them in a vegetable steamer and steam them until just done (when a knife easily pierces them), about 15 minutes. Set aside.

While the potatoes are steaming, place the next 9 ingredients (the spices) in a small sauté pan and roast them over medium heat, tossing constantly, until they begin to pop and emit a roasted aroma. Put the roasted spices into a clean coffee grinder and grind them to a powder. Set aside in a small bowl.

Place one corner of the bottom of a large saucepan directly over a moderate flame, holding the pot at an angle so that the bottom edge forms a "valley" in the flame. Place the ghee in this valley; when it is hot, add the curry leaves, cumin seed, hing, and turmeric. Let the mixture pop and fizzle for 5 seconds or so, then set the pot flat on the burner and add the coconut milk, cooked beans, gingerroot, lemon juice, cooked potatoes, and the remaining ingredients except the tomato and herb.

Bring the mixture to a simmer and cook, stirring occasionally, for 20 to 25 minutes. Turn the heat off, cover, and leave the mixture, cool on the stove. When ready to serve, turn the heat on low and reheat gently. Garnish with small wedges of fresh tomato and cilantro or parsley leaves.

Grilled Tofu with Mustard-Dill Sauce

SERVES 4

● ●

Very simple. Very mustardy. This dish is "gourmet macrobiotic"—it highlights the best of the ingredients you're using, without trying to mask the tofu and pretend it's something that it's not. The appearance of the marinated tofu with its edges blackened by fire, coupled with a velvety dill-flecked yellow sauce, is attractive—reminiscent of the Japanese dish dengaku.

You may broil the tofu instead of fire-roasting it, but the taste will not be the same.

1	block of firm (Chinese) tofu (such as White Wave tofu)
	Tamari or teriyaki sauce
3 to 4	tablespoons Dijon mustard
2 to 3	tablespoons sake
3 to 4	tablespoons chopped fresh dill

Tofu blocks are rather like bread loaves, longer than they are wide. So pretend your tofu block is like bread and you're going to slice it. Place the long side parallel to your body. Evenly cut off ¼- to ½-inch slices, so you wind up with eight equal tofu "cutlets."

Place the tofu pieces flat on several layers of paper towels, covering them with more paper towels, then put a cutting board and a weight (like a heavy pot) on top of the cutting board. This gently removes any excess water from the tofu without squeezing and breaking it. Let the tofu stand under the weight for 5 minutes, then remove the wet paper towels and repeat the process, replacing the wet towels with dry ones, letting the tofu drain for an additional 15 minutes.

Place the drained tofu on a platter or other flat dish. Sprinkle on a generous amount of tamari, then turn the tofu over and sprinkle the other side as well. (The tofu should quickly absorb the tamari, rather like a sponge.) Let the tofu marinate for 15 minutes or so.

Meanwhile, mix the Dijon mustard, sake, and dill in a small bowl. Set aside.

Once the tofu has marinated, carefully remove two cutlets and skewer them lengthwise on metal skewers. Continue with the other cutlets.

Set a gas burner at medium high. Hold the tofu directly in the flame, turning it frequently, until the edges darken and turn black, and the tofu is hot, about 2 minutes per skewer. Continue with the other cutlets.

(If you have an electric range, roast the cutlets over a burner that has been set on High; the cooking time will be a bit longer, but you'll still have a satisfactory end result.)

Place two warm, roasted tofu pieces on a plate and spoon some of the mustard sauce on top. Serve immediately.

> *Out together—*
> *bean-curd man,*
> *noon-time glories.*
> —Issa

Rediscovering Simplicity

● ●

Cooking is a learning process, and the first recipes one usually tries are the simplest and most basic. These early endeavors teach fundamental techniques of how to cut, cook, blend, and combine ingredients for a satisfactory meal. After some mastery is achieved, fresh recipes and techniques spring up, urging the cook to attempt different combinations and unusual ingredients, sometimes treating the exotic as superior merely because it is exotic.

As one learns about new techniques, new spices, new comestibles, one is usually tempted to continue through this learning curve, finishing it all off with a complex flourish of tastes and textures. In culinary terms, the stakes have been raised higher and higher. The task now becomes not merely to put a delicious meal on the table, but to create subtleties through combinations of ingredients. But this, too, follows a curve; after those "new" techniques and ideas have been explored, the result is to either find other "new" techniques or revisit old themes.

Where does this end?

The tea-making part of the Japanese tea ceremony (*cha-no-yû*) could be described mundanely as "someone makes green tea for someone else." But for those who have studied *cha-no-yû*, nothing could be farther from the truth, yet no closer to the truth. Each step of the ceremony has been fully studied, carefully practiced, and eventually mastered to give the most serene experience to the guest. The tea garden itself, the size and architecture of the tea house, the display of seasonal flowers in the *tokonoma*, the choice of tea utensils, the traditional Japanese sweets—all have been especially chosen for the occasion to reflect that particular time of the year in a specific place in this life. The experience of the Japanese tea ceremony is all directed toward the guests: it is a gift for them, not a showcase to display one's own expertise at tea.

When one studies *cha-no-yû*, each movement of the arm has meaning. Each drop of water into a container, every shift of the hand, every nuance has been refined to give the participant the most æsthetically rewarding moment.

Eventually, one who studies the tea ceremony might say, "I began by trying to make tea. Then I realized the significance of each movement and practiced each step of the ceremony, studying the tradition of tea . By then, I was obsessed with each act: I wasn't focusing on the preparation of tea anymore, I was concentrating on myself in relation to this æsthetically complex ceremony and wondered if I was doing everything right. I was merely a dot in the lineage that went back hundreds of years, so every physical movement became terribly important. But then after awhile I got used to the ritual of the ceremony. I began making tea again."

And so it is with cooking. After discovering and exploring different cuisines and techniques, I urge you to rediscover the most basic preparations. How many times have I looked at a recipe only to think, "Too simple;" then to develop rapt attention for the subtle, simple combination of, say, peas and mint? Or tomatoes, basil, and garlic oil? Or roasted peppers and balsamic vinegar? These pristine combinations are exquisite because they compliment each other perfectly without masking any of the fresh, unique tastes they possess.

Rediscover simplicity. After the hurdles of complicated cooking, your eyes will open to a new world in the kitchen: one of ease, freshness, and satisfaction. And you'll be free just to cook again.

VEGETABLES AND SALADS

● ●

Curried Vegetables

SERVES 4

● ●

Although the ingredients list seems daunting, there couldn't be an easier curry dish. It's all prepared in one pot and it can be started and stopped any time you like, picking up where you left off without any damage to the end result. It is a simple, satisfying dish with no pretensions.

Interestingly, authentic curries contain no curry powder. True curries are made from complex blends of spices, and what we call curry powder is merely an Anglo-Indian invention that bears little resemblance to the curries of India and Southeast Asia.

2 to 3	teaspoons whole cumin seed
2	tablespoons ghee or oil
½	teaspoon ground cardamom (preferably freshly ground in a mortar and pestle)
2	dried hot chiles
½	medium onion, peeled and chopped
3	cloves garlic, minced or put through a press
1	tablespoon finely grated gingerroot
½	teaspoon turmeric
2	cups quartered mushrooms
	About 2 cups water
1	small sweet potato or yam, peeled and roughly cut into 1-inch pieces
1	large carrot, peeled and roughly cut into 1-inch pieces
½ to 1	cup cooked navy beans, whole or puréed
3	tablespoons tamari

    1   *cup 1-inch cubes green or red bell pepper*
    2   *cups 2-inch lengths green beans*
    1   *cup broccoli florets*
1 to 2   *cups 1- to 2-inch chunks summer squash*
          (zucchini, crookneck, pattypan
    2   *teaspoons arrowroot mixed with*
          2 tablespoons water, optional
      Salt to taste

Place a Dutch oven on medium heat. When it is hot, add the whole cumin seed and dry- roast for 1 to 2 minutes, until it turns a shade darker and emits a lovely, roasted aroma. Add the ghee (allowing it to melt if it is hard), the cardamom, and dried chilies. Cook for 30 seconds. Add the onion, mixing well and cook until it begins to brown, after about 5 to 8 minutes. Add the garlic, ginger-root, and turmeric, and cook for another minute. Add the mush-rooms and turn the flame to medium high, tossing to coat with the spices. After about a minute, the mushrooms should begin to brown on the edges. Add the water (careful—it will splatter when it hits the hot pot), the sweet potato, carrot, cooked navy beans, and tamari, bringing the mixture to the simmer. Reduce the flame to very low, cover the pot, and let the vegetables simmer for 15 to 20 minutes, or until the sweet potato is just cooked through. Add the green bell pepper and green beans and cook for 5 minutes. Add the broccoli and summer squash and cook for 5 to 10 minutes, or until every-thing is hot, bubbly, and all of the vegetables are cooked through.

If you've used whole navy beans, add some arrowroot mixture to thicken the sauce, if desired. Puréed beans probably won't need it.

Add salt to taste, serve the curry with plain brown basmati rice.

> *Imogayu no atsusa*   Potato gruel—
> *umasa mo aki to natta*   *Its warmth! Its good taste!*
>   *Autumn is here*
>   —Santôka

Acorn Squash Genovese

SERVES 4

● ●

Acorn squash has a luscious buttery texture, and when sautéed, can have gen-tly browned edges, giving a warm, nutty, slightly sweet taste. This particular dish is lovely as an accompaniment to mushroom risotto, orzo, or roasted tofu pieces. It is quite simple but very satisfying, a nice juxtaposition of sweet, salt, and garlic/herb flavors.

1   *large acorn squash*
1 to 3   *tablespoons olive oil*
2   *tablespoons pesto*
1 to 2   *tablespoons tamari*
½   *cup water or vegetable stock*
1 to 2   *teaspoons chopped Italian parsley, optional*

Slice the acorn squash in half lengthwise. Using a spoon, scoop out and discard the seeds and pith. With a vegetable peeler, remove the skin, working into the ridged areas so that the squash is completely peeled. Rinse the squash under running water and peel the other half. Slice the squash halves into ¼- to ½-inch widths, then slice these pieces in half or into thirds, so that each piece of squash is approximately 2 inches long.

Place a large, heavy sauté pan over a moderate flame. When it is hot, add the olive oil. When the oil has heated, add the squash, tossing to coat with the oil. Sauté for 8 to 10 minutes, tossing and turning the pieces periodically, until the squash has turned from a bright yellow orange to a dull, soft ochre. Some of the pieces should begin to brown lightly on the edges. Insert a fork into one of the larger pieces; if it feels soft on the outside but a bit firm on the inside, you are ready to proceed. If the squash is quite hard and feels raw, continue to sauté the pieces until they have softened up a bit.

Add the pesto, tamari, and liquid. Stir the mixture once and cover the pan. Let the squash cook, covered, for another 5 to 8 minutes, until it has absorbed the liquid and the pieces are quite soft.

Serve immediately with a sprinkling of chopped Italian parsley, if desired.

Taberu mono wa   *I've something to eat*
atte you mono mo atte   *And something to make me drunk;*
zassô no ame.   *Rain in the weeds.*
        —SANTŌKA

Coconut Corn and Mushrooms

SERVES 4

• •

This quick dish is very pretty, with the yellow corn, red tomatoes, and green garnish. It is also perfect for vegans, as you can use oil instead of ghee. The browned mushrooms add a "meaty" taste.

         2   tablespoons ghee or olive oil
         2   cups ¼-inch mushroom pieces
         1   tablespoon cumin seed
    2 to 3   cloves garlic, peeled and minced or put through
                 a press
         ¼   teaspoon cayenne pepper
         ¼   teaspoon turmeric
         2   teaspoons ground coriander
         ½   teaspoon salt
         2   tomatoes, peeled, seeded, and chopped
         2   ears of sweet corn, kernels removed from
                 the cob
         2   teaspoons finely minced or grated gingerroot
        1½   cups unsweetened coconut milk
         1   tablespoon lemon juice
    1 to 2   teaspoons sugar
             Cilantro or mint, for garnish

Place a large sauté pan over medium high heat. Add the oil; when it is hot, add the mushrooms and cumin seed. Cook until the mushrooms begin to brown lightly, tossing and stirring for 3 to 4 minutes. Reduce the flame to medium and add the garlic, cayenne, turmeric, coriander, and salt, and cook and stir for another 1 to 2 minutes. Add the tomatoes, corn, and gingerroot. Sauté for 2 minutes. Add the coconut milk and lemon juice. Bring the mixture to the simmer, cover, and cook for 2 to 3 minutes. Remove the cover and simmer another 3 to 5 minutes or so, until the corn is just cooked through. Taste for seasoning, adding sugar and salt as needed, and serve immediately, garnishing with cilantro or fresh mint leaves.

Meaty Mushrooms

SERVES 4

● ●

These mushrooms look vaguely like slices of browned beef and have a rich, "meaty" taste, hence their name. They are delicious as an appetizer with croûtes, as a side dish, or as part of a vegetarian pizza or sandwich. Don't be misled by the simplicity of the ingredients—you'll be surprised at the flavor!

If you wish, you may substitute other mushrooms (such as crimini, oyster, shiitake) for all or part of the white ones , but be sure always to include the portobellos, as they give a deep brown color and rich taste.

½   pound white mushrooms, or others of your
        choice
4 to 6   ounces portobello mushrooms
2   tablespoons olive oil
1   tablespoon butter
¼ to ⅓   cup red wine
½ to ⅔   cup canned crushed tomatoes (including juice)
¼   cup chopped fresh chives
2 to 3   tablespoons chopped fresh sage
        Salt and pepper to taste

Clean and cut the mushrooms into ¼-inch slices.

Place a large sauté pan over high heat; when it is hot, add the oil and butter. Once the butter has melted, add the mushrooms and then toss them in the oil. Cook over high heat until they soften and begin to exude juices, about 5 minutes. If you like, you can continue to cook the mushrooms until they have browned lightly. Otherwise, add the wine, cook for 1 minute, then add the tomatoes. Stir and heat through; reduce the heat to low and cook for an additional 5 minutes. Remove from the heat.

Add the chives, sage, and salt and pepper to taste. Serve immediately, or allow to cool.

> A single line of
> Fragrant smoke
> From the incense stick
> Trails off without a trace:
> One's heart, as well?
> —RENGETSU

Bharta
Indian Smoked Eggplant

SERVES 4

● ●

The first time I made bharta I wasn't crazy about it. It was my own fault, because I must have overcooked the eggplant; all I remember was that it tasted very smoky. Now, however, I adore it. It is sumptuously creamy in texture and delightfully subtle in taste, overall quite complex. A wonderful side dish for any Indian meal.

1   *large 10-inch eggplant, or 2 small eggplants,*
       6 to 8 inches long
1   *small onion, peeled and roughly chopped*
2   *cloves garlic, peeled*
1   *½-inch piece of gingerroot, peeled*
2   *tablespoons oil or ghee*
1   *2-inch stick of cinnamon*
1½ *teaspoons whole cumin seed*
½   *teaspoon fennel seed*
2   *teaspoons black mustard seeds*
¼   *teaspoon ground fenugreek*
2   *cups finely chopped tomatoes (canned*
       or fresh)
1 to 2 *teaspoons salt, to taste*
1   *teaspoon sugar*
1 to 3 *teaspoons tamarind paste (see Ingredients*
       page 256)
½   *cup green peas, thawed if frozen, optional*
½   *cup plain yogurt*

Put the eggplant over an open flame and roast it directly in the fire; start with the end parts so that the eggplant is standing up. Let the outside skin turn black and smoke somewhat. As soon as the ends are blackened, lay the eggplant on its side and continue in the same manner, roasting and turning, until the entire eggplant is roasted. (NOTE: as the eggplant cooks, it will become soft and mushy, and may even begin to exude juices. It will be difficult to handle and may make a mess on your stovetop, but it's well worth it.) When the eggplant is done, after about 15 minutes of roasting, place it on a plate and allow it to cool for 15 minutes. (Alternatively, you may place the eggplant in a roasting pan and broil it, turning often, until the skin is black and charred and the eggplant is soft. This method, however, will not give the same smokiness as grilling in an open flame.)

After the eggplant has cooled, slice it in half lengthwise and open it up. Using a large spoon, carefully scrape the inside flesh into a bowl, leaving as much of the blackened, outer skin as possible on the plate to discard.

Place the onion, garlic, and gingerroot in a food processor and blend to a smooth paste, pushing the mixture down with a spatula as needed. Set aside.

Heat a large skillet or wok over a moderate flame; when the pan is hot, add the oil and heat for 30 seconds. Add the cinnamon stick, cumin, fennel, and mustard seeds. Stir briefly and turn the heat to medium high; as soon as the mustard seeds are sizzling and begin to pop, turn the heat off and cover the pan. When the seeds have stopped popping (just listen—you'll be able to tell), remove the cover and add the fenugreek, stirring once. Turn the flame back to medium low and add the onion purée, keeping your face averted. Stir-fry the onion paste until it is completely done and has browned lightly, about 15 to 20 minutes, scraping the bottom and stirring often.

While the onion mixture is cooking, rinse out the food processor bowl and add the roasted eggplant. Purée in a few short, quick spurts, leaving some chunks of eggplant if desired, or continue until you have a smoother purée. Set aside.

To the cooked onion mixture, add the tomatoes, 1 teaspoon salt, the sugar, and the tamarind paste. Raise the heat to medium, and stir and cook for 10 minutes, until the tomatoes have reduced somewhat. Add the eggplant purée and stir; reduce the flame to low, and cook for 20 to 30 minutes.

DO-AHEAD NOTE: the bharta can be prepared up to this point a day or two in advance. Reheat gently before continuing.

Add the green peas at the last moment, just warming them through.

Let the bharta cool for 5 minutes. Immediately before serving, stir in the yogurt.

> In Nothing,
> everything is contained:
> limitless—
> Flowers,
> moon,
> pavilions.

Savory Yogurt Eggplant

SERVES 4

● ●

This is a smooth, satisfying side dish, perfect with rice. If you wish, you may reduce the amount of ghee to 1 tablespoon, cutting the fat content in half.

> 4 to 6   *Japanese eggplant, cut into 1-inch pieces*
>   *Salt*
> 2   *tablespoons ghee or butter*
> 2 to 3   *whole, dried, hot red chili peppers*
> 1   *cup finely diced red bell pepper*
> 1   *tablespoon fennel seed*
> 2 to 3   *teaspoons whole cumin seed*
>   *Pinch of hing*
> ¼   *teaspoon ground fenugreek*
> 2   *tablespoons grated gingerroot*
>   *About 1 cup plain yogurt (nonfat, low-fat,*
>   *or regular)*

Wash the eggplant, remove and discard the stem ends, and slice the eggplant into 1-inch rounds. Place the eggplant pieces in a steamer, salting lightly, and steam until tender, about 8 to 10 minutes. Set aside.

In a heavy pan, sauté the chile peppers and sweet pepper in ghee over medium high heat until the bell pepper is tender and may have a few brown specks. Add the fennel seed and cumin seed and cook for another 30 seconds or so. Add a big pinch of hing, the fenugreek, and gingerroot. Stir. Add the cooked eggplant, cover, and cook for 5 to 8 minutes, until everything is hot. Remove from the heat and add yogurt by tablespoonfuls, stirring well to create a smooth sauce. Serve immediately.

> *Unmoved, the melons*
> *don't seem to recall*
> *one drop*
> *of last night's downpour*
> —SODO

Nomadic Eggplant

SERVES 4

● ●

If someone were to ask me "What's the most difficult thing about writing a cookbook?" I would immediately answer, "Naming the recipes." For this recipe title, I'm envisioning a traveler in Ancient Greece boarding a boat with his favorite eggplant recipe in hand. After a long voyage, he lands on Italian soil. There the traveler finds a few vegetables he had not tasted hitherto, and those new discoveries get added to his recipe. Wanderlust, however, is a cruel mistress, so before he can say "mille grazie," he packs up his togs and travels to France, where he discovers a few more culinary treats and incorporates those, too, into his recipe.

This is a recipe that could (almost) be Greek, Italian, or French. No matter where it comes from, it is delicious. It's a particularly nice side dish in the middle of January when you're yearning for the arrival of spring, knowing full well that Old Man Winter has you firmly in his clutches. A few bites of this will remind you of the sun-filled days to come, balmy breezes, and the abundance of fresh herbs thriving in your garden.

If you happen to have ripe, fresh tomatoes on hand, use 2 cups fresh, peeled, chopped tomatoes for the canned tomatoes and juice.

1	**large eggplant, about 10- to 12-inches in length** **Pam**
2 to 3	**tablespoons olive oil**
1	**large onion, peeled and chopped into ½-inch dice**
1	**red bell pepper, chopped into ¼-inch dice**
2	**stalks celery, chopped into ¼-inch dice**
1	**teaspoon dried thyme, or 1 tablespoon chopped** **fresh thyme**
1	**teaspoon dried basil, or 2 tablespoons chopped** **fresh basil**
1½	**cups diced canned tomatoes**
⅓	**cup juice from the tomatoes**
½	**cup green salad olives, cut in half**
¼ to ½	**cup pitted black Kalamata olives** **Salt and pepper**
¼	**cup chopped Italian parsley**

Slice the ends off the eggplant. Using a vegetable peeler, peel off the skin. Slice the eggplant into ¾-inch rounds. Lay the rounds on a baking sheet and spray them on both sides with Pam. Broil the eggplant slices until they have turned reddish brown, flipping the slices as needed. When they have browned, set them aside.

Place a large sauté pan over moderate heat. When the pan is hot, add the olive oil and onion. Sauté the onion, stirring often, until it is soft and has begun to turn brown. Add the bell pepper, celery, thyme, and basil. Continue to sauté for 5 minutes. Add the tomatoes and juice. Bring the mixture to a simmer, cover, and turn the heat to low.

While the tomatoes are cooking, slice the browned eggplant into ½- to 1-squares. Add to the pan and mix thoroughly.

Cook the eggplant, covered, over low heat for 30 minutes, stirring occasionally. The dish may be made ahead of time and stopped at this point; simply let the eggplant cool, covered, and reheat before serving.

Add the green and black olives and taste for seasoning, adding salt and pepper as desired. Sprinkle the parsley over the top and serve immediately.

Variations:
- The list of variations here could go on for days. You could add: chopped capers, pepperoncini, zucchini, garlic, mushrooms, carrots, lemon, vermouth, red wine. You could substitute rosemary, oregano, or marjoram for the thyme or basil. Experiment with what you have on hand.

Kûshû keihô	*The air-raid alarm*
ruirui to shite	*Screaming, screaming;*
kaki akashi.	*Red persimmons.*
	—SANTÔKA

Smoked Ratatouille

SERVES 2 TO 3

• •

This recipe, utterly delightful in its simplicity, has a remarkable complexity of tastes.

1	*medium eggplant, 7 to 10 inches long*
1 to 2	*tablespoons olive oil*
1	*large onion, peeled and roughly chopped*
4	*cloves garlic, peeled and minced*
2	*cups canned tomato pieces with juice,*
	or crushed tomatoes
½	*cup torn fresh basil leaves (large pieces)*
½	*cup chopped fresh Italian parsley, optional*
	Salt and pepper

Hold the eggplant over an open flame and roast it directly in the fire; start with the end parts so that the eggplant is standing up. Let the outside skin turn black and smoke a bit. As soon as the end is blackened, lay the eggplant on its side and continue in the same manner, roasting and turning, until the entire eggplant is roasted. (Note: as the eggplant cooks, it will become soft and mushy, and may even begin to exude juices. In other words, it will be difficult to handle and messy—but well worth the effort.) Alternatively, you could place the eggplant on a roasting pan and broil it, turning often, until the skin is black and charred and is soft. When the eggplant is done, after about 20 minutes of roasting, wrap it in a paper towel, place it on a plate, and let it cool for 15 to 30 minutes.

After the eggplant has cooled, remove the blackened outer skin with a small knife. It shouldn't be necessary to actually peel the eggplant, as the skin has been completely charred; all that should be necessary is to remove the blackened skin from the inside flesh. You will probably need to rinse your knife and hands periodically under cool water to get off the charred skin. Once the skin has been removed, cut off the stem end, and, as best you can, since the eggplant is quite soft, cut into 1-inch cubes. Set aside.

Place a large sauté pan over medium heat. When hot, add the oil, onion, and garlic, sautéing for 5 to 8 minutes until the onion is translucent. Add the eggplant cubes and tomato and bring the mixture to a simmer. Reduce the heat to low and simmer, covered, for 20 minutes, until everything is cooked through. Add the basil and optional parsley, stirring once. Let the mixture cool. Taste for seasoning, adding salt and pepper as desired.

Serve at room temperature or warm.

Variation:

- Chop all the vegetables into ¼- to ½-inch dice and cook as directed. This will make more of a "spread" that can be used on toast or crackers. You might add some chopped black and green olives, capers, roasted bell pepper and balsamic vinegar to taste.

Hiru shizuka na   *Noon quiet—*
yakinasu   *Cooking the eggplant,*
no yaketa nioi.   *Its burnt smell.*
                                   —SANTÔKA

Bombay Beets

SERVES 4

● ●

It never occurred to me that beets were grown in India until one day I spied a recipe in one of Madhur Jaffrey's fabulous cookbooks. Now I cannot even think of eating a beet if it's not been cooked with cardamom, garlic, ginger, and tomato, laced with garam masala. If you don't like plain old beets, try this—you may have just found a new favorite vegetable.

These beets can be quite fiery, depending on how you season them. The sour cream smoothes out the tastes somewhat, so if you want very perky beets, do not add it.

1	bunch beets, approximately 4 to 6, scrubbed
1	tablespoon ghee or canola oil
2 to 3	cloves garlic, peeled and minced
1	tablespoon minced gingerroot
¼	teaspoon ground cardamom
½ to 1	teaspoon red pepper flakes
1 to 2	teaspoons whole cumin seed
1 to 2	teaspoons sugar
2 to 3	tablespoons red wine vinegar or rice wine vinegar
1	tablespoon lemon juice
1	cup chopped tomatoes, fresh or canned
¾	cup water
½ to ⅔	cup yogurt or sour cream, regular or nonfat
½	teaspoon garam masala
	Salt to taste
2	teaspoons arrowroot mixed with 2 tablespoons water, optional
	Cilantro, for garnish, optional

Remove the stems and root tip from the beets. Place the beets in a large pot and cover with water; bring to a boil over moderate heat, then reduce the heat to low and simmer the beets until done, adding water as necessary. Large beets will take longer than smaller ones, but the average beet will cook in around 30 minutes. To test for doneness, insert a small, sharp knife into a beet; if it pierces easily, the beets are done.

Drain and rinse the beets under cool water. Fill the pot with cold water and let the beets stand for 15 minutes, cooling in the pot. With a small knife, remove the outer skin of the beets under cool, running water (this is messy). Chop the beets into ½-inch cubes and put them in a bowl.

Heat the ghee in a tall saucepan over a moderate flame; add the garlic and cook until it has toasted lightly, about 30 seconds. Immediately add the gingerroot, cardamom, red pepper flakes, cumin, sugar, vinegar, lemon juice, and tomatoes. Stir and cook for 30 seconds more, then add the water and cubed beets. Bring the mixture to the simmer and cook, covered, for 20 minutes.

After the mixture has cooked, remove from the heat and add the yogurt or sour cream, mixing well; then add the garam masala.

Taste for seasoning, adding salt as necessary. (If the mixture is particularly watery, you may wish to thicken it up with some arrowroot and water at this point, adding a little bit at a time and barely bringing the mixture back to the simmering point.)

Serve immediately, garnishing with cilantro if desired, accompanied by a rice dish to soak up some of the wonderful juices.

> *The river in winter!*
> *In her boat, washing vegetables,*
> *there is a woman.*
> —BUSON

Guido's Taties

SERVES 4

● ●

This favorite recipe was a standard of a friend, John "Guido" D'Ambrisi. The finger-sized potato slices should be extraordinarily crisp and wonderfully golden brown.

> 4 russet potatoes
> ⅓ to ½ cup olive oil
> 3 tablespoons butter, melted
> About 1 tablespoon salt
> About 1 teaspoon black pepper

Preheat the oven to 375° to 400°.

Scrub (don't peel) the potatoes and slice them in half lengthwise. Slice them again in half lengthwise, forming fourths. Slice the fourths again to form long, thin rectangles or wedges. If the potatoes are extremely large, it may be necessary to cut them further. You want pieces of potato approximately 4- x ½-inches. In other words, really big French fries.

Place the potato wedges in a roasting pan along with the olive oil and butter. Toss to coat, then sprinkle in the salt and pepper evenly. Separate the potatoes in the bottom so that they are in a single layer. Bake in the preheated oven. They will sizzle and smell delicious. After about 30 to 40 minutes, check to see if the bottoms are crisp and brown; if so, turn them so an unbrowned side is now on the bottom. (If you try to turn them too soon, before they've browned sufficiently, they will crumble and fall apart, or the brown part will stick to the bottom.) Bake again until the new bottom side is browned.

After baking an hour, the other sides should be starting to brown. Turn and bake the potatoes as often as necessary, until you have beautifully crisp, brown fries. The total baking time can vary (depending on the water content of the potatoes and general environmental conditions) anywhere from 60 to 90-plus minutes.

Remove from the oven and scrape from the bottom. Serve immediately.

Variations:
- Sprinkle 3 tablespoons chopped fresh rosemary on the potatoes before baking.
- Mix 4 to 5 peeled and halved cloves of with the potatoes before baking.

> *Winter bareness—*
> *little birds seeking food*
> *in the patch of green onions.*
> —BUSON

Horseradish Mashed Potatoes

SERVES 4

● ●

4	large red potatoes, washed
	Salt
¼	cup finely grated fresh horseradish
¼	cup half-and-half
2 to 5	tablespoons unsalted butter
	Salt and pepper
	Additional half-and-half, buttermilk, heavy cream, or milk

Wash the potatoes and remove any dark spots. Do not peel them. Cut the potatoes into ½-inch cubes, and place them in a large pot of water. Add salt if desired, put the pot on the stove, and bring to a simmer. Once the potatoes are simmering, reduce the flame so that the potatoes cook steadily at a heavy simmer. Cook for 20 to 30 minutes, until the potatoes are tender when pierced with a small knife. Turn off the flame and set the potatoes aside in the hot water.

While the potatoes are cooking, peel a 4-inch piece of fresh horseradish with a vegetable peeler and grate it on a cheese grater (the side on which you'd grate Parmesan cheese), to yield about ¼ cup very finely grated horseradish—it may take a little bit of elbow grease. Put the grated horseradish in a small bowl and cover with about ¼ cup half-and-half. Set aside. (The recipe can be made ahead several hours up to this point. To continue, bring the potatoes back to the simmer again before continuing.)

Drain the still hot potatoes in a sieve or colander. Return the cooked potatoes to the pot and add the butter. Using a very large fork or a potato masher, mash until you have a smoothish mixture (it's not important that it be completely smooth). Add the horseradish by tablespoons, tasting after every addition, until you've reached the perfect amount of flavor for your taste. Add salt and pepper to taste. If you have enough horseradish but feel the potatoes are a bit dry, add more half-and-half to get a creamy, smooth dish. Serve immediately.

Variations:
- Add ½ cup freshly grated Parmesan cheese.
- Add 2 to 4 whole, peeled cloves of garlic to the potatoes as they are cooking; include these when you mash the potatoes.

Asayake yûyake	*Sunrise, sunset;*
taberu mono ga nai.	*Nothing to eat.*
	—Santôka

Pan Fries

SERVES 4

• •

    3   *russet (baking) potatoes*
   ½   *stick (4 tablespoons) butter*
        Salt, regular or kosher
        Freshly cracked black pepper

Scrub the potatoes and cut them into ⅛-inch slices. Place the slices in water if you like to remove some of the starch. If you don't want to wash the slices, don't, but be sure to use them quickly, as they'll begin to brown when exposed to the air.

Heat 2 tablespoons of the butter in a heavy 12-inch skillet over a moderate flame. When it has melted, remove the skillet from the heat. (If you've washed the potato slices, be sure to drain and dry them thoroughly before continuing.) Place a layer of potatoes in the skillet, covering as much of the bottom as possible. Sprinkle on a bit of salt and a grinding of fresh pepper. Place another layer of potatoes on top, then salt and pepper, continuing with the layering until all the potatoes are used up. Cut the remaining 2 tablespoons butter into small bits and dot the top of the potatoes with it. Place a piece of foil over the potatoes. Now put a heavy pot on top of the foil, weighing down the potatoes well. If possible, put something in the pot to make it even heavier (water, a brick, a big rock).

Place the weighted skillet over a medium low flame. (The key to making these potatoes is a low flame and an extended cooking period.) Allow to cook undisturbed for 30 minutes. The pan will sizzle, bubble, and steam will rise from underneath the foil. Occasionally check the sides of the potatoes to see if they're browning and becoming crisp. The cooking time will vary depending on the freshness of the potatoes, how well the skillet transfers heat, how heavy the weight is. The bottom may brown in as little as 25 minutes or it may take over 40 minutes. When you're satisfied that the entire bottom is crisp and brown, remove the weight and foil. Using a large metal spatula, gently but firmly scrape the potatoes from the bottom, trying to keep everything in one big piece. Since potatoes contain starch, they will stick to the bottom, but if they are truly brown, they should detach with relative ease. Once you've scraped the entire bottom and have a big, loose, potato pancake, remove the skillet from heat. Place an inverted plate over the potatoes and carefully holding the plate in place (using pot holders), quickly flip the skillet over, plopping the potato pancake onto the plate.

Carefully slide the potato pancake back into the skillet with the uncooked side down. If desired, dribble a bit of melted butter in the bottom to aid browning. Return the skillet to the flame, and replace the foil and weighted pot. The second side browns more quickly than the first, so check it after 20 minutes or so. Once the second side has sufficiently crisped and browned, remove the pancake from the skillet and slice it into wedges or halves. Serve immediately—the potatoes will soften as they cool.

Variations:
- Add 1 or 2 minced cloves of garlic as you're layering the potatoes.

- Add 1 tablespoon chopped fresh rosemary as you're layering the potatoes.
- Add both garlic and rosemary.
- For a subtle taste, use some Roasted Garlic Oil (page 235) instead of all the butter.

Spice-stuffed Okra

ABOUT 4 SERVINGS

● ●

The recipe below is inspired by Indian cuisine. The small okra pods are cleaned and sliced down one side, so you can stuff them with ground spices. The stuffed okra are stir-fried quickly and served whole.

> 1 **pint small, unblemished, pale green okra pods, about 6 to 8 pods per person**

SPICE MIXTURE:
> ½   *teaspoon cayenne pepper*
> 1   *tablespoon ground cumin seed*
> 1½   *tablespoons ground coriander*
> 1   *teaspoon salt*
> ½   *teaspoon garam masala*
> ¼   *teaspoon turmeric*
> 1 to 2   *teaspoons sugar*
>   *Big pinch of hing*
> 1 to 2   *tablespoons canola oil or ghee*
> 2 to 3   *lemons, cut for juicing*

Wash and thoroughly dry the okra pods. Using a small knife, remove as much of the cap as you can, not cutting it off completely. Set aside.

Combine the dry spices in a small bowl.

Using the small knife, make an incision down the length of each okra pod, prying this slit apart gently with your thumb. Add ½ teaspoon of the spice mixture to the cavity and set the pod aside on a plate. Continue until all the pods have been stuffed. The okra can be stuffed and stored in the refrigerator for several hours before cooking.

Place a sauté pan or a wok over moderately high heat. Add the oil or ghee. Add the okra and stir-fry for 2 to 3 minutes (a bit longer if the okra has been refrigerated), covering occasionally, until the pods are deep green and nearly tender. Once done (I prefer okra to retain some crispness, but others do not. Cook until you think it is done), serve immediately. Squirt a tablespoon of fresh lemon juice on top of each serving just before presentation.

Aging—
more haiku,
more turnip broth.
—KYOSHI

Petits Pois avec Menthe
(Peas and Mint)

SERVES 4

● ●

Don't be put off by the idea of frozen peas: they are a remarkably good alternative to store-bought fresh peas, which are often tasteless. Frozen peas are picked, cleaned, and frozen at the peak of their season, and careful thawing results in a very satisfactory vegetable. Canned peas, on the other hand, are hideous.

I first had this combination of peas and mint (a traditional English mixture) one evening with my dear friends Bill and Beverly May. Beverly had prepared a lovely, simple meal of broiled salmon, a rice pilaf, and these peas. I was utterly delighted with everything, but the peas were a minor epiphany for me, since my childhood experience with peas had always been negative (and we all know how difficult it can be to overcome childhood prejudices). I'd suddenly discovered a new vegetable—I felt incredibly stupid for having ignored the simple green pea for so many years!

1	pound baby fresh or thawed frozen small peas
3	tablespoons butter
	Salt to taste (about ¼ to ½ teaspoon)
	Sugar to taste (about 2 tablespoons)
¼ to ⅓	cup fresh spearmint (not peppermint) leaves, torn into pieces

If you're using fresh peas, shell and wash them in a sieve. Otherwise, use the frozen variety, thawed. The best way to thaw frozen peas is to put them in the refrigerator for 6 to 10 hours.

Put the butter in a sauté pan over a moderate flame. Add a pinch of salt and the sugar, letting the butter and sugar cook for 30 seconds, then add the peas. Toss and stir until the peas have heated through and are hot, about 2 minutes. Remove to a serving bowl and add the spearmint leaves. Stir once, taste for seasoning (salt and sugar) and serve immediately.

> How calming
> after rage—
> shelling of peas.
> —Hosai

Carrots

SERVES 4

● ●

Growing up I never liked cooked carrots because they were usually overcooked. As a result, I've spent a lot of years eating only eating raw carrots, until I discovered that barely cooked carrots are delicious and retain their color, taste, and texture. This side dish is fragrant, extremely easy, and a vivid accompaniment to practically any main course. Please note that the amount of added fat is up to you.

4 to 6	carrots, depending on size*
	Pam or 2 teaspoons (or more) of butter
⅛ to ¼	teaspoon allspice
	Big pinch salt
¼	cup half-and-half, water, milk, or cream
⅓	cup currants
	Sugar to taste
¼	cup chopped toasted almonds

Peel the carrots and cut off the ends. Using a hand-held grater, grate the carrots and set them aside.

Place a large sauté pan over a low flame and spray with Pam or add the butter. Add the grated carrots and allspice. Cover the pan and let the carrots begin to cook through for about 1 to 2 minutes. Stir them and add the salt. Add the liquid, cover again, and cook for another 2 minutes, or just until the carrots are soft, bright orange, and heated through. Add the currants, stir, and taste to see if you want to sweeten the vegetables. Add brown or white sugar as desired. As soon as the currants are heated through (another 30 seconds), remove the pan from the flame and add the almonds, stirring well. Serve immediately.

As a side dish, you need roughly 1 large carrot per person, but if you really like carrots you can use more and increase the other ingredients accordingly.

*Who cares to notice
carrot flowers,
explode into bloom!*
—SADO

Kyoto Spinach and Carrots

SERVES 2 TO 3

● ●

*Kyoto, a city called the "cultural center" of Japan, is known for its subtle,
slightly sweet cuisine. Delicacy is the key to Kyoto cooking.*

10 **to 16 ounces fresh spinach, stemmed and
washed**
¼ **cup very thinly sliced and chopped onion**
1 **teaspoon oil**
1 **large or 2 small carrots, peeled and sliced
⅛-inch thin on a diagonal**
2 **teaspoons sugar
Salt**
1 to 2 **tablespoons sake or white wine**
2 **tablespoons teriyaki sauce**

Place the spinach in a colander. Slowly pour a large kettle of
boiling water over it, turning the greens over occasionally, to make
sure all the spinach has been wilted by the hot water. Let stand for
30 seconds, then rinse under cold water. Squeeze out as much
excess moisture as you can, then roughly chop the blanched greens.

In a large skillet, barely sauté the onion in the oil; add the carrot
and stir. Add the spinach, sugar, a sprinkling of salt, sake, and tamari;
stir-fry until everything is hot and just done. Serve immediately.

Tarragon Spinach

SERVES 2 TO 3

● ●

*Yet another simple recipe. Very delicate—a side dish for almost any main
course.*

1 **pound fresh spinach**
1 **tablespoon butter**
½ **teaspoon salt**

½   *cup chopped green onions, or ¼ cup finely*
       chopped regular onion
1 to 2   *teaspoons fresh, fragrant tarragon, or ¼ to*
       ½ teaspoon dried tarragon*
½   *cup sour cream (regular, light, or nonfat)*
       or heavy cream

Wash the spinach and chop. Set aside.

Place the butter in a large sauté pan and heat over a moderate flame. Add the salt and onion, sautéing for 1 minute. (If you're using regular onion, sauté until it is soft and translucent, about 2 minutes.) Add the tarragon and spinach and cover. Turn the heat to medium high and let the spinach wilt on one side for 30 seconds, then stir and wilt the other side. Cook for 30 seconds and turn off the heat. Drain off any liquid that may be in the pan. Add the sour cream, stirring once to incorporate everything. Serve immediately.

> *Evening bell:*
> *persimmons pelt*
> *the temple garden.*
>   *—Shiki*

Baked Whole Garlic

● ●

Baked garlic is completely different from raw or sautéed garlic; it has a mellow, warm taste that is buttery in texture and incredibly sensual. As you can tell from the recipe, amounts are not terribly important—you just cook the garlic until it's done. There are even terra cotta garlic bakers on the market, available in gourmet food stores.

If you like baked garlic, try Roasted Garlic Oil, page 235.

> **Whole heads of garlic†**
> **Fresh or dried herbs, such as thyme, rosemary,**
>   **marjoram, basil, or oregano**
> **Olive oil**

*If you live in the American South, you may have access to a plant called Mexican marigold mint, sometimes also referred to as Mexican tarragon. Although this is not tarragon, it is a great substitute for French tarragon, and is extremely easy to grow.

†Select heads that are firm and appear fresh; don't use those that have sprouted at the top or feel a bit rubbery or papery.

Preheat the oven to 350°.

Tear off a large enough piece of foil to contain the garlic heads. Place the garlic heads in the center, then lay a few sprigs of fresh herbs (or a light sprinkling of dried herbs) on top, then drizzle the garlic with a small amount of olive oil. Wrap the foil around the garlic, folding and sealing the seams well. Place the packet in the oven.

Bake for at least 1 hour before testing to see if it is done. (Depending on the freshness of the garlic and general weather conditions, it may take anywhere from 1 hour to 1½ hours.) The garlic is done if it has: 1) become slightly shriveled and has a tan, roasted color; 2) gives off a lovely roasted smell; 3) yields easily if you squeeze it gently between your thumb and finger. It should be quite soft, but don't bake it for more than 1½ hours or you'll dry it out and lose the buttery quality you're trying to achieve.

Allow the garlic to cool on the countertop, still wrapped in the foil. Serve at room temperature by slicing off the top portion of the garlic head to expose the baked cloves; guests scoop out the garlic with a knife and spread it on bread, crackers, or cheese. Or, you can carefully break off each clove and squeeze out the baked garlic into a small bowl, leaving only the papery husk, assuming you've baked enough garlic heads to make an adequate presentation.

Variations:
- Remove all the baked garlic from the husks and place in a small bowl; mash it with a fork or spoon until completely smooth. Add salt to taste and use as a spread. If desired, add any or a combination of the following:
- a bit of fresh herb (such as 1 tablespoon chopped rosemary, basil, thyme, oregano)
- some chopped capers—use sparingly, as they are potent and can overwhelm the taste of the garlic
- for a true Mediterranean, non-vegetarian touch, a bit of anchovy paste
- ¼ teaspoon finely grated lemon zest
- 1 tablespoon or so of finely chopped green or Kalamata olives
- 1 tablespoon or so of finely chopped sun-dried tomatoes, or a teaspoon of sun-dried tomato paste

WHAT TO DO WITH YOUR SEASONED GARLIC PASTE:

- Whisk the puréed baked garlic into a freshly made mayonnaise for a subtle, luscious treat.
- Add puréed garlic to sour cream or mayonnaise as a dip, spread, or for a sauce.
- Spread seasoned garlic on slices of hot bread and sprinkle with grated Parmesan cheese; broil if desired.
- And of course, toss with hot pasta.

Sautéed Zucchini with Hot Vinaigrette

SERVES 4

● ●

1	cup all-purpose flour
2	teaspoons cayenne pepper
2	eggs
2	small to medium zucchini
2	tablespoons Roasted Garlic Oil (page 235)
	Salt to taste
¼ to ½	cup torn fresh basil leaves
⅔	cup Basic Vinaigrette (page 216)

Place the flour in a dish. Sprinkle in the cayenne and mix well. Set aside.

Beat the eggs thoroughly in a bowl. Set aside.

Wash the zucchini and remove the ends. Slice the zucchini lengthwise into ¼- to ½-inch lengths. Dredge a slice of zucchini in the flour, dip it in the egg, then dip it in the flour again. Set it on waxed paper and continue with the remaining zucchini slices.

Place a large sauté pan over a moderate flame and add the garlic oil. Lay the coated zucchini slices in the pan and allow to cook for 5 minutes on one side, until nicely browned. Turn the slices over and cook the other side in the same manner. Sprinkle a bit of salt over them. Remove the cooked slices to a warm serving platter, arranging them attractively.

Tear the basil leaves with your fingers and arrange the pieces over the cooked zucchini slices. Spoon the vinaigrette over the warm zucchini and serve immediately.

Gleam of left-over
bean-curd—
mosquitoes buzz.
—Issa

Japanese Cucumber Salad

SERVES 4

● ●

This very easy salad is one that might more appropriately be called a "quick pickle." Pickles and vinegared salads (tsukemono and sunomono) are very popular in Japanese cuisine, with pickled eggplant, cucumbers, or cabbage being served at the end of a meal with green tea, thought by some to aid digestion of fried foods.

	About 2 tablespoons sugar, to taste
3 to 4	tablespoons rice wine vinegar
3 to 4	tablespoons tamari
1	long European or Japanese cucumber, or a large regular cucumber, peeled and seeded
1	carrot or tomato
	About 1 teaspoon chopped fresh chives
1	tablespoon toasted sesame seeds

Place the sugar, vinegar, and tamari in a medium-sized bowl. Stir thoroughly until the sugar is dissolved.

Wash and remove the tip ends of the cucumber. Slice into very thin rounds (⅟₁₆-inch if possible—this is easier if you use a mandoline-type gadget). Place the cucumber rounds in the bowl with the vinegar mixture.

If using a carrot, peel and slice it into thin matchsticks, approximately 1½ x ⅛ x ⅛-inch. If you're using a tomato, remove the seeds and core and slice it into ¼-inch dice. Add to the bowl.

Stir the vegetables once so that everything is coated with the marinade. Let stand, unrefrigerated, for 30 to 60 minutes. The salt in the tamari will draw out the water in the vegetables, causing them to "wilt."

After the vegetables have marinated, use a slotted spoon to divide them among bowls. Pour a bit of the marinade in with the vegetables, but not so much that they're swimming in it.

Sprinkle the chopped chives and sesame seeds on top. Serve immediately.

Variations:
- Just after you've dissolved the sugar in the vinegar, slice a clove of garlic in half. Let the garlic marinate in the vinegar mixture for 15 minutes, then remove it. Continue as above, but eliminate the chives.
- If you don't have sesame seeds, add ¼ teaspoon toasted sesame oil instead.

Nasu kyûri   *Eggplants, cucumbers;*
Kyûri nasu   *Cucumbers, eggplants:*
bakari taberu suzushisa.   *That's all I eat—the coolness.*
                              —SANTÔKA

Fresh Mozzarella, Tomatoes, and Basil

SERVES 2

● ●

This salad is simplicity itself to make and superbly tasty. It is quite a common Mediterranean salad from Greece to Italy to France, and the inclusion of roasted garlic oil is heaven.

½ **pound fresh mozzarella cheese, cut into ¼-inch slices**
1 to 2 **ripe tomatoes, cut into ¼-inch slices**
¼ to ⅓ **cup of fresh basil, cut into ⅛-inch slices**
Roasted Garlic Oil (page 235)
Salt and freshly ground black pepper to taste

Alternate the slices of mozzarella and tomatoes on a platter. Sprinkle on the basil leaves attractively. Drizzle some of the garlic oil on top. Serve immediately, inviting the guests to add salt and pepper as desired.

Midsummer Fennel Salad

SERVES 4

● ●

This recipe is delicious and highlights fresh summer produce, hence its name. Fresh fennel (sometimes also seen in the markets as fresh bulb anise) is rather like a cross between celery and licorice in taste; in texture and appearance it resembles celery, but the taste is delicate and aromatic. Fennel is a staple in Italian and Provençale cuisine, so even if you're not a fan of anise, try it—you may be pleasantly surprised.

½	cup raw cashews, lightly toasted
1	bulb fresh fennel
1 or 2	large, ripe tomatoes
½	cup golden or black raisins
4	cups washed salad greens, including spinach, shiso, lettuces, and sorrel
⅓	cup olive oil
1	small onion, peeled and finely minced
2	cloves garlic, minced
2 to 3	teaspoons fennel seed
⅓ to ½	cup rice wine vinegar
2 to 3	tablespoons freshly minced herbs, one or more of the following: thyme, lemon balm, sorrel, salad burnet, shiso, savory, basil
1	teaspoon salt
1	tablespoon black olive purée (in small jars, sometimes called olive paste)

Roast the cashews. Either put them in a toaster oven set at 325° for 15 to 20 minutes, tossing occasionally, until they turn a shade darker, or put them in a small skillet and toss them over a medium flame until they turn slightly darker. Remove the nuts as soon as they have toasted.

Slice off the rooty bottom and the top of the fennel, so that you have a compact bulb. Slice the bulb in half. Wash it under cool water, prying open the layers as you go. Shake off any excess water. Take the fennel bulb apart by pulling the layers away from the center (much like a celery stalk). Cut the fennel into thin ¹⁄₁₆- to ⅛-inch slices, and put the slices in a large salad bowl.

Wash and chop the tomatoes; add this to the salad bowl. Add the cashews, raisins, and cleaned salad greens. Set aside.

In a small saucepan, heat the olive oil over a moderate flame. When it is hot, add the onion and garlic, cooking and stirring for 1 to 2 minutes, until the onion has softened. Allow to cool.

In a medium-sized bowl, place the fennel seed, vinegar, mixed herbs, salt, and olive purée. Mix thoroughly. When the onion mixture has cooled somewhat, add it to the vinegar bowl and toss well. Pour this dressing over the salad greens and toss. Serve immediately.

Old-fashioned Summer Pickle

SERVES 4 TO 6

This recipe probably originated when the summer's harvest of tomatoes and cucumbers had come in and there was no time to can them all. Hence this quick way to use up vegetables at the height of their flavor. There's no cooking involved (if you don't count dissolving sugar in water), so the kitchen stays cool and you have an easy accompaniment to lunch or dinner.

2	cups water
1	cup sugar
1	tablespoon salt
1	cup cider vinegar
3 or 4	ripe tomatoes, cut into wedges or bite-sized pieces
1 or 2	cucumbers, peeled, seeded, and sliced into ¼-inch rounds
½ to 1	small onion, peeled and sliced into thin half-rings

Place the water, sugar, and salt in a small saucepan and bring to a simmer, stirring until the sugar and salt have dissolved completely. Let the mixture cool.

Pour the sugar mixture into a large ceramic or glass bowl and add the cider vinegar. Add the tomatoes, cucumbers, and onions. Refrigerate for 5 hours before eating.

NOTE: after eating all vegetables, you may simply add more vegetables and marinate them as above, but the taste will be somewhat diluted, since the marinating liquid will now have acquired some of the water from the cucumbers and tomatoes.

I recommend that you make fresh pickling liquid every other batch.

Variations:
- Use celery salt (or another seasoned salt) instead of regular salt.
- Add finely sliced red and green bell pepper to the pickle.

> *Autumn gale—*
> *tossing sponge cucumber,*
> *shuddering melon.*
> *—Meisetsu*

Salad Dressings

• •

There are thousands of recipes for salad dressings, but I always come back to a few basic dressings that seem to fit the bill. Basic vinaigrette, blue cheese, ginger-miso, and shoyu dressings are my top four (not necessarily in that order).

Basic Vinaigrette

MAKES ABOUT ⅔ CUP

• •

	Juice of ½ lemon
3	*tablespoons red wine vinegar*
½	*teaspoon salt*
1 to 3	*teaspoons sugar*
1	*clove garlic, peeled and crushed*
1	*teaspoon Dijon mustard*
	Freshly ground black pepper
½ to 1	*teaspoon dried basil, or 2 tablespoons chopped fresh basil*
¼	*cup chopped parsley*
⅓	*cup extra virgin olive oil*

Put the lemon juice, vinegar, salt and sugar in a jar with a lid. Add the crushed garlic, shake to blend, and let the mixture stand for 30 minutes.

Remove the garlic and add the remaining ingredients, shaking the jar well to blend. Refrigerate until needed.

Variation:
- If you wish, add some mayonnaise or heavy cream to the vinaigrette to make a creamy dressing.

Blue Cheese Dressing
MAKES ABOUT ¾ CUP

● ●

	Juice of ½ lemon
1	*clove garlic, crushed*
1 to 2	*teaspoons sugar*
1	*1- to 2-inch chunk of blue cheese (Roquefort or Danish blue)*
2	*tablespoons chopped fresh parsley*
½	*teaspoon dried basil or 1 tablespoon chopped fresh basil, optional*
⅓	*cup half-and-half, cream, or plain yogurt*
⅓	*cup mayonnaise (regular or low-fat)*
	Salt to taste

Put the lemon juice in a bowl. Add the crushed garlic clove and leave it in the juice for 30 minutes. Remove the garlic and discard.

Add the sugar to the lemon juice, blending well, then add the blue cheese. Using a fork, mash the cheese with the lemon juice to a pastelike consistency. Add the remaining ingredients, blending well. If the mixture seems thin, add some half-and-half.

Ginger Miso Dressing
MAKES ABOUT ⅔ CUP

● ●

1	*1-inch square piece of gingerroot, peeled and roughly chopped*
2	*tablespoons miso (mugi miso recommended)*
¼	*cup rice wine vinegar*
¼	*cup water*
1 to 2	*teaspoons honey, to taste*
	Juice of ½ lemon
½	*teaspoon toasted sesame oil*

Place all of the ingredients into blender and blend until smooth, about 1 minute. Keep the dressing refrigerated for up to 5 days.

VARIATIONS:
- Add 1 tablespoon chopped cilantro to the dressing.
- Add ½ teaspoon hot chili oil or Tabasco for a spicier taste.
- Add 1 tablespoon toasted sesame seeds at the end for texture.
- Add 1 tablespoon poppy seeds for a more traditional dressing.
- Add ¼ cup plain yogurt or buttermilk for a creamier dressing.
- Use orange juice instead of lemon juice.

Shoyu Salad Dressing

MAKES ABOUT ½ CUP

This is so ridiculously simple that it's embarrassing, but it's also absolutely wonderful. Incredibly light, it highlights the freshness of a salad without masking the taste.

⅓ cup tamari or soy sauce
¼ cup mild light vinegar, such as rice wine vinegar
½ teaspoon toasted sesame oil
1 easpoon to 1 tablespoon sugar
1 clove garlic, peeled and cut in half

Combine all the ingredients and allow to stand for at least 30 minutes. Remove the garlic and pour the dressing over salad greens.

VARIATION:
- Omit the garlic and add ½ teaspoon grated gingerroot.

Zippy Poppyseed Dressing

MAKES ABOUT ¾ CUP

• •

¼ to ⅓ cup canola or rice bran oil
1 teaspoon toasted sesame oil
1 tablespoon finely grated gingerroot
½ cup rice wine vinegar
2 to 4 tablespoons hoisin sauce (Ingredients page 253)
2 tablespoons sugar
1 teaspoon salt
½ cup cilantro leaves, not packed
1 to 2 teaspoons red pepper flakes
1 to 2 tablespoons poppy seeds

Place the canola oil, sesame oil, gingerroot, rice wine vinegar, hoisin sauce, sugar, salt, and cilantro leaves in a food processor. Process until the cilantro is finely chopped, around 30 seconds. Add the red pepper flakes and poppy seeds; process once briefly to mix. Refrigerate until needed.

Creamy Basil Dressing

MAKES ABOUT 1 CUP

• •

1 cup fresh basil leaves, not packed
1 tablespoon lemon juice
½ cup sour cream (regular, light, or nonfat)
3 tablespoons mayonnaise (regular, light, or nonfat)
1 to 2 teaspoons Dijon mustard
¼ teaspoon finely minced garlic, optional
1 to 2 teaspoons sugar
  About ¼ cup milk, half-and-half, or heavy cream
  Salt
  Freshly cracked black pepper

Combine the ingredients in a food processor or blender and blend until completely smooth. Thin out mixture with milk to reach the desired consistency. Taste for seasoning, adding salt and pepper if needed.

Herb Mayonnaise

MAKES ABOUT ⅔ CUP

● ●

This blend can be used as a dipping sauce for artichokes as well as a delicious spread for sandwiches or tempeh burgers.

	Juice of ½ lemon
1	teaspoon sugar
½	teaspoon salt
1	teaspoon Dijon mustard
1	tablespoon chopped fresh basil
1	tablespoon chopped fresh parsley
1	teaspoon chopped fresh tarragon
⅓	cup mayonnaise
2	tablespoons plain yogurt (regular or low-fat)
2	tablespoons sour cream (regular, low-fat, or nonfat)

Combine all the ingredients, mixing well. Keep refrigerated until needed.

Ears
Hear and eyes
See,
Then what does
Mind do?

30-Second Dressing

MAKES ABOUT ½ CUP

● ●

When you want a simple salad dressing, this couldn't be easier, considering that it takes a grand total of thirty seconds to prepare and uses three basic ingredients you probably already have on hand. Try it on sliced cucumbers, fresh tomatoes, or shredded carrots.

The poppy seeds are included only for appearance, since they don't give much taste to the dressing. If you're using a fresh herb (such as the suggested Mexican marigold mint), then you may want to skip the poppy seeds.

1	tablespoon sweet Russian mustard
¼	cup rice wine vinegar
¼	cup mayonnaise

1   *teaspoon poppy seeds, optional*
1   *teaspoon freshly chopped tarragon or Mexican*
      marigold mint, optional

Put the mustard, vinegar, and mayonnaise in a jar with a lid, and shake well. Add the optional ingredients and shake again. Refrigerate until needed. This keeps about a week.

Variations:
- Add 2 to 3 tablespoons grated Parmesan cheese.
- Add 2 to 3 tablespoons crumbled blue cheese.
- Add 1 teaspoon grated gingerroot and ½ teaspoon toasted sesame oil.

DESSERTS, COOKIES, AND MISCELLANEOUS

Desserts

Fresh Pumpkin Pie

MAKES ONE 9- TO 10-INCH PIE

The difference between canned pumpkin and fresh pumpkin is shocking. Don't think that puréeing your own pumpkin is a fussy and unnecessary step, as it makes a HUGE difference in the end product.

1	partially baked 9- to 10-inch pie shell (page 244)
1	cup puréed pumpkin, preferably fresh*
⅓	cup packed brown sugar
3	eggs, beaten
½	cup heavy cream
½	cup milk, half-and-half, or soy milk
3	tablespoons brandy, Cognac, or whiskey
2	tablespoons finely shredded fresh gingerroot

*TO MAKE FRESH PUMPKIN PURÉE: *Peel and seed a small pumpkin (if available; otherwise peel part of a larger pumpkin. You will need about 2 cups of pumpkin cubes.) Cut into 1-inch cubes and steam, covered, for about 20 to 30 minutes until it has changed from a bright yellow orange to deep orange. You should be able to pierce the cubes easily with a small knife. Remove from the steamer and purée in a blender or food processor until smooth.*

1	teaspoon ground cinnamon
¼	teaspoon ground allspice
¼	teaspoon ground cloves
¼	teaspoon freshly ground nutmeg
¼	teaspoon salt
1	tablespoon vanilla extract

Preheat the oven to 350°.

In a large bowl mix the pumpkin purée and sugar well, removing any lumps from the brown sugar. Add the eggs and blend again, making sure the eggs are well incorporated into the mixture. Add the remaining ingredients and mix well.

Pour the mixture into the partially baked pie shell and place in the lower third of the preheated oven. Bake for 45 minutes, until the pie has risen around the edges; the center will still look as if it is not set. To test, insert a small knife in the center; if it comes out with little globules clinging to it (as opposed to a thick liquid the consistency of melted ice cream adhering to the knife) then it is done. Remove from the oven and allow to cool. The pie will firm up and set as it cools; overcooking the pie will result in a heavy, eggy-tasting pie.

Serve cold, at room temperature, or warmed slightly, with lightly whipped cream. If desired, garnish with pecan halves around the rim.

Steamed Miniature Chocolate Cakes

SERVES 4

● ●

These luscious little cakes are elegant, fun, and fantastically delicious. The almonds (if not ground to a complete powder) tend to settle near the bottom, so when the cake is unmolded you have a layering of almonds on top and a smooth, mousselike confection underneath. There are several steps in the cake's preparation, but none are difficult, and the cakes can easily be made ahead of time, saving the chocolate sauce for the last minute. Steaming the cakes maintains incredible moistness.

If you like chocolate and orange, use some Grand Marnier instead of the brandy. If you like cherry-chocolate combinations, use some kirschwasser.

    Pam or butter
    Sugar
¼ *cup (½ stick) unsalted butter*
1   *teaspoon instant coffee*
1   *tablespoon Cognac, brandy,*
        Grand Marnier, or kirschwasser
1   *teaspoon vanilla*
½   *teaspoon almond extract*
    Pinch salt
2½ to 3 *ounces semisweet chocolate, broken*
        into bits
½   *cup lightly toasted ground almonds*
¼   *cup fresh white bread crumbs (about*
        1 slice white bread without crusts)
2   *eggs at room temperature*
3 to 4 *tablespoons sugar*

FOR THE CHOCOLATE SAUCE:
¼ to ½ *cup heavy cream or half and half*
4   *ounces Ghirardelli sweet dark chocolate,*
        broken into bits

FOR THE WHIPPED CREAM TOPPING:
½   *cup heavy cream*
1   *tablespoon sugar*
½ to ¾ *teaspoon cinnamon*

Either spray 4 ramekins or custard cups with Pam or grease them with some butter; sprinkle some sugar in each cup and rotate the molds to coat the insides evenly. Invert the cups to remove any excess sugar; set the prepared molds aside.

Place the ¼ cup butter in a small saucepan over moderate heat; stir until melted, then remove from the heat. Add the instant coffee, Cognac, vanilla, almond extract, and salt; stir the mixture until the coffee has dissolved and is thoroughly mixed with the butter and flavorings. Add the chocolate pieces and stir once; let the chocolate melt.

While the chocolate is melting, process the almonds in a food processor or blender until they are finely ground. Remove them and process the bread; combine the almonds and bread crumbs and set aside.

Stir the chocolate until it is completely melted and smooth; it may be necessary to return the pan to a very low heat for a minute or so; be extremely careful just to warm the pan, not get it hot. Continue stirring until you have a completely liquid sauce. Set the melted chocolate aside and keep it barely warm.

Place the whole eggs and sugar in a large bowl. Begin beating with a hand-held mixer over low speed to break up the eggs; when the mixture becomes somewhat frothy, turn the mixer to high and continue beating for 4 to 5 minutes, until the eggs have quadrupled in volume, are light and pale lemon-colored, and form a slowly dissolving ribbon when the mixture is folded back on itself. Pour the warm chocolate mixture into the egg mixture and sprinkle the bread crumbs and almonds on top; fold (don't stir) the chocolate, almonds, and bread crumbs into the egg mixture with a spatula until everything is incorporated.

Divide the batter equally among the prepared custard cups; place the cups in the Dutch oven.* Pour just enough boiling water in the pan to come halfway up the sides of the molds; place the pot over a very low flame, maintaining the temperature just below the simmering point. Cover the pan and steam the cakes for 20 to 25 minutes until they have risen slightly and appear to have set. Remove the lid from the pan and allow the cakes to sit in the hot water for 15 more minutes. Remove the cakes and allow them to cool completely on a wire rack. (The cakes may be made a day ahead of time and refrigerated. When ready to serve, place them in a preheated 300° oven for 15 to 20 minutes until they are no longer cold and are perhaps slightly warm.)

At serving time, carefully run a small spatula around the outside of each cake. Place a small dessert plate over each cake and invert it. Let the cakes drop into the center of the plates. Prepare the chocolate sauce and whipped cream.

For the chocolate sauce: Put the heavy cream in a small saucepan and bring it just to the boil; remove from the heat and add the

---

Sometimes it is difficult to find a single pot big enough to hold all four custard cups in one layer; if this is a problem for you, here is an alternative method for steaming the cakes. Before you prepare the recipe, place a large roasting pan on top of the stove over one or two burners and arrange the empty custard cups in the pan as if you were getting ready to steam the cakes. Add enough water to come halfway up the sides of the cups, then remove them, dry them off, and prepare them as directed in the recipe. Tear off enough aluminum foil to cover the roaster (it may be necessary to tear off two sheets and seal them together as one). Place the foil on top of the roasting pan as if it were a lid, crimping the edges well on three sides for now, as you'll need to keep one side open to insert the ramekins. Before steaming, turn the burners to low and bring the water almost to the simmer. Maintain this temperature carefully as you steam the cakes.

sweet dark chocolate. Stir with a whisk until the chocolate has completely melted. Keep slightly warm.

For the whipped cream topping: Place the heavy cream, sugar, and cinnamon in a small bowl and beat either with an electric mixer or hand-held beater until thick and whipped.

Pour some chocolate sauce over each steamed cake, trying to enrobe each cake with a layer of warmed sauce. Garnish each dessert with a dollop of cinnamon whipped cream on top or on the side.

Apple Cake

MAKES 1 CAKE

● ●

This variation of a recipe from my grandmother was once named "Depression Cake," because (one can only assume) it used ingredients available during the Depression. To me, this cake is the quintessential autumn dessert, because it is full of the sweet-tart taste of fresh baking apples and the warm spiciness of cinnamon and cloves. It is not at all cakelike, but a nut-and-fruit-studded dessert that is irresistible served warm with a dollop of whipped cream. I urge you to use an appropriate apple for this dessert; if you happen upon some newly picked Jonathans you must make this recipe!

1	cup flour
1	teaspoon baking soda
1	teaspoon cinnamon
½	teaspoon cloves
¼	teaspoon allspice
½	teaspoon salt
¾ to 1	cup brown sugar
½	cup (1 stick) butter, melted
1	egg
1	teaspoon vanilla extract
2	cups diced fresh baking apples (Jonathan, McIntosh, Rome, Granny Smith, Jonagold)
1	cup raisins (golden or regular), or currants
½ to ⅔	cup pecan halves

Preheat the oven to 375°.

In a bowl, combine the flour, soda, cinnamon, cloves, allspice, and salt, stirring well. Set aside.

In a large bowl, thoroughly mix the sugar, melted butter, egg, and vanilla. Sprinkle in the flour-spice mixture and stir well. Add the raisins and nuts, stirring again. The batter will barely coat the apples, nuts, and raisins.

Spoon the batter into a greased (or sprayed with Pam) and floured 8 x 8-inch baking dish, smoothing it down so that there is some semblance of evenness and it fills the bottom of the pan.

Bake in a preheated 375° oven for 15 minutes; then reduce the heat to 350° and bake 25 to 30 minutes longer, until it is just done. The cake will be brown and moist; allow it to cool completely before cutting and serving. Do-ahead note: this is equally delicious cold or room temperature, and can be prepared a day ahead and reheated when you want it.

> *Now spring is complete—*
> *A mountain breeze*
> *Catches up the*
> *remaining blossoms in*
> *Billowing white clouds.*
> —RENGETSU

Cookies

Mocha-Nut Thins

MAKES ABOUT 2 DOZEN COOKIES

● ●

There's nothing particularly thin about these marvelous cookies except their shape—they're not unduly sweet and are exceptional after dinner with cappuccino. These are unquestionably an "adult" cookie.

1	cup (2 sticks) butter, softened
¾	cup brown sugar
½	teaspoon salt (you may wish to eliminate this if you're using salted butter)
1	teaspoon vanilla
1	teaspoon brandy, rum, or whiskey
1½	tablespoons powdered (not granules) instant coffee
1½	cups all-purpose flour
½	cup whole wheat flour
1	cup toasted walnuts or raw pecans
½	cup chocolate chips
½ to 1	cup granulated sugar

Preheat the oven to 350°.

Cream the butter, sugar, and salt together in a large bowl until fluffy. Add the vanilla, brandy, and powdered instant coffee and blend again, making sure the instant coffee is fully incorporated and there are no lumps. Add the flours and stir well to get a uniformly mixed batter. Set aside.

Place the nuts in a food processor and grind in short spurts until most of the nuts are approximately the size of half a grain of rice. (Be careful not to overprocess or you'll wind up with nut butter.) Put the nuts in a bowl.

Place chocolate chips in the processor bowl (without cleaning) and process in short spurts until they are approximately ½ to ¼ their original size. Put the chocolate chips in the same bowl with the nuts.

Add half of the chocolate mixture to the batter and stir; add the remaining half and mix again until everything is fully incorporated.

Take 2 tablespoonfuls of batter between your hands and roll into a ball; flatten it slightly between your palms so you have a round disk approximately ½ inch thick. Place the disk on a greased or Pam-sprayed baking sheet. Continue until you have filled all the baking sheets, keeping the disks 1 inch apart.

Lay a paper towel on a flat surface and pour the granulated sugar in the center. Lightly moisten the bottom of a flat-bottomed glass and set the glass in the sugar, coating the bottom with sugar. Press a disk of cookie batter with the bottom of the sugared glass until it is ¼-inch thick. Return the glass to the sugar, coating the bottom again, and continue pressing the cookies until all the cookies have been pressed.

Bake for 8 to 10 minutes, until the cookies have just set; they should not brown. If you gently press the center of a cookie, it will be slightly firm and not mushy. When the cookies are done, remove them from the oven and let cool 1 minute on the baking sheets before removing to cooling racks.

Dangerous
(Pecan Sandies)

MAKES ABOUT 2 DOZEN COOKIES

● ●

During the publication process of my previous book, Let There Be Lite!, *I mailed some of these cookies as a present to my publisher. In the enclosed note I wrote, "These cookies should be called Dangerous, because they're dangerous to have around." Hence the name.*

These fantastic, nut-packed, shortbreadlike cookies are wonderful for any season or reason, and as a bonus they are firm enough to mail as a gift. If you like pecans, you'll love them. If you love pecans, you'll be hard-pressed not to eat a dozen cookies at one sitting.

2	**cups pecan halves**
1	**cup (2 sticks) unsalted butter, softened**
½	**cup sugar**
½	**teaspoon salt**
2	**teaspoons vanilla**
2	**teaspoons brandy or whiskey**
1½	**cups all-purpose flour (or a mixture of whole wheat and white flour)**
	Extra sugar for topping

Preheat oven to 350°.

FOOD PROCESSOR METHOD:

Pick over the pecans to make sure there are no pieces of shell stuck to the nut meat. Place the pecan halves in a food processor and chop in short, quick spurts until the nuts are reduced to small pieces about the size of grains of rice. (Be careful not to overblend or you'll wind up with pecan butter.) Remove the pecans from the processor bowl and set aside.

Without cleaning the bowl, place half of the butter and the sugar in the processor and blend until completely smooth; add the remaining butter and salt and blend until smooth as well. While the processor is running, add the vanilla and brandy. Stop when the liquids are integrated into the mixture, after a few seconds.

Scrape the mixture in a large bowl. Gradually stir in the flour until the batter is completely smooth, then add the pecan pieces, mixing well.

Using two spoons, place 1-inch mounds of dough on ungreased cookie sheets, trying to keep them fairly neat; if you like, you can roll the dough into neat, round balls between your hands, then press them down slightly. (Note: this dough doesn't melt and spread out the way some cookie doughs do; what you put on the sheet is pretty much what you'll wind up with. I personally like the more home-style craggy cookie to the rolled-and-neat cookie, not only because it looks less fussy but because it gives the sugar topping nooks and crannies in which to hide.)

Sprinkle the tops of the cookies with some granulated sugar—not much, just a dusting, maybe 1/4 teaspoon per cookie.

Bake at 350° for 15 minutes or so, until the cookies are lightly firm and may have browned just slightly at the edges. Be careful not to overbake or you'll lose some of the delicacy of the taste. Let the cookies cool for 1 minute on the baking sheets before moving them to cooling racks. When they are cool, store them in an airtight container.

HAND METHOD:

Pick over the pecan halves for shells. Chop into small pieces either by hand, in a processor, or in a nut chopper.

Cream the butter, sugar, and salt in a large bowl until smooth; add the vanilla and brandy. Gradually mix in the flour until completely smooth, then add the pecan pieces, mixing again until they are incorporated.

Form and bake as directed above.

Biscotti di Prato
Italian Almond Cookies

ABOUT 4 DOZEN COOKIES

● ●

These are those delicious, hard Italian "cookies" that are outstanding for dunking into cappuccino or wine. They are double-baked, which accounts for their extraordinary crispness.

2	cups (roughly 1 pound) blanched, toasted almond slivers*
4	cups all-purpose flour
2	cups sugar
	Pinch of salt
	Big pinch of ground saffron
1	teaspoon baking soda
5	eggs
½ to 1	teaspoon almond extract

Place the almond slivers on a baking sheet and toast for 10 to 15 minutes in a preheated 350° oven, just until they are lightly browned and emit a lovely, toasted aroma. Don't wait until they are quite brown, as nuts continue to darken as they cool.

If you don't have blanched almonds, toast whole, raw almonds instead—the almond skin will give deep brown flecks to the biscotti.

*Egg glaze (1 whole egg beaten with
1 tablespoon water)*

Preheat the oven to 375°.

Place 1 cup of the toasted almonds in a food processor and grind them fine, but not so fine that you get almond butter. Place the ground almonds in a large bowl and add the flour, sugar, salt, saffron, and soda. Mix well. Add the remaining almond slivers to the bowl, stirring once. (If you've used whole almonds, chop the remaining almond pieces into irregular shapes and add them now.)

Break the eggs into a smaller bowl and add the almond extract. Beat well, then add to the flour mixture, stirring until the flour has absorbed most of the liquid in the eggs.

Put the dough on a lightly floured flat surface and begin kneading it gently until you have a uniformly moist dough—it will not be terribly moist (like a bread dough), but will be stick together and be malleable. (A plastic pastry scraper is useful for this.) You will also be breaking some of the almond slivers as you knead the dough, but this, too, is fine—it adds a necessary rough-hewn quality to the biscotti.

Divide the dough evenly into 3 or 4 pieces. Roll each section into a long cylinder about 1 inch in diameter. Place the cylinders on a prepared baking sheet. Using a pastry brush, paint the tops of the cylinders with the egg glaze. Bake in the center of the preheated oven for 20 to 25 minutes, or until they are lightly browned. Remove from the oven and let cool for 5 minutes. Reduce the oven to 325°.

Carefully remove the cylinders from the baking sheets and place them on a flat surface (or a cutting board, if you have one large enough to support the long cookie cylinders). Slice the cylinders at a 45° angle into ½- to 1-inch sections. Place the cut pieces on the baking sheets and return them to the oven again, baking for another 15 to 25 minutes. Turn the biscotti once or twice during this final period to ensure even baking.

Remove the biscotti from the oven and let them to come to room temperature. Note that the biscotti will harden as they cool—if they seem a bit soft after baking 45 to 50 minutes, don't worry. Store the cooled biscotti in an airtight container.

*Tormenting my
siesta—song
of rice planters.*
—Issa

Miscellaneous

Spiced Cornbread

FILLS ONE 8- TO 9-INCH SKILLET

● ●

Try this when you are in the mood for cornbread but want something different.

1	*cup self-rising flour**
1	*cup yellow or white cornmeal*
1 to 2	*tablespoons sugar*
3	*tablespoons finely minced onion*
½	*cup chopped cheese, such as Cheddar, smoked Gouda, or Monterey Jack*
1	*teaspoon whole cumin seeds*
4	*small hot green or red chile peppers, seeded and minced*
1	*egg*
1	*cup buttermilk*
¼	*cup plain yogurt or sour cream*
2	*tablespoons oil—1 tablespoon for the wet ingredients, 1 tablespoon for the skillet*

Preheat the oven to 375°.

Mix the flour, cornmeal, sugar, minced onion, chopped cheese, and cumin seeds in a bowl.

Wash and dry the hot peppers. If you want the cornbread to be quite spicy, go ahead and mince them as they are. If you want a less fiery experience, carefully remove the seeds from the peppers under gently running water before mincing them. Add the peppers to the dry ingredients and stir everything well. (Be sure to wash your hands and cutting board well after mincing any hot pepper.)

Put the egg, buttermilk, yogurt, and 1 tablespoon of the oil in a small bowl. Beat with a whisk or fork until everything is mixed.

Place an 8- or 9-inch skillet on a high flame until it is quite hot. Remove from the heat and add 1 tablespoon oil, turning the pan around by the handle so that the oil coats the bottom well. Pour

*If you don't have self-rising flour, use 1 cup all-purpose flour, 1 teaspoon salt, 1 teaspoon baking soda, and 1 tablespoon baking powder.

any excess oil into the wet ingredients (it will sizzle). Quickly mix the wet and dry ingredients until they are fully blended, then pour the batter into the hot skillet. Bake in the upper portion of the pre-heated oven for 25 to 30 minutes, until the bread has risen and is lightly browned on top. Test for doneness by gently pressing the center of the cornbread with your fingertips; if it feel lightly firm, it is done. If it feels a bit spongy and soft, bake for another 5 to 10 minutes.

Remove the cornbread from the oven and flip it onto a plate, skillet side up. Slice into wedges and serve immediately.

Samishii yoru	*A lonely night;*
no amarimono no	*Eating the leftover food,*
taberu nado.	*And*
	—SANTŌKA

Scones

ABOUT 6 SERVINGS

● ●

Scones, despite being de rigueur nibbling food for afternoon tea, make a lovely breakfast bread that can be prepared in very little time. Scones are often made into individual breads about 3-inches in diameter, but I prefer to make one large round scone that is cut into wedges before it is baked; this gives a more homemade, "family" feeling to the finished product. Of course you can always make individual scones by rolling out the dough and cutting it into 3-inch rounds—the choice is yours. (Do-ahead note: For a quick breakfast treat, mix all the dry ingredients in a bowl the night before and store the butter/flour mix-ture in the refrigerator. The following morning all you have to do is mix the wet ingredients, blend, and bake.)

6	tablespoons (¾ stick) unsalted butter, melted
½	cup whole wheat flour
1½	cups all-purpose flour
¼	cup sugar
½	teaspoon salt
1	tablespoon baking powder
½	cup dried currants, dried sour cherries, or raisins
2	eggs
5	tablespoons milk, half-and-half, heavy cream, or soy milk
½	teaspoon vanilla extract
1	tablespoon sugar

Preheat the oven to 400°.

Melt the butter in a small saucepan over low heat. Set aside.

Place the whole wheat flour, all-purpose flour, sugar, salt, and baking powder in a large mixing bowl. Stir well. Add the melted butter and, using a fork, blend the butter completely into the dry ingredients so that the mixture seems a bit heavy and will clump together somewhat. Add the dried fruit and mix.

Beat the eggs in a bowl with a fork. Add the milk and vanilla, blending completely. Pour all but 1 tablespoon of the egg mixture into the dry ingredients and mix until everything is moist and sticking together.

Put the dough on a lightly floured surface; knead it for 15 to 30 seconds, then form it into a large, round disk about ¾-inch thick. (You can either use a rolling pin or your hands; your hands give a more homemade, rustic look.) Carefully move the dough to the center of a baking sheet sprayed with Pam. Pour the remaining tablespoon of the butter on top, and using your fingers or a pastry brush, moisten the top of the dough. Sprinkle on 1 tablespoon of sugar.

Using a long knife, cut the dough partway into sixths. Do not completely separate the wedges—just make deep indentations in the dough.

Bake in the upper middle of the preheated oven for 20 to 25 minutes, until the top has browned lightly and the scone has firmed up in the center.

Remove from the oven and allow to cool for 5 minutes. Break apart where the scone is scored. Serve immediately with extra butter, jams, preserves, or clotted cream.

Variations:
- Mix 1 teaspoon cinnamon with 1 tablespoon sugar and use this as the topping before you bake the scone.
- Use ½ teaspoon almond extract instead of vanilla extract. Reduce the dried fruit to ¼ cup and add ¼ cup toasted slivered or sliced almonds.

Hitori Shôgatsu	Alone on New Year's Day—
no mochi mo sake mo	There is mochi and sake
ari soshite.	And . . .

—Santôka

Roasted Garlic Oil
Two Versions

ABOUT ¾ CUP

● ●

This oil is great for pasta, salads, or simply as a dip for fresh bread. Since the taste of roasted garlic is delicate and subtle, it takes a large proportion of garlic to oil, but if you like roasted garlic, this is certainly no problem.

Interestingly, the baked garlic does not separate when it is submerged in the olive oil. After cooking, it easily and cleanly strains out, leaving only the garlic-flavored oil with no residue. Then the garlic is fine to use as you would regular baked garlic, so not only do you get great-tasting garlic oil, you get the garlic as well!

VERSION I:
This version is more delicate in taste than the second one.

2 entire baked heads of garlic (see Baked Whole
 Garlic, page 209)
1 cup extra virgin olive oil

Bake the garlic as directed in Baked Whole Garlic on page 209. Allow it to cool, then remove all the garlic from the papery husks. Lightly mash the garlic in a small saucepan and add the oil. Place over low to medium low heat and gently warming until the garlic has begun to sizzle. Let the garlic cook actively in the oil for 10 to 15 minutes, stirring occasionally. Let cool.

Once the oil has cooled, strain it into a clean jar and keep refrigerated until needed. Don't throw away the garlic! Use for any of the spreads listed on page 210.

Use the oil within 2 weeks.

VERSION II:

1 large head of garlic, peeled and chopped into
 ¼-inch dice
¾ cup olive oil

Put the garlic in a small saucepan and add the olive oil. Put the pan over very low heat, cover, and cook for 7 minutes. Remove the cover; the garlic should be cooking very gently. Small bubbles should be rising; if it is cooking at a furious pace, lower the heat (if possible) or periodically lift the pan from the heat source to keep the garlic cooking *gently*. Cook for another 8 to 10 minutes, stirring often, until the garlic pieces are very delicately colored, *not* brown. They should be pale gold and not toasted, and if you press the pieces against the side of the pan, they will be quite soft.

Remove from heat and allow the oil to cool. Strain the oil into a jar and reserve the garlic pieces. Cover the oil and refrigerate. Use the strained, cooked garlic bits for pasta or as a spread for toast, sandwiches, garlic mayonnaise, baked potatoes, or steamed vegetables.

Use the oil within 2 weeks.

Variations:
- Hot Garlic Oil: add 1 to 3 teaspoons crushed red pepper flakes to the oil before cooking.
- Garlic Rosemary Oil: add 2 to 3 tablespoons chopped fresh rosemary to the oil before cooking.
- Garlic Lemon Oil: add 2 teaspoons freshly grated lemon zest to the oil before cooking.

Spiced Ghee

ABOUT 2 CUPS

Ghee is usually described as "Indian clarified butter," but this is rather misleading because to most Western cooks clarified butter connotes French clarified butter, which is a different thing entirely. Ghee (sometimes also spelled ghi or gee) is butter that is brought to the boil, then the heat is reduced and any excess liquid cooks off. The solid proteins in the butter brown slightly, and the entire process takes a minimum of 25 to 30 minutes. French clarified butter, however, is quick and simple: you melt the butter and immediately scrape off any film from the top, then strain out only the clear, golden part, leaving any residue in the bottom of the pan.

"What's the difference?" you ask.

Ghee has a more concentrated, nuttier flavor than French clarified butter; it can be used as you would a cooking oil, utilizing it for deep-frying or sautéing without the fear of burning, since ghee smokes at 375°. Ghee is an animal fat, however, and as such contains cholesterol and saturated fats, so even though it can be used as you would canola or corn oil, it isn't the same.

"So why use it?"

Ghee has taste and character totally different from regular vegetable fats, and cannot be replicated. When used in small quantities, it isn't any more or less harmful than a pat or two of butter. Ghee will keep for a minimum of two months unrefrigerated (like any vegetable oil), or for four to six months in the refrigerator, or it can be frozen. You can find ready-made ghee in some grocery stores for a scandalously high price, but it is quite simple to prepare, and a pound costs the same as a pound of butter.

The ghee you will find in markets is plain, unspiced, unsalted ghee. If you want plain ghee, follow the directions below, but eliminate all the spices; the procedure is exactly the same. Spiced ghee, though, isn't really "spiced" in the true sense; even though there are a lot of whole spices in this recipe, the taste is very subtle, more "scented" than "spiced." At any rate, the smell of ghee cooking gently on the stove is intoxicating.

For more information about ghee, see Yamuna Devi's Lord Krishna's Cuisine: The Art of Indian Vegetarian Cooking (Bala Books, Dutton Publications).

1	pound (4 sticks) unsalted butter
3	¼-inch slices of fresh gingerroot
1 to 2	teaspoons roasted cumin seed
1	3-inch cinnamon stick
8	whole cloves
8	whole black peppercorns
1	tablespoon whole green or white cardamon pods
1	teaspoon fennel seed
3 to 5	whole dried red peppers, optional
3	whole black cardamom pods, optional
6 to 10	fresh curry leaves, optional

Place the butter in a wide, deep saucepan and melt it over low heat. When it has melted completely, add the spices, turn the heat to medium high, and bring the mixture to a boil. Boil for 15 to 20 seconds, then reduce the heat to low (or very low, depending on your range), keeping the butter just barely bubbling.

Let the mixture cook for about 30 minutes, undisturbed and uncovered. It will start with a froth on the surface that will begin to turn nut brown; if you can see through this foam to the bottom of the pan, you will also notice that the milky liquid there will eventually disappear (this is the water-whey from the butter cooking off). The clear yellow fat that makes up the bulk of the liquid will gradually change from a bright canary yellow to a deeper, golden yellow. When the particles floating on top of the ghee are nut brown (after 30 or more minutes), remove them gently with a spoon. You will easily see the bottom of the pan. If there is little or nothing left in the bottom except spices and the remaining liquid is a warm, golden yellow, not a dark, nut yellow, the ghee is done. Remove it from the heat.

Line a small, hand-held strainer with clean cheesecloth and set the strainer over a 2-cup jar. Gently pour or ladle the ghee through the cheesecloth into the jar. Discard the spices. Let the ghee cool to room temperature, then cover it. Refrigerate if desired.

Variation:
- The combination of spices listed is quite exhaustive; if you don't have them all, feel free to use what you have. Spiced ghee can be made with nothing but butter and a tablespoon of cumin seed, if you like.

Mushroom Duxelles

• •

Mushroom duxelles have an incredibly wonderful taste that cannot be replicated by any other method than the tried-and-true one, which is rather labor-intensive. However, it is well worth the effort, as duxelles freeze perfectly and are an elegant, rich addition to many French meals, particularly those enrobed in a creamy velouté sauce and served au gratin. Duxelles blend magically with egg dishes, giving you new alternatives for omelets, quiches, soufflés, timbales, as well as plain old scrambled eggs.

1	pound mushrooms, white, crimini, or any combination available
2	tablespoons butter
1	tablespoon olive oil
¼	cup finely minced shallots or green onions
1	small clove garlic, peeled and finely minced
¼	cup port
¼	cup strong Mushroom Soup Stock (page 28)
2	tablespoons tamari
1 to 2	teaspoons herbes de Provence
1	tablespoon finely chopped fresh parsley
	Salt to taste

Wipe the mushrooms clean with a damp towel and roughly chop them. Place 2 cups of the chopped mushrooms in a food processor and process in short, quick spurts until they are finely minced, being careful not to make mushroom purée. Remove from the work bowl and continue until all of the mushrooms have been minced. Place about 1 cup of the finely minced mushrooms in the corner of a clean kitchen towel. Wrap the towel around the mushroom bits and squeeze them firmly; quite a bit of purplish-brown liquid will exude from the mushrooms. Save this mushroom juice for soup stocks or sauces. Put the squeezed, dry mushrooms in a separate bowl. Continue squeezing the mushroom pieces until all of them are dry.

Over a moderate flame, heat the butter and olive oil until the butter is sizzling. Add the shallots and garlic, and stir for 1 minute. Add the mushrooms, breaking apart the lumps with a spatula or wooden spoon.

As the mushrooms cook, they will first begin to exude some liquid and turn a grayish brown, after 2 to 4 minutes of cooking. As they continue to cook, the liquid will begin to evaporate and the mushroom will begin sticking to the bottom of the skillet. Continue cooking and scraping until the pieces are completely dry and have browned, about 15 to 25 minutes. As soon as they have browned and smell heavenly, add the port, stock, tamari, and herbs (keep your face averted as this will splatter). Continue cooking and stirring until the liquid has been absorbed and reduced, another 5 minutes. You should have a pan full of tiny, deep brown pieces of mushrooms. Taste for seasoning, adding salt as needed. Allow the duxelles to cool. Refrigerate or freeze if not using immediately.

Crêpes

ABOUT 12 CRÊPES

● ●

Crêpes are really simple to prepare, especially if you use instant flour—you can have the entire recipe prepared from start to finish in about 30 minutes. Crêpes should be 5 to 7 inches in diameter. Depending on the thickness of your batter and the amount of batter used, about ⅓ cup of batter should make one crêpe.

1	*cup "instant" flour (like Wondra)**
⅔	*cup milk*
¾	*cup water*
3	*eggs*
	Big pinch salt
2 to 3	*tablespoons melted butter or canola oil*

Blend all the ingredients with a whisk in a large bowl. Allow to stand, covered, for 15 minutes.

Heat a crêpe pan (or a sauté pan) over moderately high heat; when it is quite hot (after 1 to 2 minutes), reduce the flame to medium. Spray the pan with Pam and pour ⅓ cup of the batter in the center. Immediately rotate the pan, spreading out the batter in as even a circle as possible. Set the pan back on the flame and let the crêpe cook for 1 minute, or until the batter turns from a raw ocher to a dull tan in color. Use a spatula to get underneath the crêpe and flip it over: the cooked side should be a speckled light tan. Let the other

If you don't have instant flour, you may use regular all-purpose flour, but the batter will need to stand for at least 2 to 3 hours before you can cook the crêpes.

side cook for 30 to 45 seconds. Remove to a cooling rack. (It is not necessary to spray the pan with Pam for every crêpe—perhaps every other to every third time would be sufficient.)

Continue until all the batter is used. Stack the cooled crêpes and seal them in foil.

Use them immediately or refrigerate until needed; after refrigeration, you may freeze them perfectly for a month or two. Crêpes do not need to have waxed paper layered between them when they are being stored for refrigeration or freezing.

Lemon Olive Oil

MAKES ½ CUP

● ●

This is simplicity itself to make and perks up many pasta and vegetable dishes without overwhelming them with lemon.

⅛   cup olive oil
2 to 4   teaspoons very finely grated lemon zest (use
      the smallest holes on a standard box grater)

Mix the lemon zest into the olive oil and let stand for at least 1 hour before using. It will keep, refrigerated, for 1 week.

> *Sukkari karete*   *Completely dried up,*
> *mame to natte iru.*   *They've become beans.*
>   —SANTŌKA

Basic Tomato Sauce

MAKES ABOUT 3 CUPS

● ●

Even though I've made this sauce a thousand times, I'm still amazed at how wonderful it is for being so utterly simple. The tastes compliment each other, with the bright, fresh taste of tomato shining through. Since you make it yourself, you can control the chunkiness of the sauce; personally, I love biting into a large hunk of tomato.

1   tablespoon finest quality olive oil
1 to 2   teaspoons fennel seeds
2 to 3   large cloves garlic, minced or put through a
      garlic press
¼   cup dry white vermouth or dry white wine
3½ to 4   cups Italian plum tomatoes (fresh, canned, or a
      mixture), peeled, seeded, drained, and chopped*

*One good way to make this is to use one 28-ounce can of Italian crushed tomatoes, supplementing with chopped, fresh tomatoes (or chopped canned tomatoes).

Freshly ground black pepper
Salt to taste

Place a large, heavy saucepan over medium high heat; when hot, add the oil and fennel. Sauté the fennel for a few seconds, then add the garlic, stirring and sautéing for 30 seconds. Add the vermouth, keeping your face averted as it will splatter; then add the tomatoes. Bring the mixture to a simmer, then reduce the heat to low. Cook for 20 minutes, or until the ingredients have blended thoroughly and the wine has cooked off. (If you're using all fresh tomatoes, this process will take considerably longer, as you'll have to cook the tomatoes and then reduce their juices, increasing the cooking time to about 60 minutes. Note that fresh tomatoes may require the addition of a bit of sugar to reduce their acidity.) The sauce will not be thick, like bottled pasta sauce, but it should not be watery either. It will thicken a bit as it cools.

Add fresh pepper and salt to taste, and serve or store.

Basic White Sauce
Béchamel or Velouté Sauce

MAKES ABOUT 1 CUP

● ●

The only difference between béchamel and velouté is the liquid; a béchamel uses milk, whereas a velouté uses stock (chicken, clam, fish, vegetable). The following proportions are for a fairly thick sauce; for a thin sauce, see the chart below the recipe.

2 to 3	*tablespoons butter*
2	*tablespoons flour*
1	*cup boiling milk or stock*
½ to 1	*teaspoon salt*
⅛	*teaspoon cayenne pepper*
⅛	*teaspoon freshly grated nutmeg*

Melt the butter in a small saucepan over moderate heat. Add the flour and stir, allowing the mixture to bubble and froth, and being careful it does not brown. After the mixture (called a *roux*) has cooked for 30 to 45 seconds, remove the pan from the heat and add the boiling liquid all at once, stirring with a whisk. The mixture will bubble and thicken within 10 seconds; return the sauce to the heat and boil, stirring constantly with your whisk, for another 30 to 45 seconds. Remove the sauce from the heat and add the salt, pepper, and nutmeg. If you're not going to use it immediately, dot the top of the hot sauce with a bit of butter; when the butter has melted, make sure the entire surface is coated. Cover the pan until needed.

To reheat, place the cooled sauce over a moderate to low flame and stir constantly with a whisk until it has warmed.

PROPORTIONS TO INCREASE OR DECREASE THE AMOUNT OF SAUCE:
- For a thick sauce, use 1 tablespoon flour per ½ cup liquid
- For a medium sauce, use 1½ teaspoons flour per ½ cup of liquid
- For a thin sauce, use 1 teaspoon flour per ⅓ cup of liquid

To enrich thick white sauces, you can always add heavy cream, sour cream, butter, crème fraîche, finely chopped vegetables, or herbs.

Yeast Brown Gravy

ABOUT 2½ CUPS

● ●

This recipe is a variation of a sauce from Edward Espe Brown's Tassajara Recipe Book *(Shambhala Publications). It is quite rich and savory, yielding a lovely deep brown gravy for any main course, from vegetarian meat loaf to stuffed peppers to curried rice.*

3	cups hot Vegetable Stock, Mushroom Stock, or water
2 to 3	tablespoons nutritional yeast
2 to 3	tablespoons flour
2 to 3	tablespoons butter
1	teaspoon toasted sesame oil
1	clove garlic, peeled and minced or put through a garlic press
2 to 3	tablespoons tamari
2 to 3	teaspoons Dijon mustard
¼ to ⅓	cup red wine or port
1 to 2	tablespoons tomato paste
1 to 2	tablespoons Chilean mushroom powder (see Ingredients page 254), optional
	A big pinch EACH of basil, thyme, and marjoram, optional
¼ to ½	cup half-and-half, cream, or ⅓ cup sour cream
	Salt and pepper

Place the stock in a pot and bring it to the simmer.

Place the nutritional yeast and flour in a large sauté pan; stir with a spoon. Put the pan over a moderate flame, stirring and toasting. After about 5 minutes, the yeast will give off a toasted aroma and the flour will turn a light nut brown.

Remove the pan from the heat and add the butter, sesame oil, and garlic; let the butter melt before you return the pan to a low flame. Cook with the butter and flour mixture for 1 minute, stirring well. You will have a thick roux.

Pour in 1 cup of the hot stock, stirring with a whisk to get out any lumps. Add the remaining stock, the tamari, mustard, wine, tomato paste, optional mushroom powder, and herbs; whisk well. Bring the mixture to the simmer and cook, uncovered, for 30 minutes. Stir occasionally, pushing down and blending in any film that may rise to the surface. As the sauce cooks, it will begin to reduce and thicken. (If you have reduced the sauce too much and it is quite thick, thin it out with milk or water.) When the sauce coats the back of a spoon well, turn off the heat. Add the half-and-half, cream, or sour cream and blend well. Taste for seasoning, adding salt and pepper as needed.

Variation:
- For curried rice, add 1 tablespoon fragrant curry powder to the sauce and pour the gravy over hot, cooked white rice along with steamed vegetables as desired.

Pie Crust
Pâte Brisée

FOR ONE 9-INCH PIE SHELL

● ●

Pâte brisée is standard pie crust. This recipe is a good all-purpose dough, and perfect for dessert pastries if you increase the sugar content by a few tablespoons.

Gluten refers to the characteristic of wheat flour molecules to bind and glue themselves together, forming an elastic, stretchable bond. Wheat flour is perfect for yeast breads, wherein yeast grows and forms gas pockets, causing the bread dough to rise and stretch without breaking. The gluten is activated in flour when it is kneaded, so the more you work with your dough the more elastic it will become. The idea with pie crust (which should be light and flaky) is to work as quickly as you can, rolling or kneading as little as possible so that the gluten molecules will not be activated.

Heat is another bugbear with pastry doughs. As soon as your dough becomes soft and limp it is impossible to work with. It must at that point be refrigerated until it is cold again. Experience has taught me that you'll achieve better results if you bake cold, refrigerated pie shells, not shells that have just been rolled and molded. It may require you to plan an extra step and add another hour or two of refrigeration, but trust me, it will be well worth the effort.

> 1½   *cups all-purpose flour*
> ½   *cup cake flour*, whole wheat pastry flour, or*
>   *more all-purpose flour*
> 1 to 2   *tablespoons sugar, to taste (more if making a*
>   *dessert pastry)*
> ½   *teaspoon salt*
> 1½   *sticks (12 tablespoons) cold unsalted butter, cut*
>   *into ¼-inch cubes*
>   *About ½ cup ice water*

Put the flour(s), sugar, and salt in a food processor. Blend for a couple of seconds to mix everything, then add the cold, cubed butter. Blend in short, quick spurts (about 5 times) until the processor has chopped up the butter somewhat. Add the water, blending just long enough so that the dough forms a shaggy ball, about 10 seconds at the most. Do not overblend.

Remove the dough from the processing bowl (there will undoubtedly be dry, with floury residue in the bottom) and place on a flat, smooth surface. In 3 or 4 motions, quickly blend the dough with your hands so that any dry portions are mixed in with the wetter portions. The dough should not be damp or wet—there should be just enough water so that it sticks together when pressed. Wrap the dough tightly in plastic wrap and refrigerate for 2 hours, or until it is firm. (You can freeze the dough at this point if desired.)

Lightly flour your work surface and roll the chilled dough ⅛ inch thick to whatever size you desire.

Partially Baked Pie Shells:

If you are partially baking a pie shell (for quiches, tarts, and the like), put the dough in the pie pan, cutting off excess dough, and trimming the edge as you think best. Refrigerate the shell until it is cold. Before baking, prick the shell all over with the tines of a fork or a roller-pricker. Lay a piece of waxed paper or kitchen parchment in the pie shell and put some dry beans (or other weight) on top. Bake the shell at 400° for 12 to 15 minutes, or until the edges of the dough are turning a golden yellow. If you think the shell needs a bit further cooking, put it back in the oven for another 3 to 5 minutes to dry out a bit more. Remove the shell from the oven and carefully remove the waxed paper and beans. (You can use these beans over and over again.) The partially baked pie shell will not be completely done, nor will it be brown; it should still be pale.

*If you wish, you may substitute whole wheat flour or whole wheat pastry flour for all or part of this measure. I would discourage adding more than ½ cup whole wheat flour, though, since more would result in a tougher, heavier crust.

MAKING DOUGH BY HAND:

Of course the above recipe can be made by hand. Just blend the flours, sugar and salt in a bowl. Quickly blend in the butter with a fork or pastry blender until the dough has the consistency of cornmeal. Add the water, mixing quickly, until the dough forms a ball. Wrap in plastic wrap and continue as above.

Savory Tart Crust

FOR ONE 9-INCH CRUST

● ●

This crust is a bit nuttier and firmer than the previous recipe, so it keeps its shape well in fluted molds. Be careful when adding liquid to any pie crust; you need to add just enough water to hold the mixture together. If you add too much liquid, the dough will become wet and will be quite tough.

1½	*cups all-purpose flour*
1½	*cup whole wheat flour*
1	*tablespoon sugar, to taste*
1	*teaspoon salt*
1	*stick cold unsalted butter, cut into ¼-inch cubes*
2	*egg yolks*
	About ½ cup ice water

Put the flours, sugar, and salt in a food processor. Blend for a couple of seconds to mix everything, then add the cold, cubed butter. Blend in short, quick spurts (about 5 times) until the processor has chopped up the butter somewhat.

Place the egg yolks in a measuring cup and add enough ice water to make ½ cup total liquid; blend with a fork.

Drizzle half of the liquid over the flour mixture, and blend for 2 seconds. Drizzle in the remaining liquid and blend again. Check the dough to see if it needs more water. If the mixture still looks quite dry, add a tablespoon more water and blend. Pinch some of the dough between your fingers; if it feels a bit dry but sticks together, you've added enough water. Remember that the liquid will be absorbed into the flour as the dough rests.

Remove the dough from the processing bowl (there will undoubtedly be a dry, floury residue in the bottom of the bowl) to a flat, smooth surface. In 3 or 4 motions, quickly blend the dough with your hands so that any dry portions are mixed with the wetter portions. Wrap the dough tightly in plastic wrap and refrigerate for 2 hours, or until it is firm. (You can freeze the dough at this point if desired.)

Lightly flour your work surface and roll the chilled dough ⅛ inch thick to whatever size you desire. Partially bake the shell as directed on page 245.

Savory Tart Crust can also be made by hand. Blend the flours, sugar and salt in a bowl. Quickly blend in the butter with a fork or pastry blender until it has the consistency of cornmeal. Add the egg yolk and water mixture, blending quickly, until the dough forms a ball. Wrap in plastic wrap and continue as above.

Variations:

- Add dried or fresh herbs to the crust for additional flavor for savory tarts. For example, perhaps a tablespoon of chopped fresh rosemary, oregano, tarragon, or chives, or 2 teaspoons dried basil, summer savory, or herbes de Provence.
- Finely grate the zest of 1 lemon and add it to the flour mixture.
- Add 2 teaspoons chili powder or ground (or whole) cumin seed.

Yin-Yang

● ●

A PATH EXISTS BECAUSE THE GOAL IS NOT YET ATTAINED

While I was in college studying theater, I took a circus techniques class. This early morning class met two or three times a week and practiced (among other things) juggling and acrobatics, but the most difficult task, and one that I never accomplished, was walking the tightrope. On one side of the huge rehearsal room was a practice tightrope raised about 18 inches off the floor, surrounded with gym pads—a safety feature, should anyone fall. Since at a height of 18 inches I didn't have to worry about falling and breaking my neck, one would have thought that the lack of height (and fear) would have enabled me to master the balancing act easily. Not so.

I found this rather odd. I had perfected balancing acts while practicing yoga; standing on my head, shoulders, one foot, hands—so I thought the feat of transferring these skills from one method to another would be simple. How many hundreds of times had I seen circus performers quickly and nonchalantly walk across a rope strung up 50 feet, let alone higher, and here I was a mere 1½ feet off the ground, unable to cross!

Time after time I tried to cross that rope, sometimes getting eight inches out before falling and other times not even getting six inches. Yet what was interesting was the idea of balance itself: on solid ground I could deftly balance for quite some time, but once up on a slightly moving object (the rope) I was lost. In other words, while stable, I could balance; while unstable, I could not. I had not found my center.

If you use the rope as a metaphor for life, we must all try to find some balance while we're constantly in motion. It's easy to lead a balanced, quiet life if you live hermetically, but once you're thrown in all of the difficulties and trials that life has to offer—whew!

Being unstable is part of the great balancing act. You must be able to adjust as you go. Walking a tightrope entails balancing your body, arms, legs, and head in conjunction with the movement of the rope; when the rope begins moving, you must find the inner-most center of your being in order to focus on what (and where) you can balance. In the midst of imbalance, it is your core of being that allows you to remain still and serene on top.

The yin-yang symbol usually associated with Taoism is commonly seen in martial arts centers, Asian markets, New-Age gifts, health food stores. Many people regard this ancient Chinese symbol as representing the balance of life. Indeed, with its many mutations it could be seen as the center point of a balancing act: male/female, dark/ bright, heavy/ light, good/ bad, heaven/ hell, hedonism/ asceticism, full/ empty, health/ illness, spiritually nourished/ spiritually deprived, life/ death.

Yet the yin-yang is not merely opposites coupled in balance: they are in fact one. Without dark there is no light. Without evil there is no good. Without life there is no death. They are symbiotically intertwined, one gaining ground one second, the other rebounding the next, yet not two warring factions, but one unified entity. The yin-yang symbol is physically represented as a stationary object, but this balanced image is in fact merely the representation of an ideal state: the yin-yang should really be viewed as constantly changing, continually in motion, with one side gaining on the other, then vice versa. Only in perfection is this Tao symbol truly static and immovable. The calm yin-yang is the point of perfection: the serene balance between "opposites."

Just as in life, sometimes we feel good about what is happening and other times we mourn. Neither state is permanent, just a temporary, transient experience. The difficult task is to find the middle ground, the point of perfect rest amidst the rushing onslaught of life. By balancing on the tightrope of life you walk The Middle Path.

INFORMATIONAL DIGRESSIONS

● ●

Is "fresh" always better?

No.

Well, sometimes no. For example, in mid-December I would opt for canned tomatoes that have some semblance of summer flavor rather than use the pale pink, hothouse-grown tomatoes from the produce section. A saucepan full of these mealy "fresh" tomatoes will be disappointing—fresh foods are always best when they are in season. Of course this holds true for fruits as well. Strawberries in season are exquisite, but forced, hothouse strawberries are hard, bland, and sour. Firm, out-of-season peaches are tart, so why bother? Why waste money on any produce that isn't flavorful?

What is a "medium" onion?

Frequently I've heard people remonstrate about recipes that call for "one medium onion"—What, they ask, is a medium onion? Or a large bell pepper? And why do you specify a quantity of onion in one recipe, yet use an indiscriminate term like "medium" in another?

The surface answer is elementary. First, if the recipe hinges on the quantity of onion, then I specify exactly how much to add. If you're making a cup of parsley sauce, you don't want to overpower the herb with the taste of onion, hence that amount is exact and specified. However, sometimes the exact quantity of something isn't terribly important, so an inexact amount is fine. A basic vegetable soup, for example, isn't affected by a large, medium, or small onion, therefore "one medium onion" is fine.

Secondarily, though, I think it's important to get used to the idea of employing vegetables as they come, to release yourself from being chained to specified amounts. Learning how to cook entails using what you have, and onions aren't all the same size, nor are carrots or peppers or celery stalks—the list goes on. The point is not to get too caught up in a recipe's amounts but to understand the concept. If a recipe calls for ½ cup onion and you've not got any yellow onions but you *do* have a bunch of scallions on hand, go ahead and substitute the green onions for the yellow onion. It won't be exactly the same, but it may be better.

Nuts, Seeds, and Legumes

What is the real difference between a seed and a nut? For many years I lived with a Southern pecan tree in my backyard, so I can say with absolute confidence that a pecan will turn into a seedling if allowed to germinate and grow. And a seed, as we all know, is what we stick in the earth to foster a plant, so if one plants a nut to grow a seedling, is there really a difference between seed and a nut?

Nuts are dry fruit seeds; ergo, not all seeds are nuts. The seed of a carrot, for instance, contains no edible "meat" and isn't enclosed in a woody shell; therefore it is unquestionably a seed. A pecan is not only a seed, but has the added distinction of being a nut.

So what should we know about seeds and nuts?

First, they're extremely nutritious. Seeds may contain the B-complex vitamins, vitamins A, D, and E, plus protein, phosphorous, calcium, and a host of other minerals including fluorine, iodine, potassium, magnesium, and zinc. Nuts, being seeds, are identically nutritious. The only problem is with their fat content. Though seeds and nuts are good sources of vegetarian protein, unfortunately they're loaded with oil as well. For instance:

> 12 pecan halves contain 11 grams of fat
> 2 tablespoons pine nuts contain 7.3 grams of fat
> 18 Virginia peanuts contain 9.2 grams of fat
> 8 to 10 English walnuts contain 9.7 grams of fat
> 8 to 10 black walnuts contain 8.7 grams of fat
> 2½ tablespoons sunflower seeds contain 7.1 grams of fat
> 2½ tablespoons pumpkin seeds contain 8.2 grams of fat

Generally speaking, the fats found in nuts are primarily polyunsaturated; however, because of the large amount of fats, nuts and seeds are generally used to boost the protein in a vegetarian dish, not used as the sole source of vegetarian protein.

So, to achieve any semblance of moderation, nuts must be used with great restraint—a troublesome feat indeed when faced with a bowlful of seasoned cashews. Nuts (seeds) are sources of protein, energy, and roughage and have been a part of man's diet for millennia.

When purchasing fresh nuts and seeds, be sure to smell them carefully to check for freshness, as the large quantity of oils contained in their flesh are sure indicators of advanced age or improper storage. If you buy some nuts and they have an "off" smell, return them immediately for a full refund.

In English, a legume is a specific type of seed (but not nut) borne of a splitting pod. Though legumes may resemble nuts because of their fleshy meat, their "meat" is contained in pods, not in leathery, woody hulls. Legumes are very nutritious, being high in protein and low in fat (with two exceptions)

> ½ cup cooked split peas contain .3 grams of fat
> ½ cup cooked lentils contain .475 grams of fat
> ½ cup cooked navy beans contain .56 grams of fat

Soybeans are one exception, being comparatively high in fat, containing 5.1 grams of fat per ½ cup serving. Peanuts, as mentioned earlier, are another exception.

Legumes generally aren't edible in their raw state, though nuts are. Legumes must be cooked before being eaten (even peanuts get a roasting before they hit the supermarket shelves). And not all legumes are edible—we do not eat indigo or mimosa, so in English, the word legume is *not* a universal term for vegetable, as in French, though often beans and peas are lumped into the "vegetable" category, an error that must be corrected sooner or later by "eatists" everywhere.

INGREDIENTS AND TECHNIQUES
• •

"We are all saints in the making."

ancho chile - Ancho chiles are dried poblano peppers. These shriveled, flat pods are nearly black in color and can be found in cellophane packages, in bulk bins, or as a produce item in some supermarkets. Roasting ancho chiles before using improves their taste. Using tongs, hold one chile by the stem above an open flame, turning frequently until it changes from black to a dark red brown and possibly begins to smoke. Being very careful, since the chile is hot, quickly remove the core and seeds, then chop the chile into small pieces using a very sharp knife. Put the chopped ancho in a bowl and add enough water to cover, allowing it to rehydrate for 20 minutes before using.

arame - An edible seaweed that looks like shriveled, hard, black rubber bands. It is sold in a dried form in small plastic pouches that weigh next to nothing. To rehydrate arame, soak it in warm water for 30 minutes. It's amazing to see the difference between dried and rehydrated seaweed—the dried form is brittle and gnarled, and the rehydrated version is smooth and dull green. Additionally, a small amount of dried seaweed rehydrates to an amazingly large amount, so if a recipe says, "1 tablespoon dried seaweed," don't put in ¼ cup.

asafetida - see **hing**.

bain-marie - A hot water bath. In a bain-marie, a filled, uncooked mold (or molds) are placed in a roasting pan and boiling water is added to come halfway up the sides of the mold(s). This entire contraption is put in the oven and baked. The water, besides ensuring a moist, more even baking process, helps insulate the delicate dish from overcooking on the outside before the inside is done. Occasionally, as is the case with chawanmushi, the bain-marie can be cooked on top of the stove in a large, covered Dutch oven, but the oven method is generally used.

basmati rice (white and brown) Basmati is a variety of rice originally grown in the north India and Pakistan regions; this aromatic, fine-grained rice is much superior to regular long-grained rice in taste and smell. Brown basmati, emitting a popcornlike aroma, is also much more flavorful than regular brown rice. For my money, the best white basmati is found in large burlap bags in any Indian market, in sizes of 5 kilos (11 pounds), 10 kilos, or 20 kilos.

black salt - A specific spice only available in Indian markets. This salt isn't really black but light gray, and contains trace minerals including a bit of sulfur. I recommend purchasing the smallest amount possible, as it's not something you use a great deal of—a small pinch per recipe is enough.

blanch - A process wherein a raw vegetable is placed into boiling water for about 30 seconds to a minute. The partially cooked vegetable is then immediately removed from the hot water, drained, and rinsed in cold water to stop the cooking process. Spinach, chard, kale, and greens are nearly cooked by blanching, but firmer vegetables (like carrots, pea pods, green beans) maintain their firmness during blanching while their color brightens.

brewer's yeast - see **nutritional yeast**

broccoli rabe - see **rapini**

canola oil - Sometimes erroneously called rapeseed oil. Plant scientists removed a toxic gene from the rapeseed plant and the hybridized result is what we call canola. Canola oil is one of the healthiest oils, because it has a high amount of monounsaturated fat and is low in polyunsaturated and saturated fats. It has a fairly bland taste, so it works well for salads and sautéing.

Chilean mushrooms - see **mushroom powder**

chili paste with garlic - This paste can be found in Thai, Vietnamese, and Chinese markets under various names and with various differences. The dull red paste basically contains garlic, dried red chiles, vinegar, and oil (sometimes toasted sesame oil). Some Thai versions contain dried shrimp paste as well. It is quite hot and spicy, so use caution for the uninitiated.

cilantro - A green, leafy herb sold in bunches alongside parsley in the produce section. Whether it is called Chinese parsley, Mexican parsley, or green coriander, it's all the green leafy part of the coriander plant. Dried ground coriander is not a substitute for cilantro, because ground coriander is the dried seed pod of the coriander plant, not the leaf. Some recipes suggest parsley as a substitute for cilantro, but I think fresh spearmint leaves are more successful.

coconut milk - This is not the sweetened, condensed coconut milk found in the bakery or liquor section of your supermarket, nor the water found inside a fresh coconut. Canned coconut milk may be stocked in the Asian section of your supermarket, or it is easily available in Thai, Vietnamese, or other Southeast Asian markets. Surprisingly, coconut milk doesn't whack you over the head with the taste of coconut. It is an integral staple of Thai cooking, so if you like Thai food, you've undoubtedly had coconut milk many times. For those watching their fat intake, light coconut milk is available in cans—all natural, just coconuts and water.

five spice powder - A blend of ground spices from China, containing star anise, ginger, cinnamon, fennel, and pepper. Five-spice powder is commonly combined with garlic and gingerroot, and it should be used with a delicate hand, as too much will overpower the taste of the dish.

folding - Folding is a technique of mixing, usually something heavy (like a white sauce or chocolate) into something light (such as beaten eggwhites or whipped cream), wherein you deflate the mixture as little as possible. The technique is thus: using a rubber spatula, plunge the spatula directly down to the very center bottom of the bowl, turning your wrist slightly to scoop the heavy material sitting at the bottom. Then bring the spatula up along the side of the bowl to the top, turning the bowl ¼ turn with each fold. Continue this procedure until the heavy mixture is folded into the light mixture. Once again—just take the spatula in hand, plunge it down the center, turn it so that it scoops up the heavy material, then bring it up along the side of the bowl to the top. That's it!

garam masala - A "house blend" spice for Indian cooking. There are thousands of garam masala recipes, with every family having a slightly different version.

for Chinese dishes,

in Japanese markets
ing, as all it requires
tight container.

okery. Fresh lemon-
gourmet supermar-
een onion, is about
ch in diameter, and
ove the bottom inch
n and using a very
can. Lemongrass is
han a green onion.
ntil the lemongrass

l yeast spread adds
ite can be found in
res, some specialty
ite are sources for

from soybeans but
ound in the refrig-
or flavoring ingre-
se it can be made
lty (rather like an
lty.

und mushrooms.
ensive, a common
or grinding is the
ealth food stores.
it is necessary to
mushroom pieces
e an earthy brown
y add a few tea-
mushroom taste.

itritional yeast is
nutritional yeasts
nutritional infor-
ed.

lest oil known to
st 20 years. Most
n to regular, from
e choices of olive
ay olive oil other
all olive oils are
stes best to you;
ie will be fruitier
nary adventure.
l they have been

, and in fact isn't even close.
ecipe. Here's a quick version:

ods)

t them over medium high heat
e the spices in a coffee or spice
n an airtight jar.

i the produce section. Look for
d, fibrous ones. Though dried
, it is **not** a substitute for fresh

Mediterranean Provence region
hyme, marjoram, savory, rose-
/or fennel seeds. Though com-
et market and some supermar-

in that imparts onion/garlic fla-
all that is needed. I have limited
is easier to measure than the
ly from brand to brand, keep an
has been used for centuries and
i markets.

hese paste made from pumpkin,
in the refrigerator, hoisin sauce
bisin sauce, you could substitute
d with a bit of tamari.

i nearly all supermarkets in the
constituted exactly the way you
harkets, however, you can pur-
ike readymade wasabi). This is
refrigerator. Although the dry,
t mustard, they aren't quite the

same, hence, I would have both on hand, the Chinese typ⸱
the Japanese for Japanese dishes.

kombu - A sea kelp used primarily for soup stock, available⸱
and health food stores. Do not wash or rinse kombu before u⸱
is to be wiped with a lightly dampened cloth. Store in an ai⸱

lemongrass - A stalk used for seasoning in Southeast Asian ⸱
grass is sold in small bundles in Asian groceries and in som⸱
kets. Lemongrass, looking somewhat like a skinny, woody ⸱
12- to 18-inches long; the bottom portion is usually about $\frac{1}{2}$-⸱
the upper portion dwindles away into dry stems. To use, ren⸱
or so, and then remove the outer layer. Starting at the bott⸱
sharp knife, slice rings off (like green onions) as thinly as yo⸱
quite sturdy and it's easier to slice into paperthin rounds ⸱
After you've sliced off a series of ultrathin rings, mince them ⸱
pieces are as fine as you can get them.

Marmite (and **Vegemite**) - This salty, dark brown, concentrat⸱
a hearty, "meaty" note to vegetarian dishes. Marmite/ Vege⸱
English and Australian specialty markets, some health food s⸱
grocery stores, or even in Indian markets. Marmite and Veg⸱
vegan-vegetarian vitamin B-12.

mince - A term meaning "to chop very finely".

miso - Miso is a Japanese fermented bean paste, usually mad⸱
sometimes made from chickpeas or other beans. It is normall⸱
erated section of a natural foods store and can be used as a m⸱
dient in soups or as a subtle seasoning for soup stocks. Bec⸱
from different beans, it has different tastes, from dark and ⸱
intense soy sauce) to pale yellow and slightly sweet, but stil⸱

mushroom powder - Any powder made from dried, g⸱
However, since some dried mushrooms are outrageously e⸱
dried mushroom that is not very good for eating but excelle⸱
dried Chilean mushroom, found in the bulk bins of many ⸱
Since no one actively markets and sells mushroom powd⸱
make it yourself, which is fine, as it's very simple. Place dri⸱
in a clean coffee grinder and grind. After 45 seconds you'll h⸱
powder, which can be stored in a glass jar indefinitely. Si⸱
spoons or tablespoons to any dish you think may benefit fro⸱

nutritional yeast - Not to be confused with brewer's yeast ⸱
specifically grown as a nutritional supplement; as such, ma⸱
are fortified with B-12. If you are a vegan, be sure to check ⸱
mation carefully to ensure that the yeast you're buying is fo⸱

olive oil and extra virgin olive oil - Olive oil, probably the⸱
man, has made amazing inroads in the American diet in the⸱
supermarkets now sell a vast range of olive oils, from extra vi⸱
Italy, Greece, Spain, France, California, Portugal —there are ⸱
oil than ever before. For my money, there is no reason to bu⸱
than extra virgin, the first cold pressing of the green olive. ⸱
the same, so experiment with different types and see whic⸱
most extra virgins should have a fruity, green, olive-y taste. ⸱
than others, so finding the "perfect" oil for you will be a ⸱
However, all oils are quite susceptible to the conditions in w⸱

stored. If you even suspect that the oil you've purchased is rancid, take it immediately to your supermarket and demand a refund. Even the most expensive oil can go rancid if stored improperly.

rapini (broccoli rabe) -Rapini is found in the gourmet or specialty section of many supermarkets, though its popularity has caused some markets to carry it as a regular item in the produce section. Rapini, sold in bunches, looks like a cross between broccoli and turnip greens, with pencil-thick stems, lush leaves, and tiny knobs of broccoli florets at the top. Rapini has a complex taste of greens combined with a slight bitterness—not unpleasantly bitter, but simply complex. To use rapini: wash thoroughly under cool water. Cut off the tough bottom ½-inch or so and peel the stalk upward as best you can with a small, sharp knife. If the bottom is particularly tough, this will be simple; the cellulose in the outer skin will pull effortlessly up the stalk, leaving you with a pale green center stem. If the stem breaks easily as you peel, then you will need a minimal amount of peeling, as the stalk is tender. Use all of the remaining rapini, chopping the stem, leaves, and florets. Blanch, stir-fry, or steam rapini as you would broccoli.

rasam - a South Indian spice blend, usually used with bean-based soups. Rasam powder can be bought ready-made at an Indian market, or you can make your own; as ingredients vary, feel free to experiment.

To prepare Rasam Powder:

1	teaspoon flavorless oil, such as canola
2	teaspoons black mustard seeds
$\frac{1}{3}$	cup whole coriander seeds
6 to 10	dried hot red chiles
1	teaspoon black peppercorns
1	teaspoon fenugreek seeds
1	tablespoon whole cumin seeds
3	whole cloves, optional

Place the oil in a heavy pan over medium high heat. Add the mustard seeds. When they begin to pop, add the remaining ingredients and reduce the heat to medium. Stir constantly and continue to cook for 3 minutes until the spices brown. Remove the spices from pan, cooling for a few minutes, then place in a clean coffee grinder.

Grind the mixture to a powder. Put the rasam powder in a small, air-tight jar.

sake - Japanese rice wine. I doubt that there is a good substitute for sake, but you might try dry sherry.

shiitake mushrooms - Japanese mushrooms found fresh in the gourmet section of better supermarkets and also available in dried form in Asian markets. (You'll also find dried shiitakes in the macrobiotic section of your health food store, but at a greatly inflated price.) If dried shiitakes are unavailable, substitute dried Chinese black mushrooms.

TIME-SAVING HINT: if you're adding dried shiitakes to a soup or stew, it's really not necessary to rehydrate them before you add them to the pot. Just break off the tough stem and slice the dried mushrooms—it's quite easy. Add the sliced mushroom pieces to the pot—the liquid from the stock will rehydrate the mushrooms.

soy sauce (shoyu) - see comments below.

tamari, (erroneously called soy sauce, shoyu) - Though tamari and soy sauce look and taste very similar, and in fact are both fermented soy bean products, they are manufactured differently. Tamari is the old-fashioned, "original" soy sauce, containing only soy beans, salt, and water (sometimes alcohol is listed in the ingredients, but this is part of the brewing process and acts as a preservative). Tamari is a more labor-intensive product than soy sauce, which accounts for its higher cost. However, the cost is not gratuitous, for it is a better product, since tamari contains less salt and has a richer, subtler quality than shoyu.

tamarind - Tamarinds are surfacing all over America, much the way gingerroot is now commonplace. Tamarinds are used in Mexican, Middle Eastern, Indian, and Southeast Asian cuisines, and have a pleasant sweet/sour taste. They are longish, hairy brown pods containing hard, large seeds and a fleshy seed pod—one uses the seed pod to make tamarind paste. Though you can make tamarind paste from scratch, there are commercially made pastes that are not only inexpensive but contain nothing more than tamarind—no preservatives, fixatives, or flavorings. I think the tamarind paste found in small plastic tubs in Indian markets is quite tasty, as is the "fresh tamarind" paste found in Southeast Asian markets. The Indian variety looks like Marmite—thick, brown, heavy—whereas the Asian variety is thin, light brown, and pulpy. Both are reasonably priced and keep indefinitely in the refrigerator after being opened. If you cannot find tamarind paste, substitute a mixture of lime juice and sugar in equal amounts.

tempeh - Tempeh is a soybean product found in 4 x 6 x 1-inch cakes, usually in the frozen or refrigerated section of your natural food store.

toasted sesame oil - This is the common Chinese sesame oil, nut brown in color and extraordinarily flavorful. Toasted sesame oil should be purchased in as small a jar as possible, not only because it can go rancid quickly, but because it is used in very small quantities—hence, a large jar of it would go bad before you could use it up. The pale, clear "regular" sesame oil is not a substitute for toasted sesame oil.

toasted sesame seeds - These are exactly what you think they are. Raw sesame seeds (either bleached and white or natural and light tan in color) are placed in a sauté pan. Put the pan over a moderate flame and stir the seeds constantly until they emit a roasted aroma, have turned a shade or two darker; they may begin to pop. Immediately remove from the pan and let them cool.

tofu - Tofu is known as soybean curd, soy curd, dofu (dôfu), or simply "bean curd." It is sold in blocks and is practically tasteless, so it takes on whatever flavor it is cooked with.

Vegemite- see **Marmite**

wakame - An edible seaweed much like arame. See **arame.**

wasabi - A form of Japanese horseradish, wasabi is usually found in Japanese restaurants, an innocuous-looking pale green blob on the plate. Its appearance is misleading, for it is quite powerful, and too much of it can result in the feeling that you've just had the top of your head blown off. Wasabi comes in a powdered, dry form and also in a prepared, wet form in a tube. The tube variety, found in Asian and Japanese markets, is easier, since all you do is squeeze out however much you wish. The dry version is quite simple to prepare; place 1 teaspoon or so in a very small bowl and add just enough water to make a paste, stirring with your finger. Turn the bowl upside down on a countertop for 5 minutes before using. Scoop out the wasabi and use as you would the readymade kind.

yeast - see **nutritional yeast**

INDEX

● ●

O

P